AAT

CENTRAL ASSESSMENT KIT

Intermediate Units 4 and 5
Financial Records and Cost Information

August 1998 first edition

This new Central Assessment Kit for *Units 4 and 5 Financial Records and Cost Information* follows the revised Intermediate Standards of Competence which are assessable from 1 June 1998. It contains:

- Guidance from the AAT on **assessment strategy**
- The **AAT's Sample Central Assessment** for each Unit
- A **Question Bank** for each Unit containing exercises taken from actual central assessments set by the AAT under the previous version of the Standards

All Samples and Questions have full answers included in this Kit.

FOR 1998 AND 1999 ASSESSMENTS

BPP Publishing
August 1998

First edition August 1998

ISBN 0 7517 6126 5

British Library Cataloguing-in-Publication Data
A catalogue record for this book
is available from the British Library

Published by

BPP Publishing Limited
Aldine House, Aldine Place
London W12 8AW

http://www.bpp.co.uk

Printed in Great Britain by
WM Print Ltd
Frederick Street
Walsall
West Midlands WS2 9NE

We are grateful to the Lead Body for Accounting for permission to reproduce extracts from the Standards of Competence for Accounting and to the AAT for permission to reproduce two of their specimen central assessments..

Page

HOW TO USE THIS CENTRAL ASSESSMENT KIT (v)

ORDER FORM

REVIEW FORM & FREE PRIZE DRAW

Contents

HOW TO USE THIS CENTRAL ASSESSMENT KIT

Aims of this Central Assessment Kit

To provide the knowledge and practice to help you succeed in the central assessments for Intermediate Unit 4 *Financial Records and Accounts* and Unit 5 *Cost Information*.

To pass the central assessments you need a thorough understanding in all areas covered by the standards of competence.

To tie in with the other components of the BPP Effective Study Package to ensure you have the best possible chance of success.

Interactive Texts
These cover all you need to know for devolved assessment for Unit 4 *Financial Records and Accounts* and Unit 5 *Cost Information*. Until you are ready to tackle assessment style questions at the end of your course, you only need to take these books to class. Icons clearly mark key areas of the texts. Numerous activities throughout the texts help you practise what you have just learnt.

Central Assessment Kit
When you have understood and practised the material in the Interactive Texts you will have the knowledge and experience to tackle this Central Assessment Kit for Units 4 and 5. This contains the AAT's sample Central Assessments for Unit 4 and Unit 5 plus relevant questions from the AAT's central assessments set under the previous version of the standards.

Recommended approach to this Central Assessment Kit

- To achieve competence in Units 4 and 5 (and all the other units), you need to be able to do **everything** specified by the standards. Study the Interactive Texts very carefully and do not skip any part of them .

- Learning is an **active** process. Do **all** the activities as you work through the Interactive Texts so you can be sure you really understand what you have read.

- After you have covered the material in the Interactive Texts, work through this **Central Assessment Kit**.

- The Kit is made up of three different types of question:

  o **Practice questions** are designed to help you practise techniques in particular areas of the Standards at a lower level than you will experience in the central assessments themselves. They are 'warm-ups' which you may find it particularly useful to do if it is some time since you studied the Interactive Text and the activities it contains.

  o **Full central assessment standard questions** give you plenty of practice in the type of question that comes up in the central assessment. Many are taken from central assessments set by the AAT under the previous version of the Standards. All have full answers provided in this Kit.

  o The AAT's **Specimen Central Assessments** for these Units with full answers provided by the AAT, modified by BPP where appropriate.

- The structure of the main body of this Kit follows that of its companion Interactive Text, with banks of both practice and full central assessment standard questions for each area of the Standards. You may opt to do all the practice questions from across the range of the Standards first, or you may prefer to do questions of both levels in a particular area of the Standards before moving on. In either case, it is probably best to leave the Specimen Central Assessment until the last stage of your revision, and then attempt it as a 'mock' under 'exam conditions'. This will help you develop some key techniques in selecting questions and allocating time correctly. For guidance on this, please see **Central Assessment Technique** on page (xi).

- This approach is only a suggestion. You may well adapt it to suit your needs.

Remember this is a **practical** course.

- Try to relate the material to your experience in the workplace or any other work experience you may have had.

- Try to make as many links as you can to your study of the other Units at Intermediate level.

Changes to the 1998 Standards for Unit 4 (formerly Units 4 and 5)

The revised Standards for Unit 4 (assessable from 1 June 1998, with the first Central Assessment in December 1998) have become more specific as to what is required from you. It expressly includes the function and form of profit and loss accounts and balance sheets for sole traders, partnerships, manufacturing and club accounts, although you do not actually have to prepare them. It is important that you know which ledger accounts end up in which sections of the P & L and balance sheet.

It states, clearly which SSAPs are relevant, and expressly emphasises that double entry accounting is assessable (in Section A of the Central Assessment). Confidentiality of business transactions is also stressed. There is slightly more detail in the capital acquisition and disposal element (which used to be a separate Unit), namely on methods of funding and organisational implications of purchasing or disposing of fixed assets. There is rather less emphasis on incomplete records. Partnership accounts do *not* include appropriation.

Changes to the 1998 Standards for Unit 5 (formerly Unit 6)

The revised Standards for Unit 5 (assessable from 1 June 1998, with the first Central Assessment in December 1998) have become more specific as to what is required from you.

The main change is the inclusion of the element *Prepare and present standard cost reports* which was formerly Element 11.1 in Unit 11 *Preparing Information For Cost Analysis and Control*, and will involve the following.

- Presenting information in reports.

- Calculating the following variances as specifically stated in the guidance to Element 5.3.
  - o Materials (price and usage)
  - o Labour (wage rate and efficiency)
  - o Overheads (expenditure, volume, efficiency and capacity)

- Explaining the significance and possible causes of variances.

- Calculating and reporting on control ratios of efficiency, capacity and activity (production volume).

The focus of the new Elements 5.1 and 5.2 is now upon whether or not a cost is **direct** or **indirect**. Other changes include the following.

- Process costing is no longer included in the standards.

- There is more emphasis on the understanding of cost behaviour.

- Activity based costing systems have now been expanded to include cost pools.

- Bases of allocating and apportioning overhead costs to responsible cost centres are now clearly spelt out: **direct; reciprocal allocation;** and the **step-down** method.

The Standards for both Units are reproduced in full in the Interactive Text for each Unit and in the combined Devolved Assessment Kit for these Units.

ASSESSMENT STRATEGY

A central assessment is a means of collecting evidence that you have the **essential knowledge and understanding** which underpins competence. It is also a means of collecting evidence across the **range of contexts** for the standards, and of your ability to **transfer skills**, knowledge and understanding to different situations. Thus, although central assessments contain practical tests linked to the performance criteria, they also focus on the underpinning knowledge and understanding. You should in addition expect each central assessment to contain tasks taken from across a broad range of the standards.

Unit 4 Central Assessment

Each central assessment will last for three hours and will be divided into three sections. The first section will contain the scenario on which most of the tasks will be based. Although the extensive use of computers in accounting should be recognised, in order to meet the requirements of the standards it will be necessary to base the tasks on an organisation or organisations using manual systems of accounting. Where records are kept, these will consist of a general ledger, where double entry takes place, a sales ledger and a purchases ledger. Candidates can assume that the debtors' control account and creditors' control account will be contained in the general ledger forming part of the double entry. The individual accounts of debtors and creditors will be in the debtors' ledger and creditors' ledger and will therefore be regarded as memoranda accounts. Care should be taken by candidates in central assessments when identifying specific accounts. This is particularly important with the debtors' control account and creditors' control account. Merely labelling these 'debtors' and 'creditors' will not be acceptable. Systems used in central assessments may also refer to day books, and candidates should be familiar with the purpose and use of these as books of original entry.

Section 1

This section will include one or more accounting exercises from the following:

- **Trial balance**

  Example task: Preparation of a trial balance from a list of balances given.

- **Extended trial balance**

  Example tasks: Completion of the adjustments columns from information given. Extension of relevant figures into profit and loss and balance sheet columns.

  Note. Exercises involving the extended trial balance will not necessarily include all of the columns. Tasks could, for example, be based entirely around the initial balances and the adjustments columns. In this case the remaining columns would not be required for the assessment.

- **Identification and correction of errors**

  Examples tasks: Candidates are given a number of transactions and entries made. Errors and correcting journal entries are to be identified.

- **Suspense accounts**

  Example tasks: Suspense account required to balance a trial balance. Correcting entries to be identified to eliminate the suspense account balance.

- **Bank reconciliation statements**

  Example tasks: Preparation of a statement to reconcile the opening balances and preparation of a further statement to reconcile the closing balances of a cash book and a bank statement.

- **Control accounts**

  Example tasks: Preparation of a debtors' control account from information given and reconciliation with the total of the sales ledger balances.

Section 2

This section will consist of a number of short-answer questions designed to assess knowledge, understanding and communication skills. The tasks will be drawn from across the whole range of the standards for the unit and may require brief explanations, calculations, accounting entries, selection from a number of given possible answers or similar responses. One or more of the tasks will require a memo, letter or notes to be written.

Section 3

This section will comprise one or more practical exercises concerned with the processing, restructuring and production of information for different types of organisations. Candidates will be expected to be able to produce:

- Manufacturing accounts from data given

- Information from data given and/or incomplete records for sole traders, partnerships and clubs

The processing, restructuring and production of information includes, for example:

- Calculation of opening and/or closing capital (accumulated fund for clubs).

- Restructuring the cash and/or bank account.

- Preparation of total debtors' account and total creditors' account to calculate, for example, sales and purchases.

- Production of simple statements showing the calculation of gross profit and/or net profit and listing assets, liabilities and capital (or equivalent for clubs); these statements to summarise figures or to ascertain missing items of information.

- Use of mark-up and margin. (The use of other accounting ratios is outside the scope of this unit.)

- Production of other statements and/or restructured ledger accounts, for example to calculate expenses paid, expense profit and loss figures, accruals and prepayments, profit or loss on the sale of an asset, provisions and subscriptions for the period.

Unit 5 Central Assessment

The central assessment will consist of three sections. Sections 1 and 2 will assess elements 5.1 and 5.2 and Section 3 will assess element 5.3. Section 1, which will be written as a case study, will consist of several numerical tasks that will test competency in technical skills. Section 2 will consist of short questions that will arise from the tasks in Section 1. Section 3 will consist of the preparation of a standard costing report, including the compilation of variances. Some variances might be given, and some might have been calculated in a task in Section 1. A report may be requested upon the results obtained that analyses, identifies and presents information on efficiency, capacity and activity, and expenditure. Alternatively, the assessment may call for the calculation of control ratios for efficiency, capacity and activity and a report thereon.

The central assessment will be three hours in duration and the recommended time split will be two hours for Sections 1 and 2 and one hour for Section 3.

There is a degree of overlap between the elements, where 5.1 and 5.2 require knowledge and understanding of variance reports whilst 5.3 focuses on standard cost reports. In Section 1, the calculation of sub-variances for material, labour or overheads might be assessed in a task and then the results taken forward to a cost report in Section 3. A further calculation of variances for a different cost element might be required in Section 3. There will be no repetition of tasks in Section 1 and Section 3, in so far as variance calculations for the same element of cost will not be asked for in each section.

The report in Section 3 will be the only occasion within the central assessment where a discursive testing of knowledge and understanding is required through the medium of a structured report. Consequently, the report will be expected to communicate and analyse information clearly in a manner that shows clear understanding of an organisation's accounting systems and reporting cycle. Assessment of variances in Section 1 will be through knowledge of skills, with the short questions in Section 2 bringing out relevant understanding.

The short questions in Section 2 will test knowledge and understanding by a combination of discursive tasks, short computations, graphical presentations and double entry.

There have been no major changes for the purposes of central assessment between elements 5.1 and 5.2 and the corresponding elements in the old Unit 6. What changes there have been mean that process costing will no longer be assessed, and more emphasis will be put upon the **behaviour** of given costs.

Element 5.1 includes:

- Analysis of the effect of changing activity level in unit costs.
- The distinction between fixed and variable costs.

Element 5.2 includes:

- Nature and significance of overhead costs, fixed costs and variable costs.
- Effects of changes in capacity levels.
- The distinction between fixed and variable costs.

This will mean that tasks will be set assessing knowledge and understanding in the following manner:

- Changes in unit cost at different levels of activity will be assessable.

- The effect on total costs of changing activity will be assessable.

    Competence in this might be assessed through a task that requires understanding of the high-low technique. Such a tasks would only focus on fixed and variable cost and would not take into account stepped fixed cost and semi-variable cost. Knowledge and understanding of stepped fixed costs and semi-variable costs will be assessed only through the short questions in Section 2.

- Methods of reapportionment of service cost centres to production cost centres are clearly spelt out (direct, reciprocal allocation and step down method) and these will be assessable.

- The knowledge and understanding of activity-based systems is now expanded to include cost pools. However, it must be borne in mind that this unit is an introduction to costing and will focus upon traditional methods of overhead apportionment and absorption. Knowledge and understanding of Activity-Based Costing (ABC) will only be assessed as a contrast to the traditional methods through the short questions in Section 2. A more detailed understanding of ABC is beyond the scope of this unit and the subject will be explored in more detail at Technician level.

- Overhead variance calculations as outlined will now be assessable in either Section 1 or Section 3.

- Job/batch costing will be assessed in Section 1 as a separate task calling upon data from other tasks within the Section.

- There will be no radical change in the style of tasks in Section 1 from the current format of central assessment for Unit 6 other than that there will no longer be requests for a report/memo to assess understanding. Understanding will be assessed through the short questions in Section 2.

CENTRAL ASSESSMENT TECHNIQUE

Passing central assessments at this level is half about having the knowledge, and half about doing yourself full justice on the day. You must have the right **technique**.

> **The day of the central assessment**

1 Set at least one **alarm** (or get an alarm call) for a morning central assessment

2 Have **something to eat** but beware of eating too much; you may feel sleepy if your system is digesting a large meal

3 Allow plenty of **time to get to where you are sitting the central assessment**; have your route worked out in advance and listen to news bulletins to check for potential travel problems

4 **Don't forget** pens, pencils, rulers, erasers

5 Put **new batteries** into your calculator and take a spare set (or a spare calculator)

6 **Avoid discussion** about the central assessment with other candidates outside the venue

> **Technique in the central assessment**

1 *Read the instructions (the 'rubric') on the front of the paper carefully*

Check that the format hasn't changed.

2 *Select questions carefully*

Read through the paper once, then quickly jot down key points against each question in a second read through.

3 *Plan your attack carefully*

Consider the **order** in which you are going to tackle questions. It is a good idea to start with your best question to boost your morale and get some easy marks 'in the bag'.

4 *Check the time allocation for each question*

Each mark carries with it a **time allocation** of 1.8 minutes (including time for reading and selecting questions). A 20 mark question should be completed in 36 minutes. When time is up, you must go on to the next question or part. Going even one minute over the time allowed brings you a lot closer to failure.

5 *Read the question carefully and plan your answer*

Read through the question again very carefully when you come to answer it. Plan your answer to ensure that you **keep to the point**. Two minutes of planning plus eight minutes of writing is virtually certain to earn you more marks than ten minutes of writing.

6 *Produce relevant answers*

Particularly with written answers, make sure you **answer the question set,** and not the question you would have preferred to have been set.

7   _Gain the easy marks_

Include the obvious if it answers the question, and don't try to produce the perfect answer.

Don't get bogged down in small parts of questions. If you find a part of a question difficult, get on with the rest of the question. If you are having problems with something, the chances are that everyone else is too.

8   _Produce an answer in the correct format_

The assessor will state in the requirements the format in which the question should be answered, for example in a report or memorandum.

9   _Follow the assessor's instructions_

You will annoy the assessor if you ignore him or her. The **assessor will state** whether he or she wishes you to 'discuss', 'comment', 'evaluate' or 'recommend'.

10 _Lay out your numerical computations and use workings correctly_

Make sure the layout fits the **type of question** and is in a style the assessor likes.

Show all your **workings** clearly and explain what they mean. Cross reference them to your solution. This will help the assessor to follow your method (this is of particular importance where there may be several possible answers).

11 _Present a tidy paper_

You are a professional, and it should show in the **presentation of your work**. Students are penalised for poor presentation and so you should make sure that you write legibly, label diagrams clearly and lay out your work neatly. Markers of scripts each have hundreds of papers to mark; a badly written scrawl is unlikely to receive the same attention as a neat and well laid out paper.

12 _Stay until the end of the central assessment_

Use any spare time **checking and rechecking** your script.

13 _Don't worry if you feel you have performed badly in the central assessment_

It is more than likely that the other candidates will have found the assessment difficult too. Don't forget that there is a competitive element in these assessments. As soon as you get up to leave the venue, **forget** that central assessment and think about the next - or, if it is the last one, celebrate!

14 _Don't discuss a central assessment with other candidates_

This is particularly the case if you **still have other central assessments to sit**. Even if you have finished, you should put it out of your mind until the day of the results. Forget about assessments and relax!

Unit 4
Question Bank

Country Crafts (December 1993)

The suggested time allocation for this extended trial balance exercise is 80 minutes.

Country Crafts Ltd is a small business started in 1989. It buys in craft items, for example, pottery, hand-made clothes and wooden toys from a large number of small craft producers, and then sells them to craft shops throughout the country.

The rented premises consist of a warehouse containing racks and bins to hold the craft products along with an adjoining office and garage. The company owns two delivery vans, used for both collections and deliveries, and two company cars.

The company was started by two friends, Sandip Patel and Abdul Mohim, who met on a small business training course in Leicester. Sandip has responsibility for buying and selling and has built up a network of small craftworkers who make stock for him. Abdul is responsible for the running of the warehouse and the office and the administration of the business.

In addition to the two owners, the business employs two drivers, a warehouseman, two accounts clerks and a secretary.

You are the senior of the two accounts clerks and you are responsible for the nominal ledger.

The company's accounts are currently operated using a manual system, but computerisation of the accounts should take place in the near future and some equipment has recently been purchased.

The sales ledger holds at present about 100 accounts; the company has no cash customers.

All purchases of craft products are on credit and the purchase ledger contains about 80 accounts.

There are very few cash transactions. Any that do occur, for example, window cleaning, office sundries and travel expenses, are dealt with by a simple petty cash system. A £50 float is maintained, expenditure is recorded in a simple petty cash book and at irregular intervals the expenditure is posted to the nominal ledger.

Depreciation policy

Rates:			
	Motor vehicles	25% pa	straight line
	Office furniture	10% pa	straight line
	Computer equipment	$33^1/_3$% pa	straight line

Depreciation is charged a full year in the year of purchase and is not charged for in the year of sale.

Zero scrap values are assumed.

Fixed asset information

Motor vehicles

Delivery vans	H247AFE	K174RFU
Date of purchase	9.8.90	12.8.92
Cost	£16,200	£19,800
Company cars	J168TFE	J169TFE
Date of purchase	11.9.91	11.9.91
Cost	£9,200	£9,200

Office furniture

All office furniture was purchased upon incorporation of the business on 1 September 1989.

Cost	£4,850

Computer equipment

Date of purchase	1 June 1993
Cost	£16,830

Mark-up policy

The company marks up all its products by 100% on cost.

Data

(a) Listed below is the company's trial balance at 31 December 1993.

COUNTRY CRAFTS LIMITED
TRIAL BALANCE AS AT 31 DECEMBER 1993

	Dr £	Cr £
Motor vans (cost)	36,000	
Motor cars (cost)	18,400	
Office furniture (cost)	4,850	
Computer equipment (cost)	16,830	
Motor vans (provision for dep'n)		17,100
Motor cars (provision for dep'n)		9,200
Office furniture (provision for dep'n)		1,940
Computer equipment (provision for dep'n)		
Stock	24,730	
Debtors control	144,280	
Bank		610
Cash	50	
Creditors control		113,660
Sales		282,490
Purchases	152,140	
Rent	12,480	
Heat and light	1,840	
Wages and salaries	75,400	
Office expenses	7,900	
Motor expenses	14,890	
Depreciation (motor vans)		
Depreciation (office furniture)		
Depreciation (computer equipment)		
Share capital		50,000
Profit and loss		35,850
VAT		12,640
Suspense	13,700	
	523,490	523,490

(b) Adjustments need to be made for the following.

   (i) On 2 December 1993 a new delivery van, L673NFU, was purchased for £22,600. Van H247AFE was given in part exchange, the balance of £17,600 being paid for by cheque and debited to the suspense account.

   (ii) On 4 December 1993, as a cost-saving measure, company car J168TFE was sold for £3,900 and the receipt credited to the suspense account.

   (iii) On 20 December 1993 the company had allowed a local organisation to use its car park and adjacent field for a Car Boot Sale. For this service the company was paid £250.00. This amount had been credited to the sales account.

(c) The following additional matters need to be taken into account.

   (i) Depreciation for the year ended 31 December 1993 is to be provided for.

   (ii) On 15 December 1993 a rack full of china craft products fell in the warehouse. These products, valued at £2,300 at selling price, were so badly damaged that they had to be thrown away. The Raven Moon Insurance Company have agreed to compensate for the damage except for the first £200. A claim has been submitted, but so far no payment has been received.

   (iii) The stocktake on 30 December 1993 revealed stock at cost price of £31,640.

      Two batches of stock, however, were of particular note.

      (1) A batch of Baby Beatrice mugs, value at selling price £320, were judged to be saleable for only £120.

      (2) A batch of Windsor Fire Damage plates, value at selling price £620, were judged to be saleable for only £350.

   (iv) Several small customers had been going out of business recently, probably because of the recession. The company's accountant had therefore judged it prudent to create a provision for doubtful debts representing 5% of the trade debtors figure at the year end.

(v)   Petty cash transactions for December were as follows.

December 3	Window cleaning	£10.00
December 8	Tea and coffee	£4.40
December 12	Xmas decorations	£28.60
December 20	Petty cash float replenished	£50.00

These transactions, including the withdrawal from the bank, have not yet been entered into the company's books.

(vi)   The electricity bill for the September, October, November quarter for £315 had been received on 16 December and entered into the purchase ledger. It is normal for the electricity bill for the December, January, February quarter to be double that for the previous quarter.

(vii) The rent of £7,488 per annum is paid annually in advance on 1 September.

Task 1

Prepare journal entries for the transactions listed in (b) above. Narratives are required. Use the journal form on Page 6.

Task 2

Enter all the account balances, including those adjusted in Task 1, in the first two columns of the extended trial balance. Use the blank ETB on Page 7.

Task 3

Make appropriate entries in the adjustment columns of the extended trial balance.

Task 4

Extend the figures into the extended trial balance columns for profit and loss account and balance sheet. Total all columns, transferring the balance of profit or loss as appropriate.

A suggested answer to this exercise is given on page 85.

JOURNAL

Details	DR £	CR £

COUNTRY CRAFTS Account	Trial balance Debit £	Trial balance Credit £	Adjustments Debit £	Adjustments Credit £	Accrued £	Prepaid £	Profit and loss a/c Debit £	Profit and loss a/c Credit £	Balance sheet Debit £	Balance sheet Credit £
Motor vans (cost)										
Motor cars (cost)										
Office furniture (cost)										
Computer equipment (cost)										
Motor vans (prov for depreciation)										
Motor cars (prov for depreciation)										
Office furniture (prov for depreciation)										
Computer equipment (prov for depreciation)										
Stock										
Debtors control										
Bank										
Cash										
Creditors control										
Sales										
Purchases										
Rent										
Heat and light										
Wages and salaries										
Office expenses										
Motor expenses										
Depreciation (motor vans)										
Depreciation (motor cars)										
Depreciation (office furniture)										
Depreciation (computer equipment)										
Share capital										
Profit and loss										
VAT										
SUBTOTAL										
Profit for the year										
TOTAL										

Futon Enterprises (June 1994)

The suggested time allocation for this extended trial balance exercise is 80 minutes.

Jason Sarmiento, trading as Futon Enterprises, is a sole trader assembling and selling futons. A futon is a Japanese-style bed, consisting of a slatted wooden frame and a mattress. Jason buys in the pre-cut timber and the mattresses and assembles the futons for sale through his retail shop in Lincoln and by mail order.

The assembly takes place in a small workshop to the rear of the shop and is carried out by a full-time assembler. The business also employs a driver, a secretary and you, the accounts clerk. Jason spends most of his time in the shop and dealing with the mail order side of the business.

The business accounts are currently operated using a manual system, though Jason is actively engaged in investigating computerised accounting systems.

A very simple sales ledger is operated and the purchase ledger contains about 20 accounts. There are few cash transactions. Any that do occur are handled through a traditional petty cash book. A £50 cash float is maintained and at weekly intervals the expenditure is posted to the nominal ledger and the float replenished.

Accounting policies

1   *Manufacturing*

Purchases of raw materials are posted to a materials account. The assembler's wages are posted to the production wages account. No separate production overheads account is maintained.

It has been agreed that finished goods stocks should be valued at a standard cost of production, calculated as follows per futon.

	£
Materials	36.00
Production wages	7.00
Overheads	5.00
	48.00

2   *Depreciation*

Rates:	Assembling machinery	10% per annum straight line
	Delivery van	30% per annum reducing balance
	Furniture and fittings	20% per annum straight line

Depreciation is charged a full year in the year of purchase and is not charged in the year of sale. Zero scrap values are assumed.

3   *Mark-up*

The company normally marks up all its products at 75% on standard production costs.

Fixed asset information

	Date of purchase	Cost	
		£	£
Assembling machinery	1.6.90		3,650
Delivery van (see note (b)(i) below)	1.8.93		12,400
Furniture and fittings			
Shop fittings	1.6.90	7,200	
Office furniture	1.6.90	2,350	
Reception (materials only)			
(see note (b)(ii) below)	1.9.93	1,240	
			10,790

Data

(a)   Listed below is the company's trial balance at 31 May 1994.

FUTON ENTERPRISES
TRIAL BALANCE AS AT 31 MAY 1994

	Dr £	Cr £
Delivery vans (cost)	12,000	
Delivery vans (provision for depreciation)		7,884
Assembling machinery (cost)	3,650	
Assembling machinery (provision for depreciation)		1,095
Furniture and fittings (cost)	10,790	
Furniture and fittings (provision for depreciation)		5,730
Raw materials stock	1,320	
Finished goods stock	1,440	
Sales ledger total	1,860	
Bank		320
Cash	50	
Purchase ledger total		4,265
Sales		120,240
Materials	35,465	
Production wages	12,480	
Driver's wages	11,785	
Salaries	22,460	
Employer's national insurance	4,365	
Motor expenses	2,160	
Rent	3,930	
Sundry expenses	3,480	
VAT		1,220
Inland Revenue		1,365
Drawings	12,400	
Capital		7,516
Suspense	10,000	
	149,635	149,635

(b) Adjustments need to be made for the following.

 (i)   A new delivery van was purchased for £12,400 on 1 August 1993. The old delivery van, originally purchased for £12,000 on 1 August 1990, was given in part exchange; the balance of £10,000 was paid for by cheque and debited to Suspense Account.

 (ii) The reception area was re-built in the first week of September 1993. This work was carried out by the assembler as business was rather slack at that time. He spent the whole of the first week in September on this task; his pay is £12,480 per annum.

 (iii) Jason gave two futons as Christmas presents in December 1993. An account was opened in the sales ledger to record these transactions.

(c) The following additional information needs to be taken into account.

 (i)   Depreciation for the year ended 31 May 1994 is to be provided for.

 (ii) The stocktake at 31 May 1994 has revealed the following.

 Stock of timber, mattresses and sundry materials = £1,526
 23 fully completed futons were in stock

 There was no work in progress.

 (iii) The electricity bill for £180 covering the February, March, April 1994 quarter had been received on 15 May and entered into the purchase ledger. Electricity usage is relatively even throughout the year. Electricity is included within sundry expenses.

 (iv) On 12 May the delivery van was involved in an accident, suffering minor damage. The repairs, costing £164, have been carried out and the cost included in motor expenses. A letter has been received today from the Mercury Insurance Company agreeing to compensate for all but the first £50 of the repair costs.

 (v)   A customer, T Young, who bought two futons at the regular price in July 1993, has disappeared without paying. It has been decided to write off the amount owing.

 (vi) The rent of £3,144 per annum is paid annually in advance on 1 September.

Task 1

Prepare journal entries for the transactions listed in (b) above. Narratives are required. Use the blank journal form on Page 11.

Task 2

Enter all the account balances, including those adjusted in Task 1 above, in the first two columns of the extended trial balance. Use the blank ETB on Page 12.

Task 3

Make appropriate entries in the adjustments columns of the extended trial balance. Create additional accounts as required.

Task 4

Extend the figures into the extended trial balance columns for profit and loss account and balance sheet. Total all columns, transferring the balance of profit or loss as appropriate.

A suggested answer to this exercise is given on page 88.

JOURNAL		
Details	DR £	CR £

FUTON ENTERPRISES	Trial balance		Adjustments		Accrued	Prepaid	Profit and loss a/c		Balance sheet	
Account	Debit	Credit	Debit	Credit			Debit	Credit	Debit	Credit
	£	£	£	£	£	£	£	£	£	£
Delivery vans (cost)										
Assembling machine (cost)										
Furniture and fittings (cost)										
Delivery vans (prov for depreciation)										
Assembling machine (prov for depreciation)										
Furniture and fittings (prov for depreciation)										
Stock: raw materials										
Stock: finished goods										
Sales ledger total										
Bank										
Cash										
Purchase ledger total										
Sales										
Materials										
Production wages										
Driver's wages										
Salaries										
Employer's NI										
Motor expenses										
Rent										
Sundry expenses										
VAT										
Inland Revenue										
Drawings										
Capital										
Depreciation: delivery vans										
Deprecation: assembling machine										
Depreciation: furniture and fittings										
SUBTOTAL										
Profit for the year										
TOTAL										

Kidditoys (December 1994)

The suggested time allocation for this extended trial balance exercise is 80 minutes.

Kidditoys is a retail shop which specialises in the sale of unusual toys, games and other baby products. The business was started in December 1987 and is owned and run by Sophie Stewart.

About half the sales of the business are cash sales through the shop, the remainder being on mail order. Mail order customers pay cash with order.

Sophie employs one sales assistant and one packing assistant.

Her present manual system of bookkeeping comprises a purchase ledger with approximately 30 active accounts, a nominal ledger and a petty cash book. A petty cash float of £50 is maintained for sundry expenses and is replenished as required. A further cash float of £50 is maintained in the sales till. All cash receipts are banked daily.

You are an accounting technician who is helping Sophie to prepare the business's accounts up to the trial balance stage.

Fixed asset information

	Date of purchase	Cost £	Expected useful economic life (years)
Motor van	07.08.93	12,640	5
Shop fittings	10.12.87	3,240	10
Office equipment	08.04.91	4,250	5

All fixed assets are depreciated on a straight line basis using the expected useful economic lives, above, and zero-estimated residual values.

Depreciation is charged a full year in the year of purchase and is not charged for in the year of sale.

Other information

Average mark up is 100%.

The VAT rate is 17.5%.

Data

(a) The following list of balances has been extracted from the nominal ledger at the business's year end, 30 November 1994.

	£
Sales	392,182
Sales returns	1,214
Purchases	208,217
Purchase returns	643
Stock	32,165
Wages	50,000
Rent	27,300
Rates	8,460
Light and heat	2,425
Office expenses	3,162
Selling expenses	14,112
Motor expenses	14,728
Sundry expenses	6,560
Motor vans (cost)	12,640
Motor vans (provision for depreciation) at 1.12.93	2,528
Shop fittings (cost)	3,240
Shop fittings (provision for depreciation) at 1.12.93	1,944
Office equipment (cost)	4,250
Office equipment (provision for depreciation) at 1.12.93	2,550
Cash	100
Bank current account (debit balance)	4,420
Bank investment account	68,340
Interest received	3,280
	£
Purchase ledger total	27,683
Capital	22,145
VAT (credit balance)	6,420
Suspense (see note (b)(ii))	1,958

(b) After extracting the balances listed in (a), the following six errors and omissions were discovered.

(i) Credit purchases of £954 had been correctly posted to the purchases account, but had been debited in the supplier's account (T Ditton).

(ii) The shop had been entirely re-fitted during the year. The old fittings had been sold off to the local Boy Scouts for £50. This had been debited in the bank account, but had been credited in the suspense account.

The invoice for the new shop fittings, for £9,620, had been received from Kingston Displays Ltd on 15 November. This invoice had not yet been entered into the accounts. Sophie intended to pay the invoice in January after the Christmas sales period. The new shop fittings are expected to have a useful economic life of 10 years.

(iii) Sophie paid herself a 'wage' of £2,000 per calendar month which she debited to wages account.

(iv) During the year an invoice for £843 (for zero-rated supplies) had been received from a supplier (E Molesey). When payment was made, Sophie accidentally made out the cheque for £840. Sophie noticed this error and contacted E Molesey who told her to ignore such a small sum of money. No adjustment has yet been made for this discrepancy.

(v) During the year Sophie gave away a number of toys from the shop as presents to relatives and friends. She kept a record of these, which came to £640 at selling price, including VAT, but has not so far entered the transactions into the accounts.

(vi) The company's current bank account statement arrived on 30 November 1994. This showed interest received for the month of November at £9. This has not yet been entered into the accounts.

(c) The following additional matters need to be taken into account.

(i) Depreciation for the year ended 30 November 1994 is to be provided for.

(ii) The stock in the shop at 30 November 1994 was valued at £42,120 at selling price.

(iii) Rent was £2,100 per month payable in advance. The rent for December 1994 had already been paid.

(iv) Business rates are paid half yearly on 1 May and 1 November. The business rates bill for the period 1 April 1994 - 31 March 1995 amounted to £6,240.

(v) The electricity bill for £318 covering the July, August and September quarter had been received on 15 October. This had been entered into the purchase ledger and duly paid. Electricity usage can be considered to be relatively even throughout the year.

Task 1

Prepare journal entries for the transactions listed in (b). Narratives are required. Use the journal voucher on the next two pages.

Task 2

Enter all the account balances, including those adjusted in Task 1 above, in the first two columns of the Extended Trial Balance shown on Page 18. Note that some of the balances have already been filled in for you. Create additional accounts as required.

Task 3

Make appropriate entries in the adjustments columns of the Extended Trial Balance. Create additional accounts as required.

Do not extend the figures in the extended trial balance into the profit and loss account and balance sheet columns.

Note. All final workings should be clearly shown in your finished answers.

A suggested answer to this exercise is given on page 90.

JOURNAL		
Details	DR £	CR £

JOURNAL		
Details	DR £	CR £

KIDDITOYS

Account	Trial balance		Adjustments		Accrued	Prepaid
	Debit	Credit	Debit	Credit		
	£	£	£	£	£	£
Sales						
Sales returns						
Purchases						
Purchase returns						
Stock	32,165					
Wages						
Rent	27,300					
Rates	8,460					
Light and heat	2,425					
Office expenses	3,162					
Selling expenses	14,112					
Motor expenses	14,728					
Sundry expenses	6,560					
Motor vans (cost)	12,640					
Shop fittings (cost)						
Office equipment (cost)	4,250					
Motor vans (prov for depreciation)						
Shop fittings (prov for depreciation)						
Office equipment (prov for depreciation)						
Cash	100					
Bank current account						
Bank investment account						
Interest received						
Capital						
VAT						
SUBTOTAL						
Profit for the year						
TOTAL						

Country Crafts (December 1993)

The following short answer questions are mainly based on the scenario outlined in the extended trial balance exercise Country Crafts (Page 3). You may have to refer back to the information in that exercise in order to answer the questions.

The suggested time allocation for this set of short answer questions is 40 minutes.

1   The company had bought a small item of computer software, cost £32.50 earlier in the year. This had been treated as office equipment. Do you agree with this treatment? Give brief reasons.

2   If the company had depreciated its motor vehicles at 50% per annum on a reducing balance basis, what would have been the profit or loss on the company car sold on 4 December 1993?

3   If the organisation which had rented the car park and field for the car boot sale had rented the field for a similar event in January 1994 and had paid £250 in advance, how would that transaction be treated in the 1993 accounts? Briefly explain the effect in the 1994 accounts.

4   (a)   In manual accounts transposition errors can occur, for example, a credit purchase entered in the purchases a/c as £1,234, but entered in the supplier's account as £1,423. Can such errors occur in computerised accounting systems? Give reasons.

    (b)   In manual accounts, errors of principle can occur. For example, the purchase of a piece of office machinery might be posted to the office expenses a/c. Can such errors occur in computerised accounting systems? Give reasons.

5   You have heard a rumour that one of your customers, who owes you £1,640 is about to go out of business. Should this debt be treated as a bad debt, a doubtful debt or should the rumour be ignored? Give reasons.

6   Explain fully what the balance on VAT account represents.

7   If one of the company's vans had to have its engine replaced at a cost of £1,800, would this represent capital or revenue expenditure? Give brief reasons.

8   If the company decided it needed a china coffee set to use to entertain potential customers, and it took a suitable one from the stock in the warehouse, how would you record this in the books of the company?

A suggested answer to this exercise is given on page 93.

Futon Enterprises (June 1994)

The following short answer questions are mainly based on the scenario outlined in the extended trial balance exercise Futon Enterprises (Page 8). You may have to refer back to the information in that exercise in order to answer the questions.

The suggested time allocation for this set of short answer questions is 40 minutes.

1   Assume that two of the futons had been used as a shop window display and had faded somewhat. If it had been decided that the mattress required replacing at a cost of £18 each to make the futons saleable at a price of £50 each, how would this have affected the closing stock valuation?

    Give reasons for your answer.

2   What is the net book value of the assembling machinery at 31 May 1994? Is this the amount it is estimated would be realised if the machinery were disposed of at that date?

    Briefly justify your answer.

3   Give one reason why the company might have chosen reducing balance as the method for depreciating its delivery vans.

4   If the customer, T Young, whose amount owing in (c)(v) had been written off, subsequently paid later this year, how would you account for the payment?

5   Explain what the balance on Inland Revenue Account represents.

6   If the delivery van was refitted with wooden racks by the assembler in half an hour's spare time and using materials at a cost price of £24, would this be treated as capital or revenue expenditure?

Give reasons.

7   An acquaintance wishes to use the shop to display and sell framed photographs. She will pay £40 per month for this service.

(a)   How would you account for this transaction each month?

(b)   If, at the end of the year, the acquaintance owed one month's rental, how would this be treated in the accounts?

8   The business maintains a traditional petty cash book. At the end of each week, the petty cash book is balanced, the totals of the analysis columns posted to the relevant accounts and the float of £50 replenished.

(a)   Into which account would the total of the VAT analysis column be posted and would this be a debit or credit entry?

(b)   What would the total of the VAT column represent?

(c)   If the petty cash expenditure in one week had been £37, what would be the double entry to replenish the float?

A suggested answer to this exercise is given on page 93.

Kidditoys (December 1994)

The following short answer questions are mainly based on the scenario outlined in the extended trial balance exercise Kidditoys (Page 13). You may have to refer back to the information in that exercise in order to answer this question.

The suggested time allocation for this set of short answer questions is 40 minutes.

1   Give a reason why Sophie Stewart does not have any bad debts.

2   Explain in detail what the balance on her VAT a/c represents.

3   When cash sales are banked, which accounts would be debited and credited?

4   What is the net book value of the delivery van at 30 November 1994? What does this amount represent?

5   Assume that some of the shop's window display stock, comprising four dolls, had deteriorated. In their damaged state the dolls could be sold for only £5 each. Their original sales price was £16 each.

(a)   How would this have affected the closing stock valuation at 30 November 1994?
(b)   What would have been the effect on the company's profit?

6   Occasionally Kidditoys has to pay a special delivery charge on deliveries of toys it urgently requires. How should this delivery charge be dealt with in the accounts?

7   Sophie is considering sending a quantity of goods to John King on a sale or return basis. How should the transaction be dealt with when the goods are first delivered to John King?

Give reasons for your answer.

8   The company is considering buying some new software for the office word processor at a cost of £85. It is expected to be in use for five years. How would you deal with this transaction in the accounts?

Give detailed reasons for your answer.

9   If, in preparing the extended trial balance for Kidditoys, the business was found to be making a loss:

(a)   would the loss appear in the debit or credit column of the profit and loss account balances;

(b)   how would the loss be dealt with in the balance sheet balances columns?

10 Using your figures from the extended trial balance in Part 1, complete the profit and loss a/c and balance sheet balances columns for stock, below.

Profit and Loss A/c		Balance Sheet Balances	
Dr	*Cr*	*Dr*	*Cr*

A suggested answer to this exercise is given on page 94.

Brian Hope (Sample)

The suggested time allocation for this incomplete records exercise is 60 minutes.

Data

You have been asked to help in preparing the accounts of Brian Hope. Brian started in business in 1991 doing repair and servicing of electrical equipment and he works in a rented workshop. So far he has not kept proper records of his transactions. His accounts to 31 December 1991 were prepared for him on the basis of enquiries and the closing position was then shown as follows.

	£	£
Bank balance	190	
Cash in hand	10	
Van	6,000	
Stock of materials	1,210	
Trade debtors and creditors	1,420	2,220
Vehicle repair bill owing		80
Insurance prepaid	340	
Rent prepaid	400	
Capital		7,270
	9,570	9,570

You have started by summarising the bank statements for the year ended 31 December 1992 as follows.

	£	£
Opening balance		260
Cash paid in		510
Receipts from debtors		21,120
		21,890
Payments to trade creditors (see (g) below)	3,930	
New vehicle (less trade-in)	3,600	
Vehicle running expenses	1,040	
Rent	2,640	
Insurance	960	
Other expenses	1,710	
Hope's drawings	8,000	
		21,880
Closing balance		10

You discover the following information regarding Hope's 1992 transactions in the year to 31 December 1992 and the closing position.

(a) He was paid in cash for some of the work done but cannot trace how much. However, you can find sufficient evidence to show that the debtors outstanding at the end of the year totalled £1,120 though £90 of this is probably irrecoverable. Hope does keep copies of all the invoices to his customers and these total £26,720 but he remembers allowing a customer £300 after a charge was disputed.

(b) Outstanding invoices from trade creditors at the end of the year totalled £2,460. Hope says that he is usually allowed a cash discount by one of the suppliers and the total discount for the year is estimated at £200.

(c) The rent was £200 per month until the end of August but was then increased to £240. Hope usually pays two months together in advance and has already paid (in December) for January and February 1993.

(d) At the end of the year £60 is outstanding for petrol and the insurance has been prepaid by £380.

(e) Hope changed the van at the end of December buying a new one for £8,000 with a trade-in allowance for the old one of £4,400. He thinks he agreed last year to a depreciation charge of 20% per annum on book value (but this would not apply in 1992 to the new vehicle just purchased).

(f) No adequate records of cash transactions have been kept but as indicated above it is known that customers often paid their accounts in cash and that Hope frequently withdrew cash for his own personal use. He estimates that payments for vehicle running costs of £500 have been made from cash and a similar amount for other expenses. There is no closing balance of cash.

(g) At the beginning of the year there were cheques to trade creditors unpresented at the bank totalling £70 and at the end of the year the unpresented cheques to trade creditors totalled £210.

Tasks

From the above information you are asked to draw up the ledger accounts on page 24 for each of the following showing the balances to be carried forward at the end of the year or the amounts to be transferred to the profit and loss account. (Dates need not be shown in the accounts.)

Trade debtors
Trade creditors
Rent
Vehicles
Vehicle running expenses
Insurance
Cash
Drawings

A suggested answer to this exercise is given on page 96.

TRADE DEBTORS			

VEHICLE RUNNING EXPENSES			

TRADE CREDITORS			

INSURANCE			

RENT			

CASH			

VEHICLES			

DRAWINGS			

Kuldipa Potiwal (December 1993)

The suggested time allocation for this incomplete records exercise is 60 minutes.

A friend of yours from Leicester, Kuldipa Potiwal, runs a small computer games retail and mail order business, but she does not keep proper accounting records. She has now been approached by the Inland Revenue for the details of the profit she has earned for the last year. She has provided you with the following bank account summary for the year ended 31 October 1993.

BANK ACCOUNT SUMMARY

	£
Balance at bank (1 November 1992)	
Bank overdraft	3,250
Receipts	
Cash paid in	56,000
Cheques from debtors	46,000
Investment income	1,500
Rent received	2,500
Payments	
Payments to trade creditors	78,000
Rent and rates	6,400
Postage and packing costs	2,200
Motor expenses	5,050
Administration expenses	4,600

Additional information was provided as follows.

(a) Kuldipa intends to sell all her computer games at cost plus 50%.

(b) Before paying cash receipts into the bank, Kuldipa used some of the cash received to make a number of payments.

Wages of shop assistant and driver	£350 per week
Drawings	£220 per week
Administration expenses	£750 per annum

All cash is paid into the bank daily.

(c) The investment income was interest on her private investment account.

(d) Other balances were as follows.

	31 October 1992	31 October 1993
	£	£
Delivery van (valuation)	17,500	12,500
Stock of games	12,200	13,750
Trade creditors	9,000	13,400
Trade debtors	6,000	7,200
Rates paid in advance	500	200
Rent receivable	-	250
Administration expenses owing	175	215

(e) During the year a vanload of games being delivered to credit customers was stolen. The van was recovered, undamaged, but the games have not been recovered. The insurance company has agreed to pay for 50% of the stolen games, but payment has not yet been received.

Kuldipa Potiwal calculated from the copy delivery notes that the selling price value of the games stolen was £6,000.

(f) At Christmas 1992 Kuldipa Potiwal gave games as presents to her young relatives. The selling price of these games was £480.00.

Task 1

Prepare a detailed calculation of the net profit of the business for the year ended 31 October 1993.

Task 2

Calculate the balance of Kuldipa's capital account at 31 October 1993.

A suggested answer to this exercise is given on page 97.

Fancy Flowers (June 1994)

The suggested time allocation for this incomplete records exercise is 60 minutes.

You belong to a badminton club at the local leisure centre and always have a drink with one of your friends, Sarah Harvey, in the coffee shop after a game. Sarah is the owner of a small florist's business and has been trading for a year as Fancy Flowers. She has never kept proper books of account and has asked you to calculate her profit for the first year of trading which ended on 31 May 1994.

On 31 May you carried out a stocktake which revealed the following situation.

	Cost £	Mark up %
Pot plants	280	100
Roses	240	75
Tulips	160	75
Sprays	340	100
Plant food	80	50
Vases	520	100

A quarter of the pot plants were rather withered and Sarah thought she would have to throw them away. She thought a further quarter would have to be sold at cost price.

The roses were of a very high quality and Sarah thought she could probably sell them at a mark-up of 100%.

One of the sprays, costing £80, had been prepared for a customer who had never collected. This would have to be thrown away.

A box of ten vases, selling price £6 per vase, was badly damaged and would have to be thrown away.

You also elicit the following information.

(a) All sales of the business are cash sales.

(b) A summary of the bank statements revealed the following.

	£
Cash paid into the bank	31,420
Cheque payments	
To plant and sundries wholesalers	24,180
Rent	5,000
Business rates	420
Advertising	385
Insurance	390
Electricity	780
Sundry expenses	560
Interest charged by bank	84

(c) All the cash paid into the bank resulted from cash sales, except for an initial £5,000 invested by Sarah as start-up capital in the business.

(d) Before paying the cash sales into the bank, Sarah withdrew cash for the following purposes.

	£
Wages for self	14,200
Sundry expenses	345

She also retained £60 change in a cash tin after paying the remaining cash into the bank.

(e) From her file of purchase invoices, Sarah discovered that the following were unpaid.

	£
Purchase of cut flowers for May	850
Purchase of roses (28 May)	345
Electricity (quarter ended 30 April)	360
Advertising charges for May	45

(f) She pays rent of £1,000 per quarter in advance.

(g) She regularly takes home about £10 worth of flowers (at selling price) each week.

Task 1

Prepare a valuation of closing stock.

Task 2

Calculate the profit for the first year of trading for Fancy Flowers.

Task 3

Calculate the balance on capital account for Sarah at the end of the first year of trading.

Task 4

Comment briefly on the situation revealed. Show all your workings.

A suggested answer to this exercise is given on page 99.

Manuel

The suggested time allocation for this incomplete records exercise is 60 minutes.

Manuel has been required to write up the June accounts for the bar of a small hotel in Torquay while the usual bookkeeper, Polly, is on holiday. He finds bookkeeping very puzzling and has asked for your help. He provides you with the following information relating to transactions for the month.

(a) Bar takings (cash): £200

(b) Bar sales on credit to the Major, a valued customer: £100

(c) Wages (cash) £50

(d) Cash received from the Major for last month's bar bill: £80

(e) Cash banked: £300

(f) Wages (cheque): £40

(g) Bank charges notified by bank: £35

(h) Supplies purchased on credit from Torquay Wines: £500

(i) Payment to Torquay Wines by cheque of £300 less 5% discount for early payment

(j) Wine purchased on credit from Devon Wines, a local firm, on a sale or return basis: £175

(k) £100 worth of wine from Devon Wines sold at mark-up on cost of 20%, on credit to a Mr Twychin

(l) Wines returned to Devon Wines: £75

(m) Opening bank balance: £300, cash in till: £320

Task 1

Enter the above transactions into the following ledger accounts (shown below)

    Three column cash book
    Sales
    Purchases
    Major
    Wages
    Mr Twychin
    Bank charges
    Devon Wines
    Torquay wines

Task 2

Produce a partial trial balance as far as the information allows.

Note. There will be a difference on the trial balance.

CASH BOOK						
DETAIL	DISCOUNT	CASH	BANK	DISCOUNT	CASH	BANK
	£	£	£	£	£	£

SALES			

PURCHASES			

MAJOR			

WAGES			

MR TWYCHIN			
BPP Publishing			

BANK CHARGES			

DEVON WINES			

TORQUAY WINES			

PARTIAL TRIAL BALANCE AS AT 30 JUNE

	Dr	Cr
	£	£
Bank balance		
Cash in till		
Discounts		
Sales		
Purchases		
Major		
Wages		
Mr Twychin		
Bank charges		
Devon Wines		
Torquay Wines		
Difference	————	————
	════════	════════

A suggested answer to this exercise is given on page 100.

PRACTICE CENTRAL ASSESSMENT 1: HIGHBURY DISCS (JUNE 1995)

SECTION 1

The suggested time allocation for this extended trial balance exercise is 80 minutes.

You have been working for some months now as an accounting technician with Highbury Discs. The business specialises in recording and distributing compact discs of choral and organ music. Recordings are made on location and artists are paid a fixed fee plus a royalty based on the number of discs sold. Royalties are calculated and paid quarterly in arrears. The owners of the recording location are paid a fee for the hire of the location.

Anthony Sedgewick, the proprietor of Highbury Discs, uses only a minimum of high quality recording equipment, believing that a wise choice of recording venue and the optimal placing of a single microphone are the dominant factors in producing a good recording. All production work is subcontracted to independent operators. This approach has resulted in a number of recordings which have been highly praised in the specialist hi-fi press. The business sells to a number of UK stores, one of which acts as an agent for overseas sales.

The business rents a unit on an industrial estate. The premises are used for administration, distribution and the storage of recording equipment and stocks of compact discs.

The financial year for the business ended on 31 May 1995.

The following alphabetical list of balances has been taken from the business ledger as at 31 May 1995.

	£
Artists' fees and royalties	41,120
Bank and cash	1,420
Capital	26,449
Drawings	14,500
Employer's national insurance	3,619
Equipment (cost)	38,200
Equipment (provision for depreciation)	19,100
Loan	10,000
Loan interest	1,350
Mastering and production costs	143,400
Motor expenses	6,330
Motor vehicles (cost)	29,800
Motor vehicles (provision for depreciation)	17,880
Recording costs	12,550
Rent	13,000
Sales	307,800
Stocks of compact discs	22,500
Sundry creditors	4,080
Sundry debtors	12,500
Sundry expenses	1,270
VAT (amount owing)	3,250
Wages and salaries	47,000

Task 1

Enter the above balances into the first two columns of the extended trial balance provided on Page 33 and total the columns. The list of balances is provided on the left of the trial balance columns to help you.

HIGHBURY DISCS Account	Trial balance Debit £	Trial balance Credit £	Adjustments Debit £	Adjustments Credit £	Accrued £	Prepaid £	Profit and loss a/c Debit £	Profit and loss a/c Credit £	Balance sheet Debit £	Balance sheet Credit £
Artists' fees and royalties	41,120		4752		4752		45872			4752
Bank and cash	1,420			220					1200	
Capital		26,449							16610	26,449
Drawings	14,500		2110							
Employer's NI	3,619						3619		36	
Equipment (cost)	38,200								38,200	
Motor vehicles (cost)	29,800								29,800	
Equipment (prov for depreciation)		19,100		9550						28,650
Motor vehicles (prov for depreciation)		17,880		3576						21,456
Loan		10,000								10,000
Loan interest	1,350				150		1500			150
Mastering and production costs	143,400						143,400			
Motor expenses	6,330			2110			4220			
Recording costs	12,550						12,550			
Rent	13,000					1600	12,000		1,000	
Sales		307,800						307,800		
Stocks of compact discs	22,500						22,500			
Sundry creditors		4,080								4080
Sundry debtors	12,500		220						12720	
Sundry expenses	1,270						1270			
VAT (amount owing)		3,250								3250
Wages and salaries	47,000		13126				47,000 13126			
Depreciation										
Stock P+L				27,760				20,700		
Stock balance			27,100						27,100	
SUBTOTAL							307,057		50,052	48,787
Profit for the year	777,118						284,443			284,443
TOTAL	388,556	388,556	43,156	43,156	4902	1000	335,500	335,500	127,730	127,730

BPP Publishing   33

Task 2

The policy of the business is to provide for depreciation as follows.

Motor vehicles	30% per annum, reducing balance method, full year basis
Equipment	25% per annum, straight line method, full year basis

Depreciation for the year ended 31 May 1995 has not been recorded in the accounts.

Calculate the depreciation charge for the year ended 31 May 1995 and complete the following table.

	Depreciation charge for the year ended 31 May 1995 £
Motor vehicles	3576
Equipment	9550
TOTAL	13126

Task 3

Stocks of compact discs are valued at cost. Cost includes a share of the recording, mastering and production costs as well as any direct overheads attributable to that recording. Stocks as at 31 May 1995 have not been recorded in the accounting system. The following is an extract of the stock sheets as at 31 May 1995 along with Anthony Sedgewick's comments.

STOCK SHEETS

Title	Number of discs in stock	Total cost £	Total price to retailers £	Total recommended retail price £	Comments
Total b/f from previous pages	4,500	18,000	27,600	39,800	No problems with any of these. We'll be able to make a profit on all of these discs.
Bambino choir of Prague	1,000	3,500	8,500	12,000	This batch of CDs arrived too late for the 1994 Christmas season. We're keeping them for the 1995 Christmas season. I think they will sell very well then.
The Joyful Singers sing Wesley	400	2,000	3,600	4,800	We just cannot get rid of these. We'll have to reduce the price to retailers to £3 a disc and recommend that retailers sell them for £5.50 a disc.
Bach at St Thomas's	2,000	7,000	14,000	20,000	This has not sold at all well. We're going to withdraw these discs and repackage them as 'The King of Instruments' and sell them to a chain store for £4 a disc. The repackaging will cost £1.50 per disc.
TOTAL	7,900	30,500	53,700	76,600	

Complete the following table to calculate the value of closing stock for incorporation into the accounts.

Stock sheets	Value
	£
Total b/f from previous pages	18,000
Bambino choir of Prague	3,500 ✓
The Joyful Singers sing Wesley	1,200 ✓
Bach at St Thomas's	7,000 ✗ 5000
VALUE OF STOCK as at 31 May 1995	

$$7,000 = 400 - 150 = 250 \times 2,000 = 5,000$$

Task 4

The following additional information was discovered after the list of balances was extracted from the ledger.

(a) Royalties due to artists for the quarter ended 31 May 1995 have just been calculated at £4,500, but these have not yet been recorded in the accounts. It has also been discovered that there has been an error in the calculation of the royalties due to Arnold Willis-Brown for the quarter ended 31 December 1994. Mr Willis-Brown had been paid a £1 royalty based on sales of 28 discs. In actual fact the number of discs sold had been 280. Anthony Sedgewick has decided that the next cheque to be sent to Mr Willis-Brown should be adjusted to correct the error.

(b) A cheque for £220 received from 'The CD Shop', a credit customer, which had been correctly recorded in the accounts, has just been returned by the bank marked 'refer to drawer'. This has not yet been recorded in the accounts.

(c) Anthony Sedgewick has estimated that one third of motor expenses have been for private use.

Prepare journal entries to record the above information in the accounts. Dates are not required, but you should include narratives. Use the blank journal on Page 36.

Task 5

The following additional information is available from the business records.

(a) The loan was taken out on 1 June 1994, bears interest at 15% per annum, and is repayable in full on 31 May 1996.

(b) The rent on the business premises is fixed at £1,000 per month from 1 June 1993 to 31 May 1998.

Incorporate the following into the adjustments columns of the extended trial balance on Page 33.

(a) Any adjustments arising from the above additional information.

(b) The depreciation charge for the year and the value of closing stock you calculated as Tasks 2 and 3.

(c) Any adjustments resulting from the journal entries you prepared as Task 4.

Task 6

Extend the figures into the extended trial balance columns for the profit and loss account and the balance sheet. Total all columns, transferring the balance of profit or loss as appropriate.

JOURNAL		
Details	DR £	CR £

SECTION 2

The following short answer questions are mainly based on the scenario outlined in Section 1. You may have to refer back to the information in that exercise in order to answer the questions.

The suggested time allocation for this set of short answer questions is 40 minutes.

1   The list of account balances on Page 32 includes an amount of £3,250 as VAT (amount owing). Explain fully what this balance represents. To whom is the amount payable?

2   Included in 'Equipment' are several high quality microphones. Apart from wear and tear through usage, there could be other factors causing these microphones to depreciate. Identify and explain one such factor.

3   Highbury Discs uses DAT (digital to analogue) tapes to record performances. These are purchased wholesale for £8 each. They can be used over a number of years to make and archive recordings. The policy of the business is to charge the cost of the tapes as an expense in the year in which they are purchased. Justify this treatment.

4   Suppose that the value of this year's closing stock had been mistakenly overestimated by £1,000 and that the error had not been detected. What would the effect be:

    (a)   on this year's profit?
    (b)   on next year's profit?

5   Highbury Discs values its stock of compact discs at the end of each financial year so that the costs incurred in producing those discs are not charged until discs are sold. Name the fundamental accounting concept of which this is an example.

6   Anthony Sedgewick has asked you to write him a memorandum explaining the rules you have used to calculate the value of closing stock in Section 1, Task 3. He would like you to refer to any relevant SSAPs and/or FRSs and illustrate the rules by demonstrating how you have calculated the value of the stocks of the three compact discs referred to in the stock sheets given for Task 3. Prepare a suitable memorandum in reply to Anthony Sedgewick.

SECTION 3

The suggested time allocation for this exercise is 60 minutes.

You have been asked to help in preparing the accounts of Lynda Booth who has been trading as a painter and decorator for some years from a rented garage and workshop. Lynda is an excellent painter and decorator but does not have the expertise to maintain a double entry set of records. Your supervisor prepared Lynda's accounts last year and has provided you with a set of working accounts consisting of all accounts with start of year balances. The balances have been entered in the accounts.

You have already spent some time analysing the statements for Lynda's business bank account for the year ended 31 May 1995 and have the following summary.

	£	£
Opening balance		323
Payments in		
Lottery winnings (see note (a), page 253)	10,000	
Cash takings paid in	2,770	
Receipts from trade debtors	43,210	
		55,980
		56,303
Payments out		
Payments to trade creditors	30,060	
Withdrawn for personal use	12,000	
Purchase of new van	4,800	
Rent and insurance	5,330	
Motor expenses	3,400	
		55,590
		713

Your analysis of the other business documentation kept by Lynda gives you the following additional information as at 31 May 1995.

(a)   Invoices for work done for customers during the year ended 31 May 1995 totalled £52,000 (of which £2,000 was unpaid as at 31 May 1995).

(b)   Unpaid invoices for raw materials purchased from suppliers totalled £4,230.

(c)   Insurance was prepaid by £200.

(d)   Motor expenses were accrued by £209.

Your supervisor has supplied you with the following notes which were made during a meeting with Lynda Booth.

(a) Lynda was a winner in the National Lottery earlier this year. She was not a jackpot winner and certainly did not win enough to retire. She paid some of her winnings into the business bank account to help with a temporary cash flow problem.

(b) Lynda thinks that £480 of the amount collectable from customers as at 31 May 1995 will not be recovered because one of her customers has gone into bankruptcy.

(c) Lynda buys all her supplies from one supplier who offers 10% discount for prompt settlement. Lynda has been able to take advantage of that discount on all payments made during the year.

(d) Some customers paid in cash during the year but Lynda has not kept any records. We've estimated that about £600 was paid for motor expenses from these cash receipts. There was £34 in the business safe as at 31 May 1995.

(e) Lynda bought the additional motor van on 1 February 1995 because she thought the price was particularly good. She has used both vans in the business herself but feels that this van will be particularly useful next summer when she expects she will have to employ an assistant. We have agreed that the vans should be written off equally on a month for month basis over an expected life of four years. This is what we did with the first van which was purchased on 1 June 1993.

(f) There were materials costing £1,600 unused in the workshop at 31 May 1995.

Task 1

From the above information reconstruct the ledger accounts provided for the year ended 31 May 1995 on Pages 39 to 41, showing the balances to be carried forward at the end of the year and/or the amounts to be transferred to the profit and loss account for the year ended 31 May 1995.

Notes

(a) Dates are not required.

(b) The following accounts are not supplied and need not be shown.

Capital
Work done/sales
Bad debts
Discounts received/allowed

A SUGGESTED ANSWER TO THIS PRACTICE CENTRAL ASSESSMENT IS GIVEN ON PAGE 105.

BANK			
	£		£
Balance b/f	323		

CASH			
	£		£
Balance b/f	25		

MOTOR EXPENSES			
	£		£
		Balance b/f	174

MOTOR VAN(S)			
	£		£
Balance b/f	7,500		

RENT AND INSURANCE			
	£		£
Balance (insurance) b/f	180	Balance (rent) b/f	250

MATERIALS USED			
	£		£
Balance b/f	1,530		

TRADE CREDITORS			
	£	Balance b/f	£ 3,650

TRADE DEBTORS			
	£		£
Balance b/f	1,550		

DRAWINGS			
	£		£

PRACTICE CENTRAL ASSESSMENT 2: JASON BROWN (DECEMBER 1995)

SECTION 1

The suggested time allocation for this extended trial balance exercise is 80 minutes.

Jason Brown is a sole trader who operates out of a warehouse in Nottingham. He buys and sells a range of office furniture and equipment and trades under the name J B Office Supplies. Most of his sales are made on credit to businesses in the Midlands area of England, although occasionally customers will call at his premises to make purchases for cash.

You are employed by Jason to assist with the bookkeeping. This is currently a manual system and consists of a general ledger, where double entry takes place, a sales ledger and a purchases ledger. The individual accounts of debtors and creditors are therefore regarded as memoranda accounts. Day books are used and totals from the columns of these are transferred periodically into the general ledger.

The following balances were extracted from the general ledger at the end of the financial year on 31 October 1995.

	£
Purchases	170,240
Sales	246,412
Purchases returns	480
Sales returns	670
Stock at 1 November 1994	54,200
Salaries	30,120
Rent	2,200
Insurance	360
Delivery vans at cost	12,800
Provision for depreciation - delivery vans	3,520
Equipment at cost	22,800
Provision for depreciation - equipment	5,760
Bad debts	2,700
Provision for doubtful debts	1,980
Debtors control account	41,600
Creditors control account	33,643
Drawings	10,522
Capital	83,171
Bank overdraft	348
Cash	568
VAT (credit balance)	2,246
Bank interest received	1,200
Bank deposit account	30,000
Suspense account	?

Task 1

Enter the above balances into the first two columns of the extended trial balance provided on Page 43. Total the two columns whilst at the same time entering an appropriate balance for the suspense account to ensure that the two totals agree.

JASON BROWN

Account	Trial balance Debit £	Trial balance Credit £	Adjustments Debit £	Adjustments Credit £	Accrued £	Prepaid £	Profit and loss a/c Debit £	Profit and loss a/c Credit £	Balance sheet Debit £	Balance sheet Credit £
Purchases	170240						170240			
Sales		246412						246412		
Purchases returns		480						480		
Sales returns	670						670			
Opening stock	54,200						54,200			
Salaries	30,120						30120			200
Rent	2200				200		2400		130	
Insurance	360					130	230		12800	
Delivery vans (cost)	12,800								22800	
Equipment (cost)	22,800									
Delivery vans (prov for depreciation)		3520		1856						5376
Equipment (prov for depreciation)		5760		2280						8040
Bad debts	2700		2460				5160			1957
Provision for bad debts		1980	23					3940	39117	
Debtors control account	41,600			2483					10522	34903
Creditors control account		33,643	1260	1260						83171
Drawings	10522								912	
Capital		83171							568	
Bank overdraft	348									2246
Cash	568		1260						600	
VAT		8246		600	600			1800	30,000	
Bank interest received		1200								20
Bank deposit account	30,000									
Suspense account		20					4436			
Depreciation			4136							
Bank interest owing			600						58194	
Closing stock (P&L)				58185				58185		
Closing stock (B/S)			58194					23		
Provision for bad debts (adjustment)										
Prepayments/accruals										
SUBTOTAL	378780	378780	66672	66673	200	130	267156	306906	175643	135893
Profit for the year							39750			39750
TOTAL	378780	378780	66672	66673	200	130	306906	306906	175643	175643

Task 2

Unfortunately the errors causing the need for the suspense account cannot immediately be found and Jason is anxious that a draft extended trial balance should be produced as quickly as possible.

Make appropriate entries in the adjustment columns of the extended trial balance to take account of the following.

(a)   Depreciation is to be provided as follows.

Delivery vans: 20% per annum reducing balance method
Equipment: 10% per annum straight line method

(b)   The £30,000 in the bank deposit account was invested on 1 November 1994 at a fixed rate of interest of 6% per annum. A cheque for £300 interest was received by J B Office Supplies on 2 January 1995 and a further cheque for £900 on 3 July 1995.

(c)   It is thought highly unlikely that £2,460 owed by M C Miller will be recovered and towards the end of October the decision was made for the debt to be written off. To date no entries have been passed. The provision on remaining debtors should be adjusted to a figure of 5%.

(d)   Closing stock has been valued at cost at £58,394. However, this figure includes four office chairs, cost price £230 each, which have been damaged in storage. It has been estimated that if a total of £40 was spent on repairing the worst of the damage then they could be sold for £190 each.

(e)   J B Office Supplies had sent a cheque for £1,260 to Metalux Imports, a supplier on 15 October 1995. Unfortunately the cheque had not been signed and was returned in the post on 30 October. No entries have been passed.

(f)   Insurance is paid annually in advance on 1 April. The premium for the period 1 May 1995 to 30 April 1996 was £260.

(g)   The rent on the property used by J B Office Supplies was set on 1 January 1994 at £200 per month payable in arrears. The next rent review has been scheduled to take place on 1 January 1996.

Task 3

Extend the figures into the extended trial balance columns for profit and loss and balance sheet. Total all of these columns, transferring the balance of the profit or loss as appropriate.

Task 4

Subsequent to the completion of the extended trial balance a further search for the errors which necessitated the opening of the suspense account takes place. The following are found.

(a)   A cheque for £60 received from Pauline Ransome, a credit customer, had been entered in the bank account but not in the appropriate control account.

(b)   Discounts allowed totalling £125 had been credited to discounts received.

(c)   Credit purchases totalling £15,840 had been transferred from the day book into the purchases account at £15,480.

(d)   In totalling the columns of the sales day book, the 'net' column had been undercast by £570.

Prepare journal entries to record the correction of these errors. Dates and narratives are not required. Use the blank journal on Page 45.

JOURNAL		
Details	DR £	CR £
Suspence account	60	
Debitors control account		60
Being payment by P Ransome - not entered on to Debitor control account		
Discounts Allowed	125	
Discounts received	125	
suspence a		250
Being misposting of Discounts allowed £125 Reverse transcactions		
Suspence account		360
Purchase account	360	
Being transportion of figures actual 15,840 Posted 15,480 different 360		
Suspence account	570	
Sales		570
Being error of undercast on Sales Book		

SECTION 2

The following short answer questions are mainly based on the scenario outlined in Section 1. You may have to refer back to the information in that exercise in order to answer the questions.

The suggested time allocation for this set of short answer questions is 45 minutes.

1   The delivery vans figures of £12,800 shown in the trial balance is made up from two vehicles, one costing £6,000 bought on 1 November 1993 and one costing £6,800 bought

on 1 November 1994. If the first van was now to be sold on 1 May 1996 for £3,200, then assuming that depreciation is calculated on a monthly basis:

(a)   What would be the book value of the van at the date of sale?
(b)   Show the disposals account as it would appear in the ledger on 31 October 1996.

MOTOR VANS DISPOSAL ACCOUNT			
	£		£

2   Jason Brown intends to launch a new computer consultancy service during 1997. He is confident that this will bring about a substantial increase in business for his financial year ended 31 October 1997. A major advertising campaign has been planned for September and October 1996. What is the argument for including the cost of the campaign in the calculation of profit for the year end 31 October 1997? Make reference in your answer to the accounting concept or concepts that relate to this matter.

3   In Task 4 of Section 1 the following errors, amongst others, were identified.

(a)   Discounts allowed totalling £125 had been credited to discounts received.

(b)   Credit purchases totalling £15,840 had been transferred from the day book into the purchases account as £15,480.

In correcting each error, would the reported profit be increased or decreased and by what amount?

4   Included in Jason Brown's stock are some standard office swivel chairs. At the beginning of October ten chairs each costing £30 were in stock. Stock movements during the month were as follows.

Stock at	1/10/95	10 at £30
Purchases	10/10/95	12 at £32
Sales	13/10/95	2
Sales	18/10/95	4
Purchases	23/10/95	10 at £31
Sales	30/10/95	6

Chairs are sold at £50 each.
Stock is valued on a FIFO basis.

Calculate the value of the following.

(a)   Sales for October.
(b)   Cost of goods sold for October.
(c)   Closing stock at the end of October.

5   'Capital expenditure is expenditure on fixed assets which appear in the balance sheet. The cost of a fixed asset does not therefore affect the calculation of profit.' State whether or not you agree with the above statement and briefly explain the reason for your answer.

6   The total sales figure to be used in the calculation of profit is £246,412.

(a)   Does this figure include or exclude VAT?
(b)   Briefly explain the reason for your answer.

7   You have received the following note from Jason Brown.

'Thank you for producing the extended trial balance showing key figures for the year. I am concerned about the profitability of the business for next year and I am considering the following changes to improve the profit figure.

(a) Running down the stock levels at the end of the financial year. This can be achieved by reducing purchases and a smaller purchases figure will increase profit.

(b) Writing off M C Millar's debt this year significantly reduce the profit. If towards the end of next year any large bad debts are identified we should delay writing them off until the following year.

(c) We should calculate depreciation on all fixed assets using both the straight line and reducing balance methods. Each year we can then use the method which gives us the highest profit.'

Prepare a memorandum to Jason Brown covering each of the points he has raised.

8 Some days after preparing the extended trial balance it was discovered that a credit sale for £96.20 had, in error, not been entered into the account of John Pearce Furniture in the sales ledger. Jason Brown is concerned about the control of errors and had contacted you for an explanation.

Write a note to Jason in the form of a memorandum, explaining why the error would not have been detected by drawing up a trial balance and how the existence of such an error would normally be detected by checking the total of the balances in the sales ledger.

SECTION 3

The suggested time allocation for this exercise is 55 minutes.

Jason's younger sister Natasha had originally intended joining him in the business as his assistant. However, when she inherited some money an opportunity arose to set up on her own buying and selling stationery and eventually she decided to go ahead with this venture. During October 1995 she purchased premises costing £74,400, fixtures and fittings at £28,800 and stock at £15,613. The stock was partly bought with her own funds and partly on credit. Her supplier, Carlton Office Supplies Ltd, offered her £10,000 credit and at this point she made full use of the facility. At the end of the month she borrowed £48,000 by way of a loan from the bank at an interest rate of 10% per annum. After these transactions had taken place she had £1,220 of surplus funds remaining and on 1 November, the date the business opened, this sum was paid into a business bank account.

All of Natasha's sales were for cash and all were at a mark up of 25% on cost. Unfortunately Natasha did not appreciate the importance of recording sales despite the fact that she had bought a computer on 1 November with the intention of using it to record business transactions. It is estimated that the computer will be used for three years after which time it will have a residual value of £250. Depreciation should be calculated on a monthly basis for the computer and for other fixed assets. (Any depreciation for October should, however, be ignored.)

During November, Natasha took out from the takings any money she needed for her own use but, again, without recording the sums involved. The following amounts were also paid out of the cash and the remainder of the takings were then deposited in the bank.

Postages   £43
Cash purchases   £187
Sundry expenses £52

Apart from the cash purchases, all other purchases of stock during November were made on credit from Carlton Office Supplies Ltd. Natasha's summarised business bank account for the period appeared as follows.

	Discount £	Bank £		Discount £	Bank £
Balance b/d		1,220	Purchase of the computer		1,402
Takings		30,408	Carlton Office Supplies	200	9,800
			Sundry expenses		61
			Insurance		384
			Carlton Office Supplies	250	12,250
			Balance c/d		7,731
		31,628		450	31,628

The insurance payment covered the period 1 November 1995 to 31 October 1996. On 30 November an invoice received from Carlton Office Supplies Ltd for £8,600 was still outstanding and this sum was therefore owed to the company. On the same date Natasha's stock was valued at £11,475. This, however, included £275 for a new electronic diary supplied for trial purposes on a sale or return basis. The £275 had not been included in any of the invoices received.

Depreciation is to be calculated at 2% per annum on cost for the premises and at 10% per annum on cost for the fixtures and fittings.

Tasks

Jason has asked you to help his sister by producing some figures for her business.

1 Calculate Natasha's original capital sum introduced into the business.

2 Draw up the account for Carlton Office Supplies Ltd showing clearly the total purchases made on credit from the company during October and November.

3 Calculate the value of the total purchases made up to the end of November, including the purchase of the initial stock.

4 Prepare a draft statement calculating the net profit for the month ended 30 November 1995 and clearly showing the total sales for the period.

5 Prepare the cash account for November showing clearly the total drawings made by Natasha during the month.

A SUGGESTED ANSWER TO THIS PRACTICE CENTRAL ASSESSMENT IS GIVEN ON PAGE 111.

PRACTICE CENTRAL ASSESSMENT 3: EXPLOSIVES (JUNE 1996)

SECTION 1

The suggested time allocation for this extended trial balance exercise is 85 minutes.

Melanie Lancton trades under the name of Explosives and operates out of a store and warehouse. She is a sole trader and has been in the clothes business for approximately ten years. Explosives deals mainly in jeans and speciality T shirts. All of the sales out of the store are for cash but the warehouse is used to supply other clothing retailers throughout the UK on a credit basis. Occasionally, orders are received on a limited scale from shops in northern France.

You are employed by Melanie to assist with the book-keeping. This is currently a manual system and consists of a general ledger, where double entry takes place, a sales ledger and a purchases ledger. The individual accounts of debtors and creditors are therefore regarded as memoranda accounts. Day books are used and totals from their various columns are transferred periodically into the general ledger.

The following balances were extracted from the general ledger at the end of the financial year on 31 May 1996.

	£	£
Stock at 1 June 1995	180,420	
Purchases	610,080	
Sales		840,560
Purchases returns		2,390
Sales returns	2,650	
Motor expenses	5,430	
Bank	20,415	
Cash	3,420	
Rent	11,000	
Lighting and heating	4,180	
Stationery and advertising	6,120	
Provision for bad debts		5,620
Debtors control account	120,860	
Creditors control account		102,860
Salaries	96,200	
Bad debts	7,200	
Drawings	31,600	
Discounts allowed	20,520	
Discounts received		18,400
Motor vehicles: at cost	60,480	
provision for depreciation		12,590
Office furniture and equipment: at cost	26,750	
provision for depreciation		3,170
VAT		10,260
Capital account at 1 June 1995		211,475
	1,207,325	1,207,325

Having extracted the above figures, the following errors were found in the books.

(a) The purchases day book totals for the month of March were as follows.

	£
Total	50,160
VAT	7,471
Net	42,689
Goods for resale	40,463
Other items	2,226

  (i) An invoice for £200 plus £35 VAT received from Just Jeans Ltd had been entered as £2,000 plus £35 VAT thus causing errors in both the net and total columns.

  (ii) The total of the net column was debited to the purchases account. An analysis of 'other items' showed £1,201 for lighting and heating and £1,025 for stationery and advertising. No entries had been passed in these accounts.

(b) A credit note received from Astra Clothing for £40 plus £7 VAT had, in error, been left out altogether from the returns outwards day book.

(c) Cash sales of £1,645 (inclusive of £245 VAT) had been entered as follows.

Dr Cash book £1,645
Cr Sales   £1,645

(d) An invoice had been received and correctly entered in the books from Kay Imports Ltd for £1,080 plus £180 VAT, total £1,260. A payment by cheque was made for £1,206 but the discount had been omitted from the discount column of the cash book.

The following adjustments also need to be taken into account.

(1) Depreciation is to be provided as follows.

Motor vehicles - 20% per annum on cost
Office furniture and equipment - 10% per annum reducing balance method

It should be noted that no depreciation is charged on assets in their year of purchase or in their year of sale. On 10 January 1996 a new vehicle had been purchased for £9,800.

(2) Rent payable on the store and warehouse is £1,000 per month.

(3) The stationery and advertising figure includes the sum of £1,560 paid to the Wise Advertising Agency for a series of newspaper advertisements covering all of Explosives' products and due to appear during the period October to December 1996.

(4) Stock has been valued on 31 May 1996 at £208,540. This figure excludes £2,300 of jeans (cost price) which had been damaged by a leak in the roof of the warehouse. The jeans were considered worthless and were thrown out. The Regal Insurance Company has agreed to pay a claim for the full cost of the jeans although as yet no payment has been received.

(5) The provision for bad debts is to be adjusted to a figure representing 5% of debtors.

Task 1

Prepare journal entries to correct the errors (a) to (d) shown on Pages 49 and 50. Dates and narratives are not required.

Use the blank journal on Page 51 for your answer.

Task 2

Enter the corrected balances into the first two columns of the extended trial balance provided on Page 52.

Note. It is the *corrected* balances that should be used, thus taking into account the journal entries prepared for Task 1. Total the two columns ensuring that the two totals agree.

Task 3

Make appropriate entries in the adjustment columns of the extended trial balance to take account of the adjustments (1) to (5) above.

Task 4

Extend the figures into the extended trial balance columns for profit and loss and balance sheet. Total all of these columns, transferring the balance of the profit or loss as appropriate.

JOURNAL		
Details	DR £	CR £

EXPLOSIVES

Account	Trial balance Debit £	Trial balance Credit £	Adjustments Debit £	Adjustments Credit £	Accrued £	Prepaid £	Profit and loss a/c Debit £	Profit and loss a/c Credit £	Balance sheet Debit £	Balance sheet Credit £
Opening stock	180 420						180420			
Purchases	606654		2360	2360			603754			
Sales		846315						846315		
Purchases returns		2430						2430		
Sales returns	2650						2650			
Motor expenses	5430						5430			
Bank	20415								20415	
Cash	3420						204		3420	
Rent	11,000				1000		12,000			1,000
Lighting and heating	5381						5381			
Stationery and advertising	7145					1560	5585		1560	
Provision for bad debts		5620		423						6043
Debtors control account	120860								120860	
Creditors control account		100959								100959
Salaries	96200						96200			
Bad debts	7200						7200			
Drawings	31600								31600	
Discounts allowed	20520						20520			
Discounts received		18454						18454		
Motor vehicles (cost)	60480								60480	
Office furniture & equipment (cost)	26750								26750	
Motor vehicles (prov for depreciation)		12590		10136						22726
Office furniture & equipment (prov for depreciation)		3170		2358						5528
VAT	1060	10512								10512
Capital		211415								211415
Depreciation			12494				12494			
Regal Insurance Company			2300	2300					2300	
Closing stock (P&L)				208540				208540		
Closing stock (B/S)			208540						208540	
Provision for bad debts (adjustment)			423				423			
Prepayments/accruals										
SUBTOTAL	1805525	1205525	223757	223757	1000	1560	1052057	1169739	475925	475925
Profit for the year							117682			117682
TOTAL	1805525	1205525								

SECTION 2

The following short answer questions are mainly based on the scenario outlined in Section 1. You may have to refer back to the information in that exercise in order to answer the questions.

The suggested time allocation for this set of short answer questions is 40 minutes.

1   Indicate with a circle the effect on the calculation of profit and on the assets in the balance sheet if capital expenditure is treated as revenue expenditure.

   (a)   Profit would be: Overstated/Understated
   (b)   The value of the assets would be: Overstated/Understated

2   Explosives makes a credit sale to Dillon Clothes for £600 plus VAT £105. (*Note.* State clearly for each entry the name of the account, the amount and whether debit or credit.)

   (a)   What double entry is made in the general ledger to record the sale?

   (b)   What double entry is made in the general ledger to record the debtor clearing the debt by cheque?

3   Expenditure on applied research may be capitalised should a company so wish.

   (a)   State whether or not you agree with the above statement. (Assume the expenditure is not on fixed assets.)

   (b)   Explain *briefly* the reason for your answer to (a), referring to the relevant statement of standard accounting practice.

4   Julie Owens is a credit customer of Explosives and currently owes approximately £5,000. She has recently become very slow in paying for purchases and has been sent numerous reminders for most of the larger invoices issued to her. A cheque for £2,500 sent to Explosives has now been returned by Julie Owens' bankers marked 'refer to drawer'. Which accounting concept would suggest that a provision for doubtful debts should be created to cover the debt of Julie Owens?

5   It is found that cash sales have, in error, been credited to purchases instead of sales. In correcting this error and adjusting the profit, would profit be increased, reduced or stay the same?

6   At the end of a previous accounting period, a suspense account with a £200 credit balance had been opened to agree the trial balance. It was subsequently found that only one error had been made, which related to cash drawings. Two debit entries had been made for the same amount instead of a debit and a credit. What entries should be passed to correct the error? (*Note.* State clearly for each entry the name of the account, the amount and whether debit or credit.)

7   You have received the following note from Melanie Lancton.

   'I have been looking at the draft final accounts you have produced. In the valuation of the closing stock you have included some of the jeans at less than cost price. The figure you used is net realisable value and this has effectively reduced the profit for the period. The closing stock will be sold in the next financial period and my understanding of the accruals concept is that the revenue from selling the stock should be matched against the cost of that stock. This is not now possible since part of the cost of the stock has been written off in reducing the closing stock valuation from cost price to net realisable value.'

   Write a suitable response to Melanie Lancton in the form of a memorandum. Your answer should include references to relevant accounting concepts and to SSAP 9.

SECTION 3

The suggested time allocation for this exercise is 55 minutes.

Melanie Lancton is considering taking over a small clothing wholesalers which belongs to Rahul Gupta. You have been asked to prepare some figures for Melanie from the records kept for the business.

You are presented with the following.

Rahul Gupta assets and liabilities at 31 May 1995

	£
Freehold buildings at cost	80,000
Less depreciation to date	16,000
	64,000
Fixtures and fittings at cost	17,500
Less depreciation to date	12,000
	5,500
Stock	33,200
Debtors	39,470
Prepaid general expenses	550
Cash	900
	74,120
Creditors	35,960
Bank overdraft	17,390
	53,350

Summary of the business bank account for the year ended 31 May 1996

	£		£
Cash sales	147,890	Balance b/d	17,390
From debtors	863,740	To creditors	607,650
Sale proceeds fixtures and fittings	1,360	General expenses	6,240
		Salaries	94,170
		Security devices	5,100
		Drawings	28,310
		Balance c/d	254,130
	1,012,990		1,012,990

Other information

(a) The profit margin achieved on all sales is 40%. At the end of the year on 31 May 1996 the stock was valued at £38,700. However, Rahul Gupta is convinced that various items have been stolen during the year. To prevent further theft the premises were fitted out with various security devices on 31 May 1996.

(b) Depreciation is calculated on a *monthly* basis as follows.

Premises	2% on cost
Fixtures and fittings	10% on cost

Fixtures and fittings purchased on 1 June 1990 for £4,000 were sold on 30 November 1995, the purchaser paying by cheque.

(c) The proceeds of cash sales are held in tills and paid into the bank at the end of the day, apart from a float which is retained on the premises to be used at the start of the following day. During May 1996 a decision was made to increase the size of the float from the £900 held at the beginning of the year to £1,000.

(d) On 31 May 1996 creditors amounted to £49,310, debtors £45,400 and £170 was owing for general expenses. During the year bad debts of £2,340 have been written off.

Tasks

1 Draw up a total debtors account (debtors control account) showing clearly the total value of the credit sales for the year ended 31 May 1996.

2 Calculate the total sales for the year ended 31 May 1996.

3 Draw up a total creditors account (creditors control account) showing clearly the total purchases for the year ended 31 May 1996.

4 Calculate the value of the stock stolen during the year.

5 Calculate the profit or loss made from the sale of fixtures and fittings on 30 November 1995.

6 Calculate the figure for general expenses which would be included in the calculation of profit for the year ended 31 May 1996.

A SUGGESTED ANSWER TO THIS PRACTICE CENTRAL ASSESSMENT IS GIVEN ON PAGE 118.

PRACTICE CENTRAL ASSESSMENT 4: CASTLE ALARMS (DECEMBER 1996)

SECTION 1

The suggested time allocation for this extended trial balance exercise is 80 minutes.

Andrew Hallgrove is the proprietor of Castle Alarms, which specialises in supplying domestic and commercial burglar alarm systems. Although the business operates throughout the UK, the offices and warehouse are located in the north of England.

You are employed within the business to assist with the bookkeeping. This is currently a manual system and consists of a general ledger, where double entry takes place, a sales ledger and a purchases ledger. The individual accounts of debtors and creditors are therefore regarded as memoranda accounts. Day books are used and totals from the various columns of these are transferred periodically into the general ledger.

At the end of the financial year of 31 October 1996, the balances were extracted from the general ledger and entered into an extended trial balance as shown on Page 56.

Task 1

Make appropriate entries in the adjustment columns of the extended trial balance to take account of the following.

(a) Depreciation is to be provided as follows.

Motor vehicles: 20% per annum straight line method
Equipment: 10% per annum reducing balance method

(b) The bank loan of £50,000 was taken out on 31 January 1996. The interest rate charged on the loan is fixed at 10% per annum.

(c) In August a system invoiced at £3,400 was installed at a local restaurant. Unfortunately no money was received in payment, the restaurant closed and the owner disappeared. A decision has now been made to write off the debt.

(d) Having written off all bad debts, the provision for bad debts is to be adjusted to 6% of remaining debtors.

(e) At the stocktake on 31 October 1996 the stock was valued at £289,400 cost price. However, this figures includes the following.

(i) Five system costing £1,200 each which have now been replaced by improved models. It is thought that in order to sell them the price of each system will have to be reduced to £1,000.

(ii) A system costing £2,000 was damaged in the warehouse. Repairs will cost £200 before it can be used in an installation.

(f) The business took advantage of an offer to advertise on local radio during October 1996 at a cost of £2,250. Although the invoice has now been received no entries have been made.

(g) Rent for the business property is £2,100 payable monthly in advance. This has been the figure payable over the last 12 months and a rent review is not due at the present time.

(h) On 30 October 1996 £5,000 cash was withdrawn from the bank for use within the business. To date no entries have been made to reflect this transaction.

(i) A credit note received from Ashito Electronics and relating to goods returned has just been found in a pile of correspondence. The credit note, dated 20 October 1996, is for £2,900 and has not been entered in any of the books of the business.

Task 2

Extend the figures into the extended trial balance columns for profit and loss and balance sheet. Total all of these columns, transferring the balance of the profit or loss as appropriate.

CASTLE ALARMS

Account	Trial balance Debit £	Trial balance Credit £	Adjustments Debit £	Adjustments Credit £	Accrued £	Prepaid £	Profit and loss a/c Debit £	Profit and loss a/c Credit £	Balance sheet Debit £	Balance sheet Credit £
Sales		1,200,000						1,200,000		
Purchases	667,820						667,820			
Sales returns	96,570						95,570			
Purchases returns		52,790		2900				55696		
Opening stock	301,840						301849			
Debtors control account	189,600		5000	3400					186200	
Cash	1,200								6200	
Bank	25,300								20,300	
Creditors control account		95,000	2900							92100
Provision for bad debts		12,000	828							11172
Bad debts	10,100		3400				13500			
Discounts allowed	6,320						6320			
Salaries	103,030						103030			
Drawings	26,170								26170	
Rent	27,300					2100	25200			
General expenses	14,310						14310			
Capital		121,860								121860
VAT		22,600								22,600
Bank loan		50,000								50,000
Interest on bank loan	2,500		1250				3750			
Advertising	11,450		2250		2250		13700			
Motor vehicles (cost)	32,600								32,600	
Equipment (cost)	48,860								48,860	
Motor vehicles (prov for depreciation)		4,100		6520						10620
Equipment (prov for depreciation)		6,620		4224						10844
Depreciation			10744				10744			
Loan interest owing				1250						
Closing stock (P&L)				288200				288200		
Closing stock (B/S)			288200						288200	
Provision for bad debts (adjustment)			828	828						
Prepayments/accruals										2250
SUBTOTAL	1,564,970	1,564,970								
Profit for the year										
TOTAL	1,564,970	1,564,970								

SECTION 2

The following short answer questions are mainly based on the scenario outlined in Section 1. You may have to refer back to the information in that exercise in order to answer the questions.

The suggested time allocation for this set of short answer questions is 30 minutes.

1   Andrew Hallgrove bought a calculator costing £10 for use in the office. Referring to the relevant accounting concept, briefly explain why the purchase would normally be treated as revenue rather than as capital expenditure, despite the fact that the calculator will probably be used for several years.

2   At the end of a particular quarter, Castle Alarms' VAT account showed a balance of £2,100 debit. Explain briefly what the balance represents.

3   Andrew Hallgrove is considering leasing a car for use by one of his stales staff. He understands that leases are classified as operating leases or finance leases and the two types affect the books of a business in different ways. Which type of lease would have to be capitalised in the books of Castle Alarms?

4   Castle Alarms makes a credit sale to Turnbull Haircare for £200 plus £35 VAT. Unfortunately, in error, the sale invoice is not entered in the sales day book.

    (a)   Would the error be detected by drawing up a trial balance?

    (b)   Briefly explain the reason for your answer to (a)

5   A motor vehicle which has been purchased by Castle Alarms for £10,450 was eventually sold for £3,000, when it had a net book value of £4,100. What is the total charge to the profits of Castle Alarms with respect to the capital cost of the vehicle, during the life of the asset?

6   Castle Alarms purchases an alarm from Ace Electronics. Ace Electronics normally sells the alarm at a price of £2,400, but Castle Alarms is given a 20% trade discount. Ace Electronics charges £10 for delivery to Castle Alarms' premises. Castle Alarms puts a price on the alarm of £2,425. What value would be placed on this particular item by Castle Alarms in valuing the stock of the business?

7   Castle Alarms purchases 20 alarm sirens from Northern Imports Ltd. The price charged for each siren is £40 plus VAT calculated at 17.5%. A 10% cash discount is offered by Northern Imports Ltd provided that payment is made within 14 days. (*Note*. State clearly for each entry the name of the account, the amount and whether it is debit or credit.)

    (a)   What double entry is made in the general ledger to record the purchase (the date of payment has not yet been determined)?

    (b)   What double entry is made in the general ledger to record Castle Alarms' clearing the debt by cheque whilst at the same time taking advantage of the discount offered?

8   Although Andrew Hallgrove has proved to be a good businessman, his knowledge of accounting is rather limited. In particular he does not understand how it is possible for a business to make a profit whilst at the same time the bank balance can remain static or even decrease. He has asked you to provide some guidance.

    Draft a memorandum to him clearly stating how profit is measured and giving examples of why the movement of the bank balance does not necessarily reflect the profits made.

SECTION 3

The suggested time allocation for this exercise is 80 minutes.

Data

(a) Andrew Hallgrove decided to open a shop selling cheap alarm systems and security equipment direct to the public. Trading was to start at the beginning of October 1996. He decided to call the shop and business 'Total Security'.

(b) On 1 September he opened a new bank account and paid in £50,000 of his own money as his investment in the business.

(c) During September he purchased shop fixtures and fittings at £22,500 and stock at £47,300. He paid £9,000 for 6 months' rent covering the period 1 September 1996 to 28 February 1997. Insurance of £480 covering the 12 months from 1 September 1996 was also paid, as were various items of general expenditure totalling £220.

(d) Since it was convenient to make some of the payments in cash he withdrew a lump sum from the bank.

(e) Unfortunately, his £50,000 investment was insufficient to cover all of the expenditure. However, he managed to negotiate a bank loan and all the monies from this were paid into the business's bank account.

(f) The interest rate for the bank loan was fixed at 12% per annum.

(g) At the end of September he had a £10,000 balance remaining in the bank account and £500 in cash.

(h) A summary of the business bank account for October 1996 is shown below.

	£		£
Balance b/d	10,000	To creditors	20,250
Cash banked	22,000	Drawings	3,500
		General expenses	500
		Stationery	320
		Customer refund	2,000
		Balance c/d	5,430
	32,000		32,000

(i) The cash banked all came from sales to customers. However, before banking the takings, £2,400 had been paid out as wages. The cash float at the end of October remained at £500.

(j) In paying his creditors he had been able to take advantage of discounts totalling £1,250. At the end of the month not all creditors had been paid, however, and he calculated that the total of the unpaid invoices amounted to £3,400.

(k) Depreciation is calculated on the fixtures and fittings at 20% per annum on cost.

(l) On 31 October 1996 a customer returned an alarm system which he had decided was not appropriate for his premises. He was given a refund by cheque.

(m) Unsold stock on 31 October was valued at £55,000, but this did not include the returned system. The profit margin on this type of system is 30%.

Tasks

1 Calculate the amount of the bank loan taken out in September, clearly showing your workings.

2 List the business assets as at 30 September 1996 together with their value. (Depreciation for September should be ignored.)

3 Calculate the value of the purchases made during October 1996

4 Prepare a draft statement calculating the net profit for the month ended 31 October 1996.

A SUGGESTED ANSWER TO THIS PRACTICE CENTRAL ASSESSMENT IS GIVEN ON PAGE 123.

PRACTICE CENTRAL ASSESSMENT 5: ELECTRONICS WORLD LTD (JUNE 1997)

SECTION 1

The suggested time allocation for this extended trial balance exercise is 75 minutes.

The company Electronics World Ltd operates out of offices and a warehouse located in Wales. The company purchases hi-fi systems, televisions and other electronic goods from manufacturers world-wide. Customers are mainly UK based shops specialising in electronic items.

- You are employed by Electronics World Ltd to assist with the bookkeeping.

- The company is relatively new and is still considering an appropriate computerised accounting system.

- The manual system currently in use consists of a general ledger, a sales ledger and a purchases ledger.

- Double entry takes place in the general ledger and the individual accounts of debtors and creditors are therefore regarded as memoranda accounts.

- Day books consisting of a purchases day book, a sales day book, a purchases returns day book and a sales returns day book are used. Totals from the various columns of the day books are transferred periodically into the general ledger.

The following balances were extracted by a colleague from the general ledger on 24 May 1997, one week before the end of the financial year, which is on 31 May 1997.

	£
Share capital	600,000
Premises	360,000
Fixtures and fittings (F and F) at cost	140,000
Provision for depreciation (F and F)	65,000
Purchases	972,140
Sales	1,530,630
Salaries	206,420
Sales returns	23,200
Purchases returns	17,350
General expenses	74,322
Insurance	16,390
Bad debts	7,506
Provision for bad debts	6,000
Debtors control account	237,855
Creditors control account	121,433
Stock at 1 June 1996	188,960
Bank	65,200
Bank deposit account	150,000
Bank interest received	3,750
Motor vehicles (MV) at cost	22,400
Provision for depreciation (MV)	3,800
VAT (credit balance)	24,720
Profit and loss	91,710

During the last week of the financial year a number of transactions took place and these are summarised below.

Purchases day book	*Total*	*VAT*	*Net*
	£	£	£
	23,970	3,570	20,400

Sales day book	*Total*	*VAT*	*Net*
	£	£	£
	35,955	5,355	30,600

Sales returns day book	Total £	VAT £	Net £
	1,410	210	1,200

Cheques issued	£
Payable to various creditors in settlement of debts	5,000

Task 1

Complete the table below to show the double entry which would have to be carried out in order to update the balances extracted on 24 May 1997, to take account of the summarised transactions shown above.

DOUBLE ENTRY TO UPDATE BALANCES EXTRACTED ON 24 MAY 1997		
Names of accounts	*Dr* £	*Cr* £
Entries from purchases day book Creditors Control Account Vat	20400 3570	23970
Entries from sales day book Sales Debitors Control Account Vat	 35955	30,600 5355
Entries from sales returns day book Debitors Control Account Vat	1200 210	1410
Entries from cheques issued Creditors Bank	5000	5000 5000

Task 2

Enter the updated balances into the first two columns of the extended trial balance provided on Page 62. Total the two columns ensuring that the two totals agree.

Note. It is the *updated* balances that should be used taking into account the effects of the entries prepared for Task 1.

Task 3

Make appropriate entries in the adjustment columns of the extended trial balance to take account of the following.

(a) Depreciation is to be provided as follows.

Motor vehicles: 20% per annum on cost
Fixtures and fittings: 10% per annum reducing balance method

No depreciation is charged on assets in their year of purchase or in their year of sale. On 12 November 1996 new fixture and fittings costing £6,000 had been purchased.

(b) The £150,000 was invested in the bank deposit account on 30 November 1996 at a fixed rate of interest of 6% per annum.

(c) The general expenses figure includes the sum of £2,400 paid to a company to clean the offices of Electronics World Ltd during the period 1 April 1997 to 30 September 1997.

(d) Stock has been valued on 31 May 1997 at £198,650. This figure excludes a television which was damaged beyond repair and had to be scrapped (no sale proceeds). Regis Insurance has agreed to cover the loss incurred in writing off the television.

Cost price of television: £420
Sales price of television: £630

(e) A cheque for £60 was issued at the beginning of May 1997 to pay for insurance cover which expired on 31 May 1997. A bank statement showed that the cheque was paid on 20 May. As yet no entries have been made in the books of Electronics World Ltd.

(f) The provision for bad debts is to be adjusted to a figure representing 5% of debtors.

ELECTRONICS WORLD	Trial balance		Adjustments		Accrued	Prepaid
Account	Debit	Credit	Debit	Credit		
	£	£	£	£	£	£
Share capital		600,000				
Premises	360,000					
Fixtures & fittings at cost	140,000					
Fixtures & fittings (prov for depreciation)		65,000		6900		
Purchases	992540		420	420		
Sales		1561230				
Salaries	206420					
Sales returns	24400					
Purchases returns		17350				
General expenses	74322					21600
Insurance	16390		60			
Bad debts	7506					
Provision for bad debts		6000		7620		
Debtors control account	272400					
Creditors control account		140403				
Stock at 1 June 1996	188960					
Bank	60200			60		
Bank deposit account	150,000					
Bank interest received		3750		750		
Motor vehicles (cost)	22,400					
Motor vehicles (prov for depreciation)		3800		4480		
VAT: credit balance		26295				
Profit and loss		91710				
Depreciation			11380			
Regis Insurance			420	420	420	
Closing stock (P&L)				198,650		
Closing stock (B/S)			198,650			
Provision for bad debts (adjustment)			7620			
Bank interest owing			750		750	
Prepayments						
SUBTOTAL						
Profit for the year						
TOTAL	2515538	2515538				1600

SECTION 2

The following short answer questions are mainly based on the scenario outlined in Section 1. You may have to refer back to the information in that exercise in order to answer the questions.

The suggested time allocation for this set of short answer questions is 50 minutes.

1   On 31 May 1997, the balances of the accounts in the sales ledger were listed, totalled then compared with the balance of the debtors control account. The total of the list of balances amounted to £274,189. Investigations were carried out and the following errors discovered.

(a)   A customer balance of £484 had been listed as £448.

(b)   A customer balance of £1,490 had been listed twice.

(c)   A discount of £100 allowed to a customer had been debited to the account in the sales ledger.

(d)   Although goods of £135 (inclusive of VAT) had been returned by a customer, no entry had been made in the sales ledger.

Enter the appropriate adjustments in the table shown below. For each adjustment show clearly the amount involved and whether that amount is to be added or subtracted.

		£
Total from listing of balances		274,189
Adjustment for (a)	add/subtract	
Adjustment for (b)	add/subtract	
Adjustment for (c)	add/subtract	
Adjustment for (d)	add/subtract	
Revised total to agree with debtors control account		

2   Stock has always been valued by Electronics World Ltd on a FIFO basis and this includes the closing stock figure of £198,650 as at 31 May 1997. It has been suggested that the closing stock figure should now be recalculated on a LIFO basis.

(a)   Assuming that the prices of electronic goods have been gradually rising throughout the year would the change suggested increase profit for the year ended 31 May 1997, decrease profit or would profit remain the same?

(b)   Which accounting concept states that the company should not normally change its basis for valuing stock unless it has very good reasons for doing so?

3   Electronics World Ltd recently arranged for a local builder to design and build an extension to the company offices. An invoice is received from the builder on completion of the work showing two main categories of expenditure: materials (bricks, doors, windows, frames etc) and labour. It has been suggested that:

'Since salaries and wages are normally shown in the profit and loss account the labour cost in the invoice should be written off as an expense whilst the cost of the materials should be debited to the premises account.'

(a)   Do you agree with the above statement?
(b)   Briefly explain the reason for your answer.

4   You are reviewing some accounting records on 10 June 1997 and discover an error in the sales day book. Although the VAT and net columns have been correctly totalled, the total column itself has been miscast. The appropriate figures have then been transferred from the day book into the ledgers.

Preparation of which of the following, if any, would be likely to detect the error?

Bank reconciliation statement/Trial balance/VAT return/None of these

5   For some months Electronic World Ltd has been purchasing a range of CD racks from Arun Divan, a small local supplier, who deals exclusively with the company. Initially

invoices received from this business did not include VAT but the last invoice did have VAT, calculated at 17.5%, added to the cost of the racks. Jackie Brown, a colleague, is confused about the regulations regarding VAT and the implications of the change. A note is left for you by Jackie raising the following specific points.

(a)   If Electronics World Ltd is now having to pay more money for the CD racks then this must affect the profits of the company.

(b)   Arun Divan has now registered for VAT. Since the increased money he receives from Electronics World Ltd is payable to HM Customs and Excise then his profitability must remain unchanged.

Prepare a memo to Jackie Brown covering both of the points raised.

SECTION 3

The suggested time allocation for this exercise is 55 minutes.

Lucy Barber previously worked full-time for a furniture manufacturing company. Approximately two years ago, however, she decided to set up a part-time business making and selling speaker stands for hi-fi systems. She now has an arrangement to sell exclusively to Electronics World Ltd and you have been asked to assist her in preparing her accounts for the year ended 30 April 1997.

The following information is available.

(a)   Tools and equipment costing £3,000 were purchased for the business on 31 July 1995.

(b)   A van costing £4,800 was purchased on 31 October 1995, again for use in the business.

(c)   Lucy Barber rents a small workshop on a light industrial estate. The rent payable was £100 a month until 31 October 1996 but then it was increased to £120 a month and this remains as the current rate. On 30 April 1996 one month's rent was owing to the landlord.

(d)   During Lucy Barber's first period of trading, which ended on 30 April 1996, all of the transactions were for cash. On 30 April 1996 the cash balance of the business was £4,250. On 1 May 1996 she opened a business bank account and a private bank account. The £4,250 was paid into the business account but no funds were paid at that time into the private account. From 1 May 1996 all business transactions passed through the business bank account with the exception of some cheques from Electronics World Ltd (see below).

(e)   From 1 May 1996 sales to Electronics World Ltd were on credit as were purchases from her supplier, Johnson Materials Ltd. Cheques received from Electronics World were all paid into the business bank account apart from three which Lucy Barber paid directly into her private account.

(f)   Throughout the year ended 30 April 1997 Lucy Barber withdrew £200 a month cash from her private account for personal spending. No other transactions passed through the account other than the three cheques paid in from Electronics World Ltd. On the 30 April 1997 the balance of the account was £600.

(g)   During the year ended 30 April 1997 she made and sold 500 pairs of speaker stands. In determining the price charged for each pair she calculated the cost of materials used for the pair then doubled this figure.

(h)   On 30 April 1997:

   (i)   £4,400 was owed to the business by Electronics World Ltd;
   (ii)   £1,500 was owed by the business to Johnson Materials Ltd;
   (iii)   materials were in stock to make 120 pairs of speaker stands.

(i)   Lucy Barber does not have a record of the materials that were in stock on 30 April 1996.

(j)   The van is to be depreciated at 10% per annum on cost. The tools and equipment are to be depreciated at 20% per annum on cost.

(k)   The following is a summary made by Lucy Barber of the entries which passed through the business bank account during the year ended 30 April 1997.

	£
Money received	
Electronics World Ltd	17,600
Money paid out	
Rent	1,300
Johnson Materials Ltd	12,000
Tools and equipment	250
Electricity	640
Telephone	560

Tasks

1   Calculate the total sales made by Lucy Barber during the year ended 30 April 1997.

2   Calculate the selling price for one pair of speaker stands.

3   Calculate the cost of materials used in making one pair of speaker stands.

4   Calculate the total cost of goods sold during the year ended 30 April 1997 (ie the cost of materials used in making the sales calculated in Task 1).

5   Calculate the cost of materials purchased by Lucy Barber during the year ended 30 April 1997.

6   Calculate the stock of materials held by Lucy Barber on 30 April 1996

7   Calculate the capital invested in the business by Lucy Barber on 30 April 1996.

8   Calculate the figure for rent which would be included in the calculation of profit for the year ended 30 April 1997.

A SUGGESTED ANSWER TO THIS PRACTICE CENTRAL ASSESSMENT IS GIVEN ON PAGE 127.

PRACTICE CENTRAL ASSESSMENT 6: DREW INSTALLATIONS (DECEMBER 1997)

SECTION 1

The suggested time allocation for this extended trial balance exercise is 75 minutes.

Colin Drew is the proprietor of Drew Installations, a firm specialising in the supply and installation of kitchens and bathrooms. The showroom, warehouse and offices are located in London and most of the work carried out by the business is in the London area.

- You are employed by Colin Drew to assist with the bookkeeping.

- The business currently operates a manual system consisting of a general ledger, a sales ledger and a purchases ledger.

- Double entry takes place in the general ledger and the individual accounts of debtors and creditors are therefore regarded as memoranda accounts.

- Day books consisting of a purchases day book, a sales day book, a purchases returns day book and a sales returns day book are used. Totals from the various columns of the day books are transferred periodically into the general ledger.

At the end of the financial year on 31 October 1997, the balances were extracted from the general ledger and entered into an extended trial balance as shown on page 67.

Unfortunately in preparing the extended trial balance it was found that the total of the debit column did not agree with the total of the credit column. A suspense account was opened as a temporary measure.

Task 1

Make appropriate entries in the adjustment columns of the extended trial balance on page 67 to take account of the following.

(a) Depreciation calculated on a monthly basis is to be provided as follows:

Motor vehicles - 20% per annum straight line method
Equipment - 10% per annum reducing balance method

On 30 April 1997 a new motor vehicle costing £12,000 had been purchased.

(b) The bank loan had originally been taken out on 30 April 1996 when the sum of £60,000 had been borrowed, repayable by six annual repayments of £10,000. The first repayment had been made as agreed on 30 April 1997. Interest is charged on the loan at 8% per annum.

(c) Rent payable by the business is as follows:

Showroom and offices - £3,000 per month
Warehouse - £2,000 per month

(d) The motor vehicle expenses include a payment of £260 paid out of the business bank account to service Colin Drew's family car which is not used in the business.

(e) Insurance includes an annual buildings policy which runs from 1 August 1997. The premium paid was £2,400.

(f) The provision for bad debts is to be adjusted to a figure representing 8% of debtors.

(g) Stock has been valued at cost on 31 October 1997 at £107,300. However, this includes some discontinued kitchen cabinets the details of which are as follows:

Cost	£2,300
Normal selling price	£3,500
Net realisable value	£1,800

Task 2

Subsequent to the preparation of the extended trial balance the following errors were found, some of which had caused the opening of the suspense account. Prepare journal entries to record the correction of the errors using the blank journal on page 68. Dates and narratives are not required.

(a) The VAT column of the sales returns day book had been overcast by £200.

(b) Motor vehicle expenses of £40 had been debited to Motor Vehicles (any adjustment to depreciation can be ignored).

(c) Sales returns of £160 had been credited to purchases returns. The VAT element of the returns had been entered correctly.

(d) Purchases of £2,340 had been transferred from the rent column of the day book and into the purchases account as £2,430.

(e) A cheque for £2,450 paid to Ashwood Kitchens, a credit supplier, had been entered in the cash book but not in the relevant control account.

31 Oct 97

DREW INSTALLATIONS	Trial balance		Adjustments		Accrued	Prepaid
Account	Debit	Credit	Debit	Credit		
	£	£	£	£	£	£
Purchases	339,500					
Sales		693,000				
Purchases returns		6,320				
Sales returns	1,780					
Carriage inwards	8,250					
Salaries and wages	106,200					
Bad debts	4,890					
Provision for bad debts		4,500	756			
Debtors control account	46,800					
Creditors control account		28,760				
Stock at 1 November 1996	113,450					
Motor vehicle expenses	5,780		260			
Motor vehicles (cost)	86,000					
Motor vehicles (prov for depreciation)		12,800		16,000		
Equipment (cost)	24,500					
Equipment (prov for depreciation)		6,700		1780		
Rent	58,000				2000	
Drawings	32,900		260			
Insurance	5,720					1800
Bank	8,580					
Bank loan account		50,000				
Bank interest paid	2,400		2000			
VAT (credit balance)		12,400				
Capital		32,750				
Suspense account	2,480					
Depreciation			17780			
Closing stock (P&L)				106800		
Closing stock (B/S)			106800			
Provision for bad debts (adjustment)				756		
Loan interest owing				2000		
SUBTOTAL	847,230	847,230				
Profit for the year						
TOTAL	847,230	847,230	127596	127596	2000	1800

Note. Only the above columns of the extended trial balance are required for this exercise.

JOURNAL		
Details	DR £	CR £

SECTION 2

The following short answer questions are mainly based on the scenario outlined in Section 1. You may have to refer back to the information in that exercise in order to answer the questions.

The suggested time allocation for this set of short answer questions is 40 minutes.

1   Colin Drew is considering part-exchanging one of the business motor vehicles for a new model. The garage has offered him £2,500 in part-exchange and he will need to pay a further £10,000 by cheque. it has been calculated that the loss on disposal on the old vehicle will be £500. The vehicle was originally purchased at a price of £9,000.

     What would have been the total depreciation charge to profits during the life of the asset excluding the loss on disposal?

2   Assume that before Colin Drew was registered for VAT, Drew Installations had purchased goods costing £400 plus VAT £70 for cash.

     Note. State clearly for both (a) and (b) the names of the accounts, the amounts and whether each entry is a debit or credit.

     (a)   What would have been the double entry made in Drew Installation's books to record the purchase?

     (b)   What would have been the double entry made in the seller's books to record the sale to Drew Installations?

3   Colin Drew is thinking of manufacturing some of the kitchen cabinets supplied to customers. He estimates that in the first year of production 15,000 units could be made, with sales of 10,000 units. Costs associated with the kitchen cabinets would be as follows:

Direct materials used	£20,000
Direct labour used	£5,000
Direct production overheads	£5,000
Selling and distribution expenses	£3,000

     If Colin Drew were to proceed on this basis, what would be the estimated value of the closing stock of 5,000 units?

4   The three figures shown on a sales invoice of £4,080 plus VAT £714, total £4,794, were mistakenly entered in the sales day book of Drew Installations as £4,800 plus VAT £714, total £5,514. Would the error be detected by drawing up a trial balance? Briefly explain the reason for your answer.

5   You have received the following note from Colin Drew.

     'I have been looking at the valuation of the closing stock prepared for the trial balance and the final accounts. It occurs to me that the current range of deluxe bathroom suites is selling so well that we are almost certain to sell the existing stock. In view of this, if we were to include the stock at selling price the costs of goods sold would effectively be reduced and the gross profit would therefore be increased. I am anxious to show as high a profit as possible and would like to have your thoughts on this proposal.'

     Write a suitable response to Colin Drew in the form of a memo. Your answer should include references to SSAP 2 and SSAP 9.

SECTION 3

The suggested time allocation for this exercise is 65 minutes.

During Colin Drew's early years in business trading as Drew Installations, he had very little administrative help and kept minimal records. A number of queries have now arisen and it has become necessary to calculate some figures relating to the year ended 31 October 1992. You have been asked to provide assistance. The information available from Drew Installations is as follows:

- Assets at 1 November 1991:

	£	£
Stock		30,400
Debtors		22,800
Motor vehicles at cost	8,750	
Less provision for depreciation	2,690	
		6,060
Equipment at cost	5,200	
Less provision for depreciation	840	
		4,360

- Liabilities at 1 November 1991:

	£
Creditors	15,600
Bank overdraft	4,300
Accrued expenses	1,000

- Payment made during the year ended 31 October 1992:

	£
To creditors	120,750
Expenses	52,800
Equipment purchased 30 April 1992	4,500
Drawings	unknown

- Receipts during the year ended 31 October 1992:

	£
From debtors	unknown

- Profit margin 50% on all sales

- Depreciation calculated on a monthly basis was provided as follows:

  Motor vehicles - 20% per annum straight line method
  Equipment - 10% per annum reducing balance method

- Assets at 31 October 1992

	£
Stock	32,700
Debtors	21,700
Motor vehicles at cost	8,750
Equipment at cost	9,700
Bank	15,850
Prepaid expenses	1,500

- Liabilities at 31 October 1992

	£
Creditors	16,850

Tasks

1   Calculate the cost of goods sold during the year ended 31 October 1992.

2   Calculate the gross profit for the year ended 31 October 1992.

3   Calculate the sales for the year ended 31 October 1992.

4   Calculate the receipts from debtors for the year ended 31 October 1992.

5   Calculate the drawings made by Colin Drew during the year ended 31 October 1992.

6   Calculate the net profit for the year ended 31 October 1992.

A SUGGESTED ANSWER TO THIS PRACTICE CENTRAL ASSESSMENT IS GIVEN ON PAGE 132.

SAMPLE CENTRAL ASSESSMENT

INTERMEDIATE STAGE - NVQ/SVQ3

Unit 4

Maintaining Financial Records

and Preparing Accounts

(AAT Specimen)

This Sample Central Assessment is the AAT's Specimen Central Assessment for Unit 4. Its purpose is to give you an idea of what an AAT central assessment looks like. It is not intended as a definitive guide to the tasks you may be required to perform.

The suggested time allowance for this Assessment is three hours. You are advised to spend approximately 80 minutes on Section 1, 40 minutes on Section 2 and 60 minutes on Section 3.

Calculators may be used but no reference material is permitted.

**DO NOT OPEN THIS PAPER UNTIL YOU ARE READY TO START
UNDER TIMED CONDITIONS**

INSTRUCTIONS

This Central Assessment is designed to test your ability to maintain financial records and prepare accounts.

The Central Assessment is in **three** sections, all of which relate to the firm Creative Catering.

You are provided with data which you must use to complete the tasks, and space to set out your answers.

You are allowed **three hours** to complete your work. You are reminded that competence must be achieved in each section. You should therefore attempt and aim to complete **every** task in **each** section. All essential workings should be included within your answer where appropriate.

A high level of accuracy is required. Check your work carefully.

Correcting fluid may be used in moderation. Errors should be crossed out neatly and clearly. You should write in black ink, not pencil.

A suggested answer to this Assessment is given on Page 135.

CREATIVE CATERING

SECTION 1 (Suggested time allocation: 80 minutes)

Data

Jane Sutton is the proprietor of Creative Catering, a firm that provides catering services for a variety of events and functions. Creative Catering's premises are located in Bristol and most of the firm's customers can be found in the west of England.

- You are employed by Jane Sutton to assist with the bookkeeping.

- The business currently operates a manual system consisting of a general ledger, a sales ledger and a purchases ledger.

- Double entry takes place in the general ledger and the individual accounts of debtors and creditors are therefore regarded as memoranda accounts.

- Day books consisting of a purchases day book, a sales day book, a purchases returns day book and a sales returns day book are used. Totals from the various columns of the day books are transferred periodically into the general ledger.

At the end of the financial year on 30 April 1998, the balances were extracted from the general ledger and entered into an extended trial balance as shown on page 74.

Task 1

Make appropriate entries in the adjustment columns of the extended trial balance to take account of the following.

(a) The stock consists of food and drink and has been valued on 30 April 1998 at £6,240. This figure includes some frozen food that had cost £860 but will have to be thrown out due to a problem with a freezer. Although the Polar Insurance Company has agreed to pay for the full cost of the food, no money has yet been received. Also included in the stock valuation figure are 20 bottles of wine. These had originally cost £8.50 each but since they are not popular they are to be sold off at £6.50 per bottle.

(b) Depreciation calculated on a monthly basis is to be provided as follows.

Motor vehicles - 20% per annum straight line method
Equipment - 10% per annum reducing balance method

(c) The sum of £20,000 was invested in the bank deposit account on 1 May 1997. The interest rate is fixed at 7% per annum.

(d) Rent payable by the business is as follows.

Up to 31 October 1997   £1,200 per month
From 1 November 1997   £1,300 per month

(e) The provision for bad debts is to be adjusted to a figure representing 5% of debtors.

(f) On 29 April 1998 Jane Sutton withdraw £5,000 from the bank account for her own use. The entries made were:

Dr   Cash   £5,000
Cr   Bank   £5,000

(g) A series of adverts were broadcast during April 1998 by Western Radio at a cost to Creative Catering of £2,750. The invoice has yet to be received from Western Radio and no entries have been made.

CREATIVE CATERING	Trial balance		Adjustments		Accrued	Prepaid
Account	Debit	Credit	Debit	Credit		
	£	£	£	£	£	£
Sales		620,700				
Purchases	410,650			860		
Purchases returns		390				
Salaries and wages	90,820					
Rent	16,300					1300
Debtors control account	51,640					
Creditors control account		33,180				
Bad debts	6,650					
Provision for bad debts		3,100	518			
Motor vehicles (cost)	60,700					
Motor vehicles (prov for depreciation)		12,600		12140		
Equipment (cost)	24,200					
Equipment (prov for depreciation)		6,300		1790		
Drawings	28,500		5000			
Cash	7,000			5000		
Bank	6,250					
Lighting and heating	2,100					
Insurance	760					
Advertising	3,470				2750	
VAT (credit balance)		8,400				
Stock at 1 May 1997	5,660					
Motor expenses	4,680					
Bank deposit account	20,000					
Bank interest received		700		700		
Capital		54,010				
Polar Insurance Company			860			
Depreciation			13930			
Closing stock (P&L)				5340		
Closing stock (B/S)			5340			
Provision for bad debts (adjustment)				518		
Deposit account interest owing			700			
SUBTOTAL	739,380	739,380				
Profit for the year						
TOTAL	739,380	739,380	26348	26348	2750	1300

Note. Only the above columns of the extended trial balance are required for this central assessment.

The bank statement shown below was received by Creative Catering on 1 June 1998 and was compared with the bank account section of the cash book also shown below.

MIDWEST BANK LTD
Bank statement

Creative Catering   **Account Number: 60419776**

Date	Detail	Debit £	Credit £	Balance £
1998				
14 May	Balance			6,300
14 May	Cheque 606842	120		6,180
14 May	Bank Giro Credit		230	6,410
15 May	Credit		320	6,730
18 May	Cheque 606844	260		6,470
19 May	Cheque 606843	440		6,030
20 May	Credit		375	6,405
21 May	Credit		2,650	9,055
22 May	Cheque 606846	1,100		7,955
22 May	Credit		860	8,815
26 May	Cheque 606848	1,650		7,165
27 May	Cheque	470		6,695
28 May	Credit		1,950	8,645

Bank account

May 15	Balance b/d	5,800	May 16	J Champion	845	620
18	P Donald	175	16	Catering Services	846	1,100
18	Mayes Ltd	200	20	Witworth Drinks	847	490
19	A Palmer	230	20	K J Foods	848	1,650
19	Rugby Club	1,260	22	D Andrews	849	470
20	Town Institute	1,390	26	Catering Services	850	260
22	P Whelan	860	27	Days Bakery	851	320
25	P Whitehead	1,950	29	K J Foods	852	1,400
28	Tennis Club	1,810	29	Balance c/d		7,365
		13,675				13,675

Task 2

Prepare a statement reconciling the £5,800 opening balance of the cash book with the £6,300 opening balance of the bank statement.

Balance of bank/cash Statement as at 14th May

£ 5800

Add: Cheque unpresented 606842 608844/43   820

Less Outstanding lodgement   320

Balance as per cash book.   6300.

Task 3

Prepare a bank reconciliation statement as at 29 May 1998.

....

....

....

....

....

....

....

....

....

....

....

SECTION 2 (Suggested time allocation: 40 minutes)

Answer each of the following questions in the space provided.

1   One of the vans used by Creative Catering was originally purchased on 1 November 1995 for £12,360. If the van was sold on 1 June 1998 for £6,500:

   (a)   **What would be the book value of the van at the date of sale?**

   £............5974.............

   (b)   **What would be the profit or loss on disposal of the van?**

   £............526............profit/loss

2   Jane Sutton is a member of the local golf club and occasionally assists with the club accounts. For the year to 31 December 1997 the club had 380 members. On 1 January 1997 six members owed the subscription for the previous year, but all of them subsequently paid the amount owing (£250 per member). At this time, no subscriptions were prepaid. On 31 December 1997 ten members had prepaid their subscription for the following year (£250 per member). During the year ended 31 December 1997, £98,000 was received in subscriptions. The amount payable for the year was again £250 per member.

   Calculate the number of members who had not paid their subscription on 31 December 1997.

   1 Jan 9+   6×250
              380×250
              10×250

   ....

   ....376........................4 members.............

   ....

   ....

3   Creative Catering provides catering for Barrett & Co, a small local business that is not registered for VAT. The sales invoice issued to Barrett & Co shows a total sum of £329, which includes £49 VAT. Barrett & Co treats the invoice as a hospitality expense in its books.

Note. State clearly for both (a) and (b) the names of the accounts, the amounts and whether each entry is a debit or credit.

(a)   **What would be the double entry made in Creative Catering's books to record the sale to Barrett & Co?**

Sales   280

Vat   49

Sales lod c/o   329

Debtars control a

(b)   **What would be the double entry made in Barrett & Co's books to record the purchase from Creative Catering?**

Creditors

Purchase ledger control   329

Hospitality   329

---

4   Jane Sutton decides to purchase some new equipment for Creative Catering on hire purchase.

When does Creative Catering record the equipment as a fixed asset in the books of the business?

| When the equipment is acquired | When the final instalment is paid | The equipment is never shown as a fixed asset |

5   A credit sale made to the Bristol Rowing Club is entered in error into the account of the Bristol Rugby Club in the sales ledger.

(a)   **Would the error be detected through use of the debtors control account?**

Yes / No

(b)   **Briefly explain the reason for your answer.**

The accounts of Bristol Rowing + Bristol Rugby are not part of the main account system — there are memorandum accounts.

6   After the end of the financial year on 30 April 1998 and after the profit for the year has been calculated, an invoice dated 20 April 1998 is found in a pile of letters. The invoice relates to a £500 purchase of soft drinks and has not been entered into the books of Creative Catering. Jane Sutton discusses the matter with you and says she is concerned that in leaving out the invoice the calculation of profit might have been affected. However, she finally decides that since all the drinks have been included in the valuation of the closing stock, none could have been sold during the year. She is therefore satisfied that all is well from an accounting point of view and tells you 'since none of the drinks were included in either the sales or purchases figure, the profits were not affected'.

She asks you to think about what she has said and to confirm her conclusions.

Write an appropriate memo to Jane Sutton covering the points she has raised relating to the calculation of profit for the financial year ended 30 April 1998. Use the headed paper on page 78 for your answer.

MEMORANDUM

To: Ref:

From: Date:

Subject:

_____

SECTION 3 (Suggested time allocation: 60 minutes)

Note. Clearly show your workings for all tasks.

Jane Sutton obtains her supplies of bread and cakes mainly from a small bakery owned by Pat Day. The goods are sold to various caterers, retailers and direct to the public through a shop attached to the bakery and also owned by Pat Day. The bakery and the shop have both recently been put up for sale and Jane Sutton is interested in buying them. She has been able to obtain some figures from the agent acting for Pat Day and these relate to the year ended 31 December 1997. Jane Sutton asks you to produce some information from these figures.

Figures for Pat Day's bakery and shop - available from the agent.

- Stocks:

	£
Stock of baking materials at 1 January 1997	1,000
Baking materials purchased	84,000
Stock of baking materials at 31 December 1997	3,000

All finished goods are sold and no finished goods are therefore held in stock.

- Staff costs

Bakery production wages	44,000
Bakery supervisory wages	25,000
Shop wages	30,000

- Business fixed assets

Bakery premises at cost 1 January 1970	100,000
Shop premises at cost 1 January 1970	80,000
Bakery equipment at cost 1 June 1990	50,000
Shop equipment at cost 1 June 1990	40,000

- Depreciation - calculated on a monthly basis:

Premises 2% per annum straight line method
Equipment 10% per annum straight line method

- Other business expenses

Bakery overheads	22,000
Shop expenses	30,000

- Sales

Two thirds of production is sold with a 50% mark-up to caterers and retail outlets. All these sales are on credit.
One third of production is passed to the shop to then be sold with a 100% mark up. All these sales are for cash.

- Debtors and creditors

Debtors at 1 January 1997	12,000
Creditors at 1 January 1997	6,000
Debtors at 31 December 1997	Unknown
Creditors at 31 December 1997	7,000
Received from debtors during the year	179,500
Paid to creditors during the year	Unknown

Task 1

Calculate the prime cost of the goods produced by the bakery during the year ended 31 December 1997.

....

....

....

....

....

....

....

....

....

....

Task 2

Calculate the total production cost of the goods made by the bakery during the year ended 31 December 1997.

....

....

....

....

....

....

....

....

....

Task 3

Calculate the total combined gross profit made by the shop and the bakery during the year ended 31 December 1997.

....

....

....

....

....

....

....

....

....

....

Task 4

Calculate the amount paid to creditors during the year ended 31 December 1997.

....

....

....

....

....

....

....

....

....

....

Task 5

Calculate the sum of money owed by debtors on 31 December 1997.

....

....

....

....

....

....

....

....

....

....

Unit 4
Answer Bank

SECTION 1

Country Crafts

Task 1

JOURNAL		
Details	DR £	CR £
Motor vans (cost) a/c	22,600	
Motor vans (cost) a/c		16,200
Motor vans (provision for dep'n) a/c	12,150	
(£16,200 × 25% × 3)		
Suspense a/c		17,600
Profit/loss on sale of fixed asset a/c		950
Being purchase of van L 673 NFU, transfer of provision for dep'n and sale of van H 247 AFE in part exchange		
Suspense a/c	3,900	
Motor cars (cost) a/c		9,200
Motor cars (provision for dep'n) a/c	4,600	
(£9,200 × 25% × 2)		
Profit/loss on sale of fixed asset a/c	700	
Being disposal of motor car J 168 TFE at a loss		
Sales	250	
Sundry income		250
Being transfer of sundry income into correct account		

Solutions to Tasks 2 to 4 are shown on the extended trial balance overleaf.

COUNTRY CRAFTS

Account	Trial balance Debit £	Trial balance Credit £	Adjustments Debit £	Adjustments Credit £	Accrued £	Prepaid £	Profit and loss a/c Debit £	Profit and loss a/c Credit £	Balance sheet Debit £	Balance sheet Credit £
Motor vans (cost)	42,400								42,400	
Motor cars (cost)	9,200								9,200	
Office furniture (cost)	4,850								4,850	
Computer equipment (cost)	16,830								16,830	
Motor vans (prov for depreciation)		4,950		10,600						15,550
Motor cars (prov for depreciation)		4,600		2,300						6,900
Office furniture (prov for depreciation)		1,940		485						2,425
Computer equipment (prov for depreciation)				5,610						5,610
Stock: opening	24,730						24,730			
Debtors control	144,280								144,280	
Bank		610		43						653
Cash	50		43	43					50	
Creditors control		113,660								113,660
Sales		282,240						282,240		
Purchases	152,140			1,150			150,990			
Rent	12,480					4,992	7,488			
Heat and light	1,840				210		2,050			
Wages and salaries	75,400						75,400			
Office expenses	7,900		43				7,943			
Motor expenses	14,890						14,890			
Depreciation (motor vans)			10,600				10,600			
Depreciation (motor cars)			2,300				2,300			
Depreciation (office furniture)			485				485			
Depreciation (computer equipment)			5,610				5,610			
Share capital		50,000								50,000
Profit and loss		35,850								35,850
VAT		12,640								12,640
Stock: closing (P&L)				31,600				31,600		
Stock: closing (B/S)			31,600						31,600	
Profit on sale of fixed asset		250						250		
Sundry income		250						250		
Insurance claim			950						950	
Stock loss			200				200			
Bad debt expense			7,214				7,214			
Provision for doubtful debts				7,214						7,214
Prepayments/accruals									4,992	210
SUBTOTAL	**506,990**	**506,990**	**59,045**	**59,045**	**210**	**4,992**	**309,900**	**314,340**	**255,152**	**250,712**
Profit for the year							4,440			4,440
TOTAL	**506,990**	**506,990**	**59,045**	**59,045**	**210**	**4,992**	**314,340**	**314,340**	**255,152**	**255,152**

Workings

1   *Profit on sale of fixed asset account*

	£
Profit on van	950
Loss on car	700
Net profit	250

2   *Insurance claim*

Cost of damaged stock (mark-up 100%) = 50% × £2,300
= £1,150 (a credit to the purchases account)
Less £200 excess = £950

Note. £200 is a 'stock loss' not covered by insurance.

3   *Stock write-off*

Baby Beatrice mugs: Cost 320/2 = £160
                                                 NRV = £120

NRV below cost ∴ write-off necessary

Windsor fire damage plate: Cost 620/2 = £310
                                                 NRV = £350

∴ No write-off necessary, NRV above cost

Closing stock ∴ £31,640 – £(160 – 120) = £31,600.

4   *Bad debt expense/provision*

Provision required: 5% × £144,280 = £7,214

5   *Prepayments and accruals*

Rent: prepayment = 8/12 × £7,488 = £4,992

Electricity: bill for 3 months to February 1994 = 2 × £315 = £630
∴ Accrual for December = 1/3 × £630 = £210

Futon Enterprises

<table>
<tr><td colspan="2" style="text-align:center">JOURNAL</td><td>Page 20</td></tr>
<tr><td>Details</td><td>DR
£</td><td>CR
£</td></tr>
<tr><td>(i) Delivery vans: cost
     Suspense account
     Delivery vans: cost (£12,400 - £10,000)
     Van disposal account

     Being correct treatment of cost of
     new van, clearing suspense account</td><td>10,000

2,400</td><td>
10,000

2,400</td></tr>
<tr><td>   Van disposal
     Delivery van (cost)
     Delivery van (provision for dep'n)
     Van disposal
     Loss on sale of van
     Van disposal

     Being disposal of old van (in part exchange)</td><td>12,000

7,884

1,716*</td><td>
12,000

7,884

1,716</td></tr>
<tr><td>(ii) Fixtures and fittings: cost
     Production wages

     Being cost of rebuilding reception area
     in production wages (£12,480 ÷ 52 = £240)</td><td>240</td><td>
240</td></tr>
<tr><td>(iii) Sales
     Sales ledger balances

     Being reversal of treatment of two futons
     given as presents (£48.00 ×2 ×175%)</td><td>168</td><td>
168</td></tr>
<tr><td>   Drawings
     Materials

     Being correct treatment of two futons
     given as presents (£48.00 ×2)</td><td>96</td><td>
96</td></tr>
</table>

	£
* Cost of van	12,000
Acc dep'n	7,884
NBV	4,116
Proceeds £(12,400	
−10,000)	2,400
Loss on disposal	1,716

FUTON ENTERPRISES

Account	Trial balance Debit £	Trial balance Credit £	Adjustments Debit £	Adjustments Credit £	Accrued £	Prepaid £	Profit and loss a/c Debit £	Profit and loss a/c Credit £	Balance sheet Debit £	Balance sheet Credit £
Delivery vans (cost)	12,400								12,400	
Assembling machine (cost)	3,650								3,650	
Furniture and fittings (cost)	11,030								11,030	
Delivery vans (prov for depreciation)				3,720						3,720
Assembling machine (prov for depreciation)		1,095		365						1,460
Furniture and fittings (prov for depreciation)		5,730		2,206						7,936
Stock: raw materials	1,320						1,320			
Stock: finished goods	1,440						1,440			
Sales ledger total	1,692			168					1,524	
Bank		320								320
Cash	50								50	
Purchase ledger total		4,265								4,265
Sales		120,240						120,240		
Materials	35,465						35,465			
Production wages (£12,480 - £240)	12,240						12,240			
Driver's wages	11,785						11,785			
Salaries	22,460						22,460			
Employer's NI	4,365						4,365			
Motor expenses	2,160			114			2,046			
Rent	3,930					786	3,144			
Sundry expenses	3,480				60		3,540			
VAT		1,220								1,220
Inland Revenue		1,365								1,365
Drawings (£12,400 + £168)	12,568								12,568	
Capital		7,516								7,516
Depreciation: delivery vans			3,720				3,720			
Depreciation: assembling machine			365				365			
Depreciation: furniture and fittings			2,206				2,206			
Loss on sale of van	1,716						1,716			
Closing stock (B/S): raw materials			1,526						1,526	
Closing stock (B/S): finished goods (£48 x 23)			1,104						1,104	
Closing stock (P&L): raw materials				1,526				1,526		
Closing stock (P&L): finished goods (£48 x 23)				1,104				1,104		
Insurance claim debtor			114						114	
Bad debts (48 x 1.75 x 2)			168				168			
Prepayments/accruals									786	60
SUBTOTAL	**141,751**	**141,751**	**9,203**	**9,203**	**60**	**786**	**105,980**	**122,870**	**44,752**	**27,862**
Profit for the year							16,890			16,890
TOTAL	**141,751**	**141,751**	**9,203**	**9,203**	**60**	**786**	**122,870**	**122,870**	**44,752**	**44,752**

Kidditoys

Details	DR £	CR £
JOURNAL — Page 20		
(i) DEBIT Suspense a/c	1,908	
CREDIT T. Ditton a/c (Purchase ledger)		1,908
Being correction of misposting		
(ii) DEBIT Suspense a/c	50	
DEBIT Provision for depreciation a/c (shop fittings) (W1)	1,944	
DEBIT Loss on sale of fixed assets a/c	1,246	
CREDIT Shop fittings (cost a/c)		3,240
Being disposal of shop fittings		
DEBIT Shop fittings (cost) a/c	9,620	
CREDIT Kingston Displays Ltd (Purchase ledger)		9,620
Being purchase of new shop fittings		
(iii) DEBIT Drawings a/c (12 × £2,000)	24,000	
CREDIT Wages a/c		24,000
Being correction of misposting		
(iv) DEBIT E. Molesey a/c (Purchase ledger)	3	
CREDIT Discount received a/c		3
Being discount received from E. Molesey after accidental underpayment		
(v) DEBIT Drawings a/c	640	
CREDIT Sales a/c		545
CREDIT VAT a/c		95
Being stock withdrawn for own use		
(vi) DEBIT Bank current a/c	9	
CREDIT Interest received a/c		9
Being posting of bank interest received credited on bank statement		

KIDDITOYS	Trial balance		Adjustments		Accrued	Prepaid
Account	Debit	Credit	Debit	Credit		
	£	£	£	£	£	£
Sales		392,727				
Sales returns	1,214					
Purchases	208,217					
Purchase returns		643				
Stock	32,165					
Wages	26,000					
Rent	27,300					2,100
Rates	8,460					2,080
Light and heat	2,425				212	
Office expenses	3,162					
Selling expenses	14,112					
Motor expenses	14,728					
Sundry expenses	6,560					
Motor vans (cost)	12,640					
Shop fittings (cost)	9,620					
Office equipment (cost)	4,250					
Motor vans (prov for depreciation)		2,528		2,528		
Shop fittings (prov for depreciation)				962		
Office equipment (prov for depreciation)		2,550		850		
Cash	100					
Bank current account	4,429					
Bank investment account	68,340					
Interest received		3,289				
Capital		22,145				
VAT		6,515				
Purchase ledger total		29,588				
Loss on sale of fixed assets	1,246					
Kingston Displays Limited		9,620				
Drawings	24,640					
Discount received		3				
Depreciation (motor vans)			2,528			
Depreciation (shop fittings)			962			
Depreciation (office equipment)			850			
Stock (closing): P&L				21,060		
Stock (closing): B/S			21,060			
SUBTOTAL	469,608	469,608	25,400	25,400	212	4,180
Profit for the year						
TOTAL	**469,608**	**469,608**	**25,400**	**25,400**	**212**	**4,180**

Workings

1   *Accumulated depreciation on shop fittings disposed of*

£324 × 6 years = £1,944

2   *Depreciation of fixed assets*

Motor van: annual depreciation charge $= \dfrac{£12,640}{5} = £2,528$

∴ Accumulated depreciation at 1.12.93 = £2,528

Shop fittings: depreciation charge $= \dfrac{£9,620}{10} = £962$

Office equipment: annual depreciation charge $= \dfrac{£4,250}{5} = £850$

Accumulated depreciation as at 1.12.93 = £850 × 3 = £2,550

3   *Business rates prepayment*

Prepayment $= £6,240 \times \dfrac{4 \text{ months}}{12 \text{ months}} = £2,080$

4   *Electricity accrual*

Accrual $= £318 \times \dfrac{2 \text{ months}}{3 \text{ months}} = £212$

SECTION 2

Country Crafts

1 The computer software has been purchased for continuing use in the business, and in that sense, could be called a fixed asset. However, many small value assets are not recorded as assets but written off directly as an expense when purchased. The decision as to how to treat the item depends on materiality, that is whether or not the item has a significant effect on the financial statements. In this particular case the expenditure on software was not material, which suggests that the item should be treated as an expense.

2

	£
Cost 1991	9,200
Depreciation 1991: 50% × £9,200	4,600
Net book value	4,600
Depreciation 1992: 50% × £4,600	2,300
Net book value	2,300
Proceeds	3,900
Profit	1,600

3 A payment in advance is *deferred income*. It would be treated as a current liability in the 1993 accounts and as income in the 1994 accounts.

4 (a) An imbalance arising from a transposition error could not occur in a computerised accounting system, because the figure is entered only once and the computer carries out the double entry.

   (b) An error of principle could occur if a computerised accounting system is used. This is because the decision as to which account an item should be posted to rests with the person responsible, not with the computer.

5 It would be wrong to treat this as a bad debt since it is only a rumour, and a bad debt is a debt that has definitely gone bad. If the business is not already making a provision for doubtful debts, it should do so now, or should investigate whether the existing provision is adequate.

6 The balance on a VAT account represents the difference between output VAT (VAT collected from customers) and input VAT (VAT paid to suppliers). As the VAT account has a credit balance, the balance represents the excess of output tax over input tax.

7 The purpose of the expenditure was to maintain the existing capacity of the asset, rather than to improve it. This is therefore revenue expenditure.

8 The correct treatment would be:

   DEBIT   Office expenses
   CREDIT   Purchases

Futon Enterprises

1 *Stock valuation*

   Cost = £48.00 × 2 = £96.00

NRV	£
Selling price (£50.00 × 2)	100.00
Costs to complete (£18.00 × 2)	36.00
	64.00

   This stock would have been valued at £64.00, reducing the total stock value by £96.00 − £64.00 = £32.00. The stock should be valued at NRV because the prudence concept requires that losses should be recognised as soon as they are foreseen. The £32.00 is such a loss. In addition, SSAP 9 requires that stock be valued at the lower of cost and NRV.

2 The net book value of the assembling machinery at 31 May 1994 is £3,650 − £1,460 = £2,190. This does not mean that the business would obtain this amount if it sold the machinery at 31 May 1994, because the depreciation charged is not meant to reflect the market value of the asset. Rather, it is a measure of the wearing out of the asset through time and use; it is allocated to the accounting periods which are expected to benefit (ie make a profit) from the asset's use.

3   One reason for the choice of the reducing balance for vans is that motor vehicles lose a great deal of their value in the first year of use. This reflects the use made of the asset at its most efficient and it is a good example of 'matching' profits against costs.

4   The payment would have been accounted for as:

DEBIT	Bank	£168
CREDIT	Bad debt expense	£168

5   The balance on the Inland Revenue account represents the income tax owed on the profits of the business (probably just for the previous year) to the Inland Revenue, less any payments already made. Obviously, a tax charge is required for the current year and this would be accounted for as:

DEBIT	Profit and loss account
CREDIT	Inland Revenue account

6   Strictly speaking, the cost of refitting, including the assembler's wages, should be capitalised as an addition to delivery vans cost, because the refitting has added value to the van. However, the amount is immaterial to the results of the business; such small amounts are best treated as revenue expenditure in the profit and loss account.

7   (a)   The transaction should be treated on a monthly basis as:

DEBIT	Bank (or cash)	£40
CREDIT	Rental (or sundry) income	£40

   (b)   The outstanding £40 would be credited to the profit and loss account and shown as a sundry debtor in the balance sheet.

8   (a)   A debit entry in the VAT accounts.

   (b)   This represents the VAT on petty cash payments which the business can reclaim from HM Customs & Excise.

   (c)
DEBIT	Cash	£37
CREDIT	Bank	£37

Kidditoys

1   Sophie's customers either pay cash in the shop or send cash with their orders. Since, therefore, she has no debtors, Sophie will not have a problem with bad debts.

2   The credit balance on Sophie's VAT account is the amount by which VAT collected on sales exceeds VAT paid on purchases and expenses. The balance is owing to HM Customs & Excise.

3
DEBIT	Bank a/c
CREDIT	Sales a/c
CREDIT	VAT a/c

4   Net book value of van $= £12,640 \times \dfrac{3 \text{ years}}{5 \text{ years}} = £7,584$

   This figure represents the cost of the van less accumulated depreciation to date. It is not an indication of the market value of the van.

5   (a)   The original sales price of each doll was £16, so the original cost must have been £8. Net realisable value at £5 is £3 lower, so the closing stock valuation will be reduced by £3 × 4 = £12.

   (b)   Profit would be reduced by £12.

6
DEBIT	Purchases
CREDIT	Creditors

7   No transaction has yet taken place; the stock still belongs to Kidditoys. No entries should be made in the accounts until a sale is made by John King.

8   The accounting treatment of the £85 spent on software depends on whether the amount is regarded as material. If it is considered material it should be capitalised:

DEBIT	Office equipment (cost)	£85
CREDIT	Bank/creditors	£85

However if, as is more likely, the amount is not to be regarded as material, the amount would be written off to office expenses as follows.

DEBIT	Office expenses	£85
CREDIT	Bank/creditors	£85

9 (a) It would appear in the credit column as a balancing figure because debits would exceed credits.

   (b) It would appear in the debit column as a deduction from capital.

10

Profit and Loss A/c		*Balance Sheet Balances*	
Dr	*Cr*	*Dr*	*Cr*
32,165	21,060	21,060	

SECTION 3

Brian Hope

Tutorial note. The three most difficult accounts to complete are trade debtors, cash and drawings. It is best to put in all the figures you know and complete the 'easier' accounts first. You should then be able to calculate, as a balancing figure, the amount for debtors who pay in cash. This will slot into the 'cash account', enabling you to calculate cash drawings as a balancing figure. The suggested time allocation for this incomplete records exercise is 1 hour.

TRADE DEBTORS

Balance b/f	1,420	Bank	21,120
		Allowance	300
Sales	26,720	Bad debt	90
		Balance c/f	1,030
		£(1120-90)	
		Cash	5,600
	28,140		28,140

VEHICLE RUNNING EXPENSES

		Balance b/f	80
Cash	500		
Bank	1,040	Profit & loss	1,520
Balance c/f	60		
	1,600		1,600

TRADE CREDITORS

Balance c/f	2,460	Balance b/f	2,220
Cash discount	200	Purchases	4,510
Bank *	4,070		
	6,730		6,730

* Payments to creditors: £(3,930 - 70 + 210) = £4,070

INSURANCE

Balance b/f	340		
		Profit & loss	920
Bank	960		
		Balance c/f	380
	1,300		1,300

RENT

Balance b/f	400		
		Balance c/f	480
Bank	2,640	Profit & loss	2,560
	3,040		3,040

CASH

Balance b/f	10	Bank	510
		Vehicle running costs	500
Debtors	5,600	Other expenses	500
		Drawings (bal)	4,100
	5,610		5,610

VEHICLES							VEHICLES

VEHICLES					DRAWINGS		
Balance b/f	6,000	Acc. dep'n	1,200		Bank	8,000	Capital	12,100
Bank	3,600	Profit & loss*	400		Cash	4,100		
		Balance c/f	8,000				
	9,600		9,600				
						12,100		12,100

* £(6,000 - 1,200 - 4,000) = £400 loss

Kuldipa Potiwal

Task 1

CALCULATION OF NET PROFIT
FOR THE YEAR ENDED 31 OCTOBER 1993

	£	£
Sales (W1)		133,590
Opening stock	12,200	
Purchases (W2)	78,080	
Closing stock	(13,750)	
Cost of sales		76,530
Gross profit		57,060
Rent received (W3)		2,750
		59,810
Expenses		
Rent and rates (W3)	6,700	
Postage and packing	2,200	
Motor expenses	5,050	
Admin expenses (W3)	5,390	
Wages	18,200	
Stock loss (£6,000 × 100/150 × 50%)	2,000	
Depreciation £(17,500 – 12,500)	5,000	
		44,540
Net profit		15,270

Task 2

CALCULATION OF CAPITAL AS AT 31 OCTOBER 1993

	£
Opening capital (W4)	23,775
Profit	15,270
	39,045
Additional capital (investment income)	1,500
	40,545
Drawings (W5)	11,760
Closing capital	28,785

This figure can be confirmed by producing a balance sheet as at 31 October 1993, although this is not required by the question.

BALANCE SHEET AS AT 31 OCTOBER 1993

	£	£
Fixed assets		
Van		12,500
Current assets		
Stock	13,750	
Debtors	7,200	
Prepayments	200	
Insurance claim (50%)	2,000	
Rent receivable	250	
Bank	6,500	
	29,900	
Current liabilities		
Creditors	13,400	
Accruals	215	
	13,615	
		16,285
Net current assets		28,785
Closing capital		28,785

Workings

1   *Sales*

CASH BOOK

	Cash £		Bank £		Cash £		Bank £
Sales	86,390	Bankings	56,000	Bankings	56,000	Bal b/f 1.11.92	3,250
		Debtors	46,000	Wages (350 × 52)	18,200	Creditors	78,000
		Investment income	1,500	Drawings (220 × 52)	11,440	Postage & packing	2,200
		Rent	2,500	Admin exps	750	Rent & rates	6,400
						Motor exps	5,050
						Admin exps	4,600
						Bal c/f 31.10 93	6,500
	86,390		106,000		86,390		106,000

Note. As cash is banked daily, there will be no cash in hand b/fwd or c/fwd.

DEBTORS CONTROL A/C

		£			£
1.11.92	Balance b/fwd	6,000	31.10.92	Bank	46,000
	Sales (bal fig)	47,200		Balance c/fwd	7,200
		53,200			53,200

Total sales = £(86,390 + 47,200) = £133,590

2   *Purchases*

CREDITORS CONTROL A/C

		£			£
	Bank	78,000	1.11 92	Bal b/fwd	9,000
31.10.93	Bal c/fwd	13,400		Purchases (bal fig)	82,400
		91,400			91,400

	£
Purchases per CC a/c	82,400
Less stolen games £6,000 × 100/150	(4,000)
Less Christmas presents £480 × 100/150	(320)
	78,080

3   *Expenses*

Rent and rates: £(6,400 + 500 − 200) = £6,700
Admin expenses: £(750 + 4,600 − 175 + 215) = £5,390
Rent received: £(2,500 + 250) = £2,750

4   *Opening capital*

	£	£
Assets		
Van	17,500	
Stock	12,200	
Debtors	6,000	
Prepayments	500	
		36,200
Liabilities		
Creditors	9,000	
Accruals	175	
Bank overdraft	3,250	
		12,425
Net assets = capital		23,775

5   *Drawings*

	£
Cash (W1)	11,440
Christmas presents* 480 × 100/150	320
	11,760

*Note. Drawings from stock are at cost price. Selling price inclusive of VAT may also be used.

Fancy Flowers

Task 1

Closing stock valuation

	Cost £	Adjust £	Total £
Pot plants	280	(70)	210
Roses	240		240
Tulips	160		160
Sprays	340	(80)	260
Plant food	80		80
Vases	520	(30)*	490
			1,440

*£6 × 100/200 × 10 = £30

Task 2

	£	£
Sales £(31,420 − 5,000 + 14,200 + 345 + 60)		41,025
Cost of sales		
Purchases £(24,180 + 850 + 345 − (£5* × 52))	25,115	
Closing stock (see *Task 1*)	(1,440)	
		23,675
Gross profit		17,350
Expenses		
Rent £(5,000 − 1,000)	4,000	
Rates	420	
Advertising £(385 + 45)	430	
Insurance	390	
Electricity £(780 + 360) + (1/3 × £360)	1,260	
Sundry expenses £(560 + 345)	905	
Interest	84	
		7,489
Profit		9,861

*£10 × 100%/200% = £5.

Note. It is not clear whether the flowers Sarah has taken have a mark-up or 100% or 75%.

Task 3

Capital account

	£
Balance at 1 June 1993	5,000
Add profit for year (see *Task 2*)	9,861
Less drawings: cash	(14,200)
goods	(260)
Balance at 31 May 1994	401

Task 4

The business is making a reasonable profit but Sarah is taking much more in wages for herself. As well as the profit for the year, she has also withdrawn a substantial part of her initial capital investment. It is unlikely that she will be able to continue drawing at this rate, particularly if the business requires more investment in future.

The gross profit figures shows a mark-up on cost of approximately 73%, or a gross profit percentage of 42%. the net profit percentage is 24%. These figures are quite healthy, although it might be wise to reduce stock write-offs in future (charge for special orders in advance?) and reduce the more discretionary expenses, such as advertising.

Manuel

Task 1

CASH BOOK

DETAIL	DISCOUNT	CASH	BANK	DISCOUNT	CASH	BANK
	£	£	£	£	£	£
Balance b/d		320	300			
Bar takings		200				
Major		80				
Bank			300		300	
Wages					50	40
Bank charges						35
Torquay Wines				15		285
Balance c/d					250	240
		600	600	15	600	600

SALES

	£		£
		Cash	200
		Major	100
		Mr Twychin	120
Balance	420		
	420		420

PURCHASES

	£		£
Devon Wines	175	Devon Wines	75
Torquay Wines	500		
		Balance	600
	675		675

MAJOR

	£		£
Balance b/d	80	Cash	80
Sales	100		
		Balance c/d	100
	180		180

WAGES			
	£		£
Cash	50		
Bank	40		
		Balance	90
	90		90

MR TWYCHIN			
	£		£
Sales	120	Balance c/d	120
	120		120

BANK CHARGES			
	£		£
Bank	35	Balance	35
	35		35

DEVON WINES

	£		£
Purchases	75	Purchases	175
Balance c/d	100		
	175		175

TORQUAY WINES

	£		£
Bank		Purchases	
Discount			
Balance c/d			

Task 2

PARTIAL TRIAL BALANCE AS AT 30 JUNE

	Dr	Cr
	£	£
Bank balance	240	
Cash in till	250	
Discounts		15
Sales		420
Purchases	600	
Major	100	
Wages	90	
Mr Twychin	120	
Bank charges	35	
Devon Wines		100
Torquay Wines		200
Difference (Note)		700
	1,435	1,435

Note. the £700 by which debits exceed credits corresponds to the opening balances as follows.

	£
Debtor (major)	80
Opening cash balance	320
Opening bank balance	300
	700

PRACTICE CENTRAL ASSESSMENT 1:HIGHBURY DISCS

SECTION 1

Task 1

See extended trial balance on Page 107.

Task 2

	Depreciation charge for the year ended 31 May 1995
	£
Motor vehicles	3,576
Equipment	9,550
Total	13,126

Task 3

Stock sheets	Value
	£
Total b/f from previous pages	18,000
Bambino choir of Prague	3,500
The Joyful Singers sing Wesley	1,200
Bach at St Thomas's	5,000
Value of stock as at 31 May 1995	27,700

Task 4

JOURNAL		Page 1
Details	**£**	**£**
(a) DEBIT Artists' fees and royalties	4,500	
CREDIT Sundry creditors		4,500
Being royalties due to artists for the quarter ended 31 May 1995.		
DEBIT Artists' fees and royalties	252	
CREDIT Sundry creditors		252
Being correction of under-calculation of royalties due to Mr Willis-Brown for quarter ended 31 December 1994		
(b) DEBIT Debtors	220	
CREDIT Bank		220
Being dishonoured cheque		
(c) DEBIT Drawings	2,110	
CREDIT Motor expenses		2,110
Being correct posting of private motoring expenses		

Tasks 5 and 6

See extended trial balance on Page 107.

HIGHBURY DISCS

Account	Trial balance Debit £	Trial balance Credit £	Adjustments Debit £	Adjustments Credit £	Accrued £	Prepaid £	Profit and loss a/c Debit £	Profit and loss a/c Credit £	Balance sheet Debit £	Balance sheet Credit £
Artists' fees and royalties	41,120				4,752		45,872			
Bank and cash	1,420			220					1,200	
Capital		26,449								26,449
Drawings	14,500		2,110						16,610	
Employer's NI	3,619						3,619			
Equipment (cost)	38,200								38,200	
Motor vehicles (cost)	29,800								29,800	
Equipment (prov for depreciation)		19,100		9,550						28,650
Motor vehicles (prov for depreciation)		17,880		3,576						21,456
Loan		10,000								10,000
Loan interest	1,350				150		1,500			
Mastering and production costs	143,400						143,400			
Motor expenses	6,330			2,110			4,220			
Recording costs	12,550						12,550			
Rent	13,000					1,000	12,000			
Sales		307,800						307,800		
Stocks of compact discs	22,500						22,500			
Sundry creditors		4,080								4,080
Sundry debtors	12,500		220						12,720	
Sundry expenses	1,270						1,270			
VAT (amount owing)		3,250								3,250
Wages and salaries	47,000						47,000			
Depreciation			13,126				13,126			
Closing stock (B/S)			27,700						27,700	
Closing stock (P&L)				27,700				27,700		
Prepayments/accruals									1,000	4,902
SUBTOTAL	388,559	388,559	43,156	43,156	4,902	1,000	307,057	335,500	127,230	98,787
Profit for the year							28,443			28,443
TOTAL	388,559	388,559	43,156	43,156	4,902	1,000	335,500	335,500	127,230	127,230

SECTION 2

1   (a)   The credit balance on the VAT account represents the excess of VAT collected on sales (output tax) over VAT paid on purchases or expenses (input tax).

    (b)   This amount is owed to HM Customs & Excise.

2   The microphones could become obsolete as a newer, better model comes onto the market.

3   A case could be made for capitalising the cost of the tapes, on the grounds that they are for use over a number of accounting periods. Highbury Discs has not, however, adopted this treatment because, at only £8 each, the cost of the tapes is not material. They have therefore been expensed in the year of purchase.

    It should be emphasised that this type of decision is not always clear cut. In particular, what is material to a small business may not be to a large one.

4   (a)   This year's profit would be overstated since closing stock is a deduction from cost of sales.

    (b)   Next year's profit would be understated since opening stock is an addition to cost of sales.

5   The accruals or matching concept.

6

MEMORANDUM

To: Anthony Sedgewick   Ref:
From: Accounting Technician   Date: 6 June 1995
Subject: *Rules for stock valuation*

The fundamental accounting concept of prudence dictates that profits are not anticipated but losses are taken into account as soon as they are foreseen.

This cautious approach is adopted in SSAP 9 *Stocks and long-term contracts* which states that stock should be valued at the lower of cost and net realisable value (NRV). Cost, here, is the cost of producing the discs, together with a share of manufacturing overheads. Net realisable value is the estimated selling price less any further costs required to sell the product or get the product into saleable form.

It should be noted further that the comparison of cost and NRV should be carried out for each item separately. It is not sufficient to compare the total cost of all stock items with their total NRV.

When net realisable value is lower than cost, net realisable value should be used. Applying this principle to the Bambino Choir discs, NRV is higher than costs, because we expect to earn a profit on them, even if this profit is delayed.

However, in the case of the 'Joyful Singers' discs, net realisable value is £3.00 each, which is lower than cost of £5.00 each. Thus we will make a loss of 400 × (£5 − £3) ie £800, which, following the prudence concept we must take to the P&L as soon as it is foreseen.

Turning now to the Bach at St Thomas's discs, we see an application of *net* realisable value. The discs cost £3.50 each. While they can be sold for £4.00, this would only be after incurring further costs of £1.50 per disc. The net realisable value of each disc is therefore £4.00 less £1.50, that is £2.50 per disc. Since this is below cost, this is the figure that must be used.

SECTION 3

Tutorial notes

(1)   Be careful when calculating the discounts received figure. The £30,060 paid to creditors is 90% of the normal price, so the discount is £30,060 × $\dfrac{10\%}{90\%}$, ie £3,340.

(2) The van owned at the beginning of the year is shown at net book value. It has been depreciated for one year, so the original cost was £7,500 × 4/3 = £10,000.

BANK			
	£		£
Balance b/f	323	Trade creditors	30,060
Cash	2,770	Drawings	12,000
Trade debtors	43,210	Motor van	4,800
Capital	10,000	Rent	5,330
		Motor expenses	3,400
		Balance c/d	713
	56,303		56,303
Balance b/d	713		

CASH			
	£		£
Balance b/f	25	Bank	2,770
Trade debtors	8,340	Motor expenses	600
		Drawings (bal fig)	4,961
		Balance c/d	34
	8,365		8,365
Balance b/d	34		

MOTOR EXPENSES			
	£		£
Bank	3,400	Balance b/f	174
Cash	600	Profit and loss	4,035
Balance c/d	209		
	4,209		4,209
		Balance b/d	209

MOTOR VAN(S)			
	£		£
Balance b/f	7,500	Depreciation charge (P&L)	
Bank	4,800	£(10,000 ÷ 4) + (4,800 ÷ 4 × $^4/_{12}$)	2,900
		Balance c/d	9,400
	12,300		12,300
Balance b/d	9,400		

RENT AND INSURANCE			
	£		£
Balance (insurance) b/f	180	Balance (rent) b/f	250
Bank	5,330	Profit and loss	5,060
		Balance (insurance) c/d	200
	5,510		5,510
Balance (insurance) b/d	200		

MATERIALS USED			
	£		£
Balance b/f	1,530	Profit and loss	33,910
Purchases	33,980	Balance c/d	1,600
	35,510		35,510
Balance b/d	1,600		

TRADE CREDITORS			
	£		£
Bank	30,060	Balance b/f	3,650
Discounts received		Purchases (bal fig)	33,980
(£30,060 × $^{10\%}/_{90\%}$)	3,340		
Balance c/d	4,230		
	37,630		37,630
		Balance b/d	4,230

TRADE DEBTORS			
	£		£
Balance b/f	1,550	Bank	43,210
Work done	52,000	Bad debts	480
		Cash (bal fig)	8,340
		Balance c/d £(2,000 – 480)	1,520
	53,550		53,550
Balance b/d	1,520		

DRAWINGS			
	£		£
Bank	12,000	Capital	16,961
Cash	4,961		
	16,961		16,961

PRACTICE CENTRAL ASSESSMENT 2: JASON BROWN

SECTION 1

Task 1

See extended trial balance on Page 112.

Task 2

(a) *Depreciation*

Delivery vans: £$(12,800 - 3,520) \times 20\% = £1,856$

Equipment £$22,800 \times 10\% = £2,280$

Total depreciation = £4,136

(b) *Interest*

£$30,000 \times 6\% = £1,800$

∴£600 accrued interest is receivable.

(c) *Bad debts*

	£
Debtors control account balance	41,600
Debt written off: M C Millar	2,460
	39,140

Provision for doubtful debts required
= 5% × £39,140 = £1,957 ∴ reduce current provision of £1,980 by £23.

(d) *Stock*

The damaged chairs must be valued at the lower of cost and net realisable value.

		£
Cost (£230 × 4)		920
NRV:	selling price (£190 × 4)	760
	less repairs	40
		720

∴ Reduce stock by £$(920 - 720) = £200$
Closing stock is £$(58,394 - 200) = £58,194$

(e) *JB Office Supplies*

This payment has not in fact been made, so the original entry must be reversed.

DEBIT	Bank overdraft	£1,260	
CREDIT	Creditors control a/c		£1,260

(f) *Insurance*

Premium prepaid = £260 × 6/12 = £130

(g) *Rent*

Total rent payable = £200 × 12 = £2,400

∴ £200 must be accrued

JASON BROWN

Account	Trial balance Debit £	Trial balance Credit £	Adjustments Debit £	Adjustments Credit £	Accrued Debit £	Accrued Credit £	Prepaid Debit £	Prepaid Credit £	Profit and loss a/c Debit £	Profit and loss a/c Credit £	Balance sheet Debit £	Balance sheet Credit £
Purchases	170,240								170,240			
Sales		246,412								246,412		
Purchases returns		480								480		
Sales returns	670								670			
Opening stock	54,200								54,200			
Salaries	30,120								30,120			
Rent	2,200					200			2,400			
Insurance	360							130	230			
Delivery vans (cost)	12,800										12,800	
Equipment (cost)	22,800										22,800	
Delivery vans (prov for depreciation)		3,520		1,856								5,376
Equipment (prov for depreciation)		5,760		2,280								8,040
Bad debts	2,700		2,460						5,160			
Provision for bad debts		1,980	23									1,957
Debtors control account	41,600			2,460							39,140	
Creditors control account		33,643		1,260								34,903
Drawings	10,522										10,522	
Capital		83,171										83,171
Bank overdraft		348	1,260								912	
Cash	568										568	
VAT		2,246										2,246
Bank interest received		1,200		600						1,800		
Bank deposit account	30,000										30,000	
Suspense account	20										20	
Depreciation			4,136						4,136			
Bank interest owing			600								600	
Closing stock (P&L)				58,194						58,194		
Closing stock (B/S)			58,194								58,194	
Provision for bad debts (adjustment)				23						23		
Prepayments/accruals							130				130	
SUBTOTAL	378,780	378,780	66,673	66,673		200		130	267,156	306,909	175,666	135,913
Profit for the year									39,753			39,753
TOTAL	378,780	378,780	66,673	66,673	200	200	130	130	306,909	306,909	175,666	175,666

Task 3

See extended trial balance on Page 112.

Task 4

See journal below.

Note. These journals clear the suspense account, as shown in the ledger account.

SUSPENSE ACCOUNT

	£		£
Debtors control a/c	60	Balance on TB	20
Sales	570	Discounts	250
		Purchases	360
	630		630

JOURNAL		Page 1
Details	**£**	**£**
(a) DEBIT Suspense a/c	60	
CREDIT Debtors control a/c		60
Being receipt from debtor not recorded in control a/c		
(b) DEBIT Discounts received	125	
DEBIT Discounts allowed	125	
CREDIT Suspense account		250
Being correction of double entry and correct account for discount allowed		
(c) DEBIT Purchase a/c	360	
CREDIT Suspense a/c		360
Being correction of purchases day book transposition		
(d) DEBIT Suspense a/c	570	
CREDIT Sales		570
Being correction of undercast in sales day book		

SECTION 2

1 (a) *Book value of van at sale*

	£
Cost	6,000
Accumulated depreciation 1.11.93 - 31.10.94 = £6,000 × 20%	1,200
	4,800
1.11.94 - 31.10.95 = £4,800 × 20%	960
	3,840
1.11.95 - 30.4.95 = £3,840 × 20%	384
Book value at date of sale	3,456

(b) *Disposals account*

MOTOR VANS DISPOSAL ACCOUNT			
	£		£
Vans: cost	6,000	Motor vans: provision for depreciation £(6,000 – 3,456)	2,544
		Cash	3,200
		Profit and loss a/c	256
	6,000		6,000

2   The argument in favour of including the advertising costs in the calculation of profit for the year ended 31 October 1997 is based on the *accruals concept*. The costs of advertising will be 'matched' with the associated revenues of the service. (However, the prudence concept might dictate that the costs should be written off against current profits if there is no guarantee that the consultancy will be profitable.)

3   (a) Decreased by £250
       (b) Decreased by £360

4   (a) *Sales for October*

$(2 + 4 + 6) \times £50 = £600$

(b) *Cost of goods sold for October*

		£
Sale 13.10.95: Cost = 2 × £30		60
Sale 18.10.95: Cost = 4 × £30		120
Sale 30.10.95: Cost = 4 × £30		120
2 × £32		64
12		364

(c) *Closing stock*

	£
10 at £32	320
10 at £31	310
	630

5   This statement is not true because fixed assets must be depreciated over their useful economic lives. The periodic depreciation charge passes through the profit and loss account as an expense, thus reducing profit. The benefit obtained from use of the asset is thus matched against its cost.

6   (a) It excludes VAT.

       (b) SSAP 5 *Accounting for VAT* requires all figures in the accounts, in particular sales and purchases, to be shown net of VAT, where VAT is recoverable.

MEMORANDUM

To: Jason Brown

From: Accounting technician

Subject: *Profit and accounting rules*

Ref:

Date: 8 December 1995

There are various problems with the changes you propose to make next year to improve profitability.

(a) At the year end the cost of sales is matched with sales to calculate profit. Where stocks are held at the year end, these must be matched against future sales (under the accruals, or matching concept), and so they are deducted from the current cost of sales. You can see then that running down stocks at the year end would therefore have no impact, for example:

	Higher year end stocks	*Lower year end stocks*
	£	£
Purchases (and opening stock)	120,000	100,000
Closing stock	30,000	10,000
	90,000	90,000

There is no effect on profit, just a lower closing stock figure in the balance sheet, and a higher cash balance (fewer purchases made).

(b) The prudence concept states that all losses must be recognised as soon as they are foreseen. It is therefore not acceptable to 'put off' writing off a debt until the following year (when in any case it would have just as bad an effect on profit).

(c) It is not acceptable to change the method of depreciation of assets from year to year because of the consistency concept. This requires items to be treated in the same way over time in order to allow comparison between accounts from year to year.

I am afraid that the only real ways to increase profitability are to increase sales and cut costs!

MEMORANDUM

To: Jason Brown   Ref:

From: Accounting Technician   Date: 8 December 1995

Subject: *Sales ledger errors*

The error discovered, that £96.20 had not been posted to the account of John Pearce Furniture Ltd, will not be discovered by a trial balance because the account in question is not part of the system of accounts. It is, rather, a 'personal' account kept as a memorandum of how much an individual owes your business, along with all other such accounts in the sales ledger.

The account within the system which relates to debtors, the debtors control account, is an impersonal, summary account which shows only the *total* owed to your business by debtors.

These accounts are both posted from the same sources (such as the sales day book and the cash book), but the debtors control account postings are in total, whereas the personal accounts in the sales ledger are posted with individual transactions.

The control account balance should therefore, in theory, be equal to the total of all the balances in the personal accounts in the sales ledger. In practice, discrepancies arise, and by comparing the two totals and investigating these discrepancies, errors can be found in both types of account and thereby corrected.

This is a good way of making sure that the figure from the control account, which appears under debtors in the balance sheet, is correct, as well as ensuring that you receive the correct amounts from the individual debtors of the business.

SECTION 3

Task 1

	£
Premises	74,400
Fixtures and fittings	28,800
Stocks £(15,613 – 10,000)	5,613
	108,813
Less bank loan	48,000
	60,813
Surplus funds	1,220
Original capital invested	62,033

Task 2

CARLTON OFFICE SUPPLIES				
	£			£
Oct 95		*Oct 95*		
		Credit purchases		10,000
Nov 95		*Nov 95*		
Bank	9,800	Credit purchases		12,500
Discount received	200	Credit purchases		8,600
Bank	12,250			
Discount received	250			
Creditor c/f	8,600			
	31,100			31,100

Task 3

	£
Carlton Office Supplies	
October	10,000
November £(12,500 + 8,600)	21,100
Cash purchases £(187 + 5,613)	5,800
	36,900

Task 4

Profit for November 1995

	£	£
Sales (balancing figure)		32,125
Cost of sales		
Purchases	36,900	
Closing stock	11,200	
		25,700
Gross profit (£25,700 × 25/100)		6,425
Discounts received		450
		6,875
Expenses		
Insurance (384 × 1/12)	32	
Depreciation		
Premises (2% × £74,400 × 1/12)	124	
Fixtures (10% × £28,800 × 1/12)	240	
Computer (1/3 × £(1,402 − 250) × 1/12)	32	
Interest (£48,000 × 10% × 1/12)	400	
Postages	43	
Sundry £(52 + 61)	113	
		984
Net profit		5,891

Task 5

CASH ACCOUNT			
	£		£
Sales	32,125	Postages	43
		Cash purchases	187
		Sundry expenses	52
		Cash banked	30,408
		Drawings (bal)	1,435
	32,125		32,125

PRACTICE CENTRAL ASSESSMENT 3: EXPLOSIVES

SECTION 1

Task 1

JOURNAL		Page 1
Details	**£**	**£**
(a) (i) DEBIT Creditors control a/c	1,800	
CREDIT Purchases		1,800
Being correction of overstatement of purchases and creditors		
(ii) DEBIT Light and heat	1,201	
DEBIT Stationery and advertising	1,025	
CREDIT Purchases		2,226
Being posting of other expenses from purchases		
(b) DEBIT Creditors control a/c	47	
CREDIT Purchase returns		40
CREDIT VAT		7
Being purchase return omitted		
(c) DEBIT Sales	245	
CREDIT VAT		245
Being correction of misposting of VAT		
(d) DEBIT Creditors control a/c	54	
CREDIT Discounts received		54
Being posting of omitted discount received		

Task 2

See extended trial balance on Page 120.

Task 3

See extended trial balance on Page 120. Workings are shown below.

(1) *Depreciation*

   Motor vehicles = 20% × £(60,480 – 9,800) = £10,136

   Office furniture and equipment = 10% × £(26,750 – 3,170) = £2,358

   Total depreciation = £(10,136 + 2,358) = £12,494

(2) *Rent*

   An accrual is required as the rent expense for the year should be £1,000 × 12 = £12,000.

(3) *Stationery and advertising*

   Advertising of £1,560 has been prepaid.

(4) *Stock and insurance*

The damaged stock is correctly excluded from the stock balance. The amount due from the insurance company is a debtor.

(5) *Provision for bad debts*

	£
Debtors control account balance	120,860

	£
Provision required £120,860 × 5% =	6,043
Current provision	5,620
Adjustment required	423

Task 4

See extended trial balance on Page 120.

EXPLOSIVES

Account	Trial balance Debit £	Trial balance Credit £	Adjustments Debit £	Adjustments Credit £	Accrued £	Prepaid £	Profit and loss a/c Debit £	Profit and loss a/c Credit £	Balance sheet Debit £	Balance sheet Credit £
Opening stock	180,420						180,420			
Purchases	606,054			2,300			603,754			
Sales		840,315						840,315		
Purchases returns		2,430						2,430		
Sales returns	2,650						2,650			
Motor expenses	5,430						5,430			
Bank	20,415								20,415	
Cash	3,420								3,420	
Rent	11,000				1,000		12,000			
Lighting and heating	5,381						5,381			
Stationery and advertising	7,145					1,560	5,585			
Provision for bad debts		5,620		423						6,043
Debtors control account	120,860								120,860	
Creditors control account		100,959								100,959
Salaries	96,200						96,200			
Bad debts	7,200						7,200			
Drawings	31,600								31,600	
Discounts allowed	20,520						20,520			
Discounts received		18,454						18,454		
Motor vehicles (cost)	60,480								60,480	
Office furniture & equipment (cost)	26,750								26,750	
Motor vehicles (prov for depreciation)		12,590		10,136						22,726
Office furniture & equipment (prov for depreciation)		3,170		2,358						5,528
VAT		10,512								10,512
Capital		211,475								211,475
Depreciation			12,494				12,494			
Regal Insurance Company			2,300						2,300	
Closing stock (P&L)				208,540				208,540		
Closing stock (B/S)			208,540						208,540	
Provision for bad debts (adjustment)			423				423			
Prepayments/accruals									1,560	1,000
SUBTOTAL	1,205,525	1,205,525	223,757	223,757	1,000	1,560	952,057	1,069,739	475,925	358,243
Profit for the year							117,682			117,682
TOTAL	1,205,525	1,205,525	223,757	223,757	1,000	1,560	1,069,739	1,069,739	475,925	475,925

SECTION 2

1   (a)   Understated

     (b)   Understated

				£	£
2	(a)	DEBIT	Debtors control account	705	
		CREDIT	Sales		600
		CREDIT	VAT		105
	(b)	DEBIT	Bank	705	
		CREDIT	Debtors control account		705

3   (a)   Disagree

     (b)   SSAP 13 *Accounting for research and development expenditure* states that both pure and applied research should be written off as incurred. Only development costs relating to new products which are technically and financially feasible may be capitalised.

4   The prudence concept suggests that Julie Owens' debt of £5,000 should be provided for as it is likely that Explosives will lose the entire amount.

5   Stay the same.

6   DEBIT   Suspense account   £200

     CREDIT   Cash   £200

     (The original credit entry should have been to cash.)

7

MEMORANDUM

To:	Melanie Lancton	Ref:
From:	Accounting technician	Date: 8 July 1996
Subject:	*Stock valuation*	

Statement of Standard Accounting Practice 9 (SSAP 9) *Stocks and long-term contracts* requires stock to be valued at the lower of cost and net realisable value (where NRV is the selling price less any further costs to be incurred to bring the stocks to a saleable condition).

Normally, the accruals concept requires the matching of income and expenditure, as you note. However, where the prudence concept and accruals concept conflict, prudence prevails (according to SSAP 2 *Disclosure of accounting policies*).

The prudence concept requires losses to be provided for as soon as they are foreseen. Here, the 'loss' is the difference between the cost and the NRV of the stock and it must therefore be written off immediately.

I hope this answers your query satisfactorily.

SECTION 3

Task 1

DEBTORS CONTROL A/C				
	£			£
1 June 1995 Balance b/f	39,470	Cash from debtors		863,740
Credit sales (balance)	872,010	Bad debts written off		2,340
		31 May 1996 Balance c/f		45,400
	911,480			911,480

Task 2

	£
Credit sales (see above)	872,010
Cash sales	147,890
Adjustment to float	100
	1,020,000

Task 3

CREDITORS CONTROL A/C			
	£		£
Cash to creditors	607,650	1 June 1995 Balance b/f	35,960
31 May 1996 Balance c/f	49,310	Purchases (balance)	621,000
	656,960		656,960

Task 4

	£	£
Sales		1,020,000
Cost of sales		
Opening stock	33,200	
Purchases	621,000	
	654,200	
Closing stock (balance)	42,200	
		612,000
Gross profit (£1,020,000 × 40%)		408,000

Stolen stock = £42,200 – £38,700 = £3,500.

Task 5

	£	£
Sales proceeds		1,360
Net book value		
Cost	4,000	
Depreciation		
10% for 66 months	2,200	
		1,800
Loss on disposal		440

Task 6

	£
Prepaid general expenses at 31 May 1995	550
General expenses paid	6,240
Owed at year end	170
Profit and loss account	6,960

PRACTICE CENTRAL ASSESSMENT 4: CASTLE ALARMS

SECTION 1

Task 1

See extended trial balance on Page 124. Workings are as follows.

(a) *Depreciation*

Motor vehicles: £32,600 × 20% = £6,520

Equipment: £(48,860 – 6,620) × 10% = £4,224

Total depreciation = £10,744

(b) *Bank loan interest*

Interest for 9 months = £50,000 × 10% × 9/12
= £3,750

Accrued interest = £3,750 – £2,500 = £1,250

(c) and (d)

Bad debts

	£
Debtors control account balance	189,600
Debt written off: restaurant	3,400
	186,200

Provision required = 6% × £186,200 = £11,172

Adjustment required = £12,000 – £11,172 = £828

(e) *Stock*

	£
Stock at cost	289,400
Reduction to NRV of 5 system £(1,200 – 1,000) × 5	(1,000)
Damaged system	(200)
	288,200

(f) *Advertising*

DEBIT	Advertising	£2,250
CREDIT	Accruals	£2,250

(g) *Rent*

Rent for year = £2,100 × 12 = £25,200

∴ £27,300 – £25,200 = £2,100 is prepaid

DEBIT	Prepayments	£2,100
CREDIT	Rent	£2,100

(h) *Cash withdrawn*

DEBIT	Cash	£5,000
CREDIT	Bank	£5,000

(i) *Credit note*

DEBIT	Creditor's control account	£2,900
CREDIT	Purchases returns	£2,900

Task 2

See extended trial balance on Page 124.

CASTLE ALARMS

Account	Trial balance Debit £	Trial balance Credit £	Adjustments Debit £	Adjustments Credit £	Accrued £	Prepaid £	Profit and loss a/c Debit £	Profit and loss a/c Credit £	Balance sheet Debit £	Balance sheet Credit £
Sales		1,200,000						1,200,000		
Purchases	667,820						667,820			
Sales returns	96,570						96,570			
Purchases returns		52,790		2,900				55,690		
Opening stock	301,840						301,840			
Debtors control account	189,600			3,400					186,200	
Cash	1,200		5,000						6,200	
Bank	25,300			5,000					20,300	
Creditors control account		95,000	2,900							92,100
Provision for bad debts		12,000	828							11,172
Bad debts	10,100		3,400				13,500			
Discounts allowed	6,320						6,320			
Salaries	103,030						103,030			
Drawings	26,170								26,170	
Rent	27,300					2,100	25,200			
General expenses	14,310						14,310			
Capital		121,860								121,860
VAT		22,600								22,600
Bank loan		50,000								50,000
Interest on bank loan	2,500		1,250				3,750			
Advertising	11,450				2,250		13,700			
Motor vehicles (cost)	32,600								32,600	
Equipment (cost)	48,860								48,860	
Motor vehicles (prov for depreciation)		4,100		6,520						10,620
Equipment (prov for depreciation)		6,620		4,224						10,844
Depreciation			10,744				10,744			
Loan interest owing				1,250						1,250
Closing stock (P&L)				288,200				288,200		
Closing stock (B/S)			288,200						288,200	
Provision for bad debts (adjustment)				828				828		
Prepayments/accruals									2,100	2,250
SUBTOTAL	1,564,970	1,564,970	312,322	312,322	2,250	2,100	1,256,784	1,544,718	610,630	322,696
Profit for the year							287,934			287,934
TOTAL	1,564,970	1,564,970	312,322	312,322	2,250	2,100	1,544,718	1,544,718	610,630	610,630

SECTION 2

1 Under the materiality concept it is acceptable to write off such items to revenue rather than capitalise them. Such a small amount depreciated over the life of the calculator would have no real impact on the balance sheet or the profit and loss account.

2 This balance represents the amount owed to Castle Alarms by HM Customs & Excise. Over the quarter Castle Alarms' VAT inputs (purchases) have been higher than its VAT output (sales) and so it can reclaim the excess VAT.

3 Finance lease only.

4 (a) No.

    (b) Errors of omission are not detected by a trial balance. Both the debits and credits in the trial balance are understated by £235.

5 The total charge represents deprecation charged plus/minus the loss/profit on disposal.

	£
Depreciation (£10,450 – £4,100)	6,350
Loss on disposal (£4,100 – £3,000)	1,100
Total charge to capital	7,450

6 Stock should be valued at the lower of cost and net realisable value (NRV).

	£
List price	2,400
Less 20% discount	(480)
Plus delivery charge	10
Value in accounts	1,930

7 (a)

			£	
DEBIT	Purchases (£40 × 20)		£800	
DEBIT	VAT (£800 × 90% × 17.5%)		£126	
CREDIT	Creditors			£926

    (b)

			£	
DEBIT	Creditors		£926	
CREDIT	Discount received (£40 × 10% × 20)			£80
CREDIT	Cash			£846

8

MEMORANDUM

To:	Andrew Hallgrove	Ref:	Bank balance and profits
From:	Accounting Technician	Date:	XX/XX/XX

The profits of a business do not represent its cash flows because of the use of *accrual accounting*. Under this method transactions are recorded, not when cash is received or paid, but when revenues have been earned or costs incurred. This means that a company can make a large sale, recording a substantial profit, but the customer may not pay immediately. The amount owing is recorded as a debtor to the business, but the cash has yet to be received.

The business may have a large amount of stock at the year end. The cost of this stock will not be matched against revenue (ie affecting profit) until the following period but, if the stock has been paid for, the business's bank balance will be adversely affected.

The bank balance will also reflect purchases of fixed assets for cash, whereas profit will only be affected by the smaller impact of depreciation.

I hope these explanations are satisfactory.

SECTION 3

Task 1

	£	£
1 September balance paid in		50,000
Payments		
Fixtures and fittings	22,500	
Stock	47,300	
Rent	9,000	
Insurance	480	
General	220	
		(79,500)
		(29,500)
Balance c/f		
Bank	10,000	
Cash	500	
		(10,500)
Loan from bank		40,000

Task 2

Business assets at 30 September 1996

	£
Fixtures and fittings	22,500
Stock	47,300
Prepayments	
Rent (£9,000 × 5/6)	7,500
Insurance (£480 × 11/12)	440
Bank	10,000
Cash	500

Task 3

TRADE CREDITORS

	£		£
Discount received	1,250	Balance b/f	-
Cash paid	20,250	Purchases on credit (bal fig)	24,900
Balance c/f	3,400		
	24,900		24,900

Task 4

Statement of net profit for October 1996

	£	£
Sales (£20,000 + £2,400)		22,400
Cost of sales		
Opening stock	47,300	
Purchases	24,900	
	72,200	
Closing stock (£55,000 + (£2,000 × 70%))	(56,400)	
		15,800
Gross profit		6,600
Discount received		1,250
		7,850
Expenses		
Wages	2,400	
Depreciation: fixtures and fittings (20% × £22,500 × 1/12)	375	
Bank interest (£40,000 × 12% × 1/12)	400	
Stationery	320	
General expenses	500	
Rent (£9,000 × 1/6)	1,500	
Insurance (£480 × 1/12)	40	
		(5,535)
Net profit		2,315

PRACTICE CENTRAL ASSESSMENT 5: ELECTRONICS WORLD

SECTION 1

Task 1

	Debit £	Credit £
Entries from purchases day book		
Purchases	20,400	
VAT	3,570	
Creditors control account		23,970
Entries from sales day book		
Debtors control account	35,955	
VAT		5,355
Sales		30,600
Entries from sales returns day book		
Sales returns	1,200	
VAT	210	
Debtors control account		1,410
Cheques issued		
Creditors control account	5,000	
Bank		5,000

Task 2

See extended trial balance on Page 128.

Task 3

For entries on the extended trial balance: see Page 128.

(a) *Depreciation*

Motor vehicles: £22,400 × 20% = £4,480

Fixtures and fittings: £(140,000 – £6,000 – £65,000) × 10% = £6,900

Total deprecation = £11,380

(b) *Interest*

Interest due = £150,000 × 6% × 6/12 = £4,500

Bank interest owing = £4,500 – £3,750 = £750

(c) *General expenses*

Prepaid £2,400 × 4/6 = £1,600

(d) *Stock*

Valued at cost = £198,650

Insurance proceeds:

DEBIT	Regis Insurance	£420
CREDIT	Purchases	£420

(e) *Insurance*

DEBIT	Insurance	£60
CREDIT	Bank	£60

(f) *Provision for bad debts*

	£
Existing provision	6,000
Provision required (£272,400 × 5%)	13,620
Additional provision	7,620

ELECTRONICS WORLD	Trial balance		Adjustments		Accrued	Prepaid
Account	Debit	Credit	Debit	Credit		
	£	£	£	£	£	£
Share capital		600,000				
Premises	360,000					
Fixtures & fittings at cost	140,000					
Fixtures & fittings (prov for depreciation)		65,000		6,900		
Purchases (£972,140 + £20,400)	992,540			420		
Sales (£1,530,630 + £30,600)		1,561,230				
Salaries	206,420					
Sales returns (£23,200 + £1,200)	24,400					
Purchases returns		17,350				
General expenses	74,322					1,600
Insurance	16,390		60			
Bad debts	7,506					
Provision for bad debts		6,000		7,620		
Debtors control account (£237,855 + £35,955 - £1,410)	272,400					
Creditors control account (£121,433 + £23,970 - £5,000)		140,403				
Stock at 1 June 1996	188,960					
Bank (£65,200 - £5,000)	60,200			60		
Bank deposit account	150,000					
Bank interest received		3,750		750		
Motor vehicles (cost)	22,400					
Motor vehicles (prov for depreciation)		3,800		4,480		
VAT: credit balance (£24,720 - £3,570 + £5,355 - £210)		26,295				
Profit and loss		91,710				
Depreciation			11,380			
Regis Insurance			420			
Closing stock (P&L)				198,650		
Closing stock (B/S)			198,650			
Provision for bad debts (adjustment)			7,620			
Bank interest owing			750			
Prepayments						
SUBTOTAL	2,515,538	2,515,538	218,880	218,880	0	1,600
Profit for the year						
TOTAL	2,515,538	2,515,538	218,880	218,880	0	1,600

SECTION 2

1   £

		£
	Total from listing of balances	274,189
(a)	Add error in customer balance (£484 – £448)	36
(b)	Subtract customer balance listed twice	(1,490)
(c)	Subtract discount misposting × 2	(200)
(d)	Subtract goods returned	(135)
		272,400

2   (a)   Profit would decrease under LIFO.

      (b)   The consistency concept would prevent the basis for valuation of stock being changed.

3   (a)   No.

      (b)   The cost of the asset shown in the balance sheet should be the full cost of bringing the asset to its present location and condition. SSAP 12 *Accounting for depreciation* requires this treatment, so that self-built assets of this nature are treated in the same way as finished assets purchased. If the company had brought a competed office building, the labour cost would be taken into account in the purchase price asked.

4   Trial balance.

5

MEMORANDUM

To:	Jackie Brown	Ref:	VAT
From:	Accounting Technician	Date:	XX/XX/XX

You have raised two queries regarding the VAT which began to appear on invoices from Arun Divan Ltd just recently.

(a)   Although Electronics World Ltd pays more money to Arun Divan for the CD racks, profit is not affected because Electronics World Ltd can claim the VAT back from HM Customs & Excise on its next VAT return. The money will therefore be recouped either by a refund of VAT or a reduction in the VAT owed. The purchase is recorded net of VAT, so that VAT is not charged against profit.

(b)   This statement is true, for the same reasons given above. It is, in effect, the other side of the same coin as in (a).

You can see from this that, as far as VAT is concerned, the only person or body who pays VAT is the final consumer (not registered for VAT) and the only person or body who gains from VAT is HM Customs & Excise (ie the government). The profitability of a company may be affected, but only to the extent that, for a final consumer, goods which have no VAT charged on them (or which are zero-rated) will be cheaper (and so more attractive) than goods with VAT charged on them.

I hope that this has cleared up your misunderstanding.

SECTION 3

Task 1

Total sales: year ended 30 April 1997

	£
Private bank account	
Balance b/f	-
Drawings (£200 × 12)	2,400
Balance c/f	600
Cheques from Electronics World	3,000

ELECTRONICS WORLD LTD

	£		£
Balance b/f	-	Cash received (business a/c)	17,600
Sales (bal fig)	25,000	Cash received (private a/c)	3,000
		Balance c/f	4,400
	25,000		25,000

Task 2

Selling price for 1 pair speaker stands

500 pairs sold for £25,000

$\therefore$ Price per pair paid $= \dfrac{£25,000}{500} = £50$

Task 3

Cost of materials for 1 pair speaker stands

Cost per pair $= \dfrac{£50}{2} = £25$

Task 4

Cost of goods sold

Total = £25.00 × 500 = £12,500

Task 5

Purchases

JOHNSON MATERIALS LTD

	£		£
Cash paid	12,000	Balance b/f	-
Balance c/f	1,500	Purchases (bal fig)	13,500
	13,500		13,500

Task 6

Closing stock at 30 April 1997 = 120 × £25 = £3,000

To find opening stock at 30 April 1996:

	£
Opening stock (balancing figure)	2,000
Purchases (Task 5)	13,500
Less: closing stock at 30 April 1997	(3,000)
Cost of goods sold (Task 4)	12,500

Task 7

Capital invested on 30 April 1996

	£	£
Assets		
Tools and equipment	3,000	
Less depreciation (£3,000 × 20% × $^{9}/_{12}$)	(450)	
		2,550
Van	4,800	
Less depreciation (£4,800 × 10% × $^{6}/_{12}$)	(240)	
		4,560
Stock		2,000
Bank		4,250
		13,360
Rent owed		(100)
Capital		13,260

Task 8

Rent to 30 April 1997

	£
1 May 1996 - 31 October 1996 (£100 × 6)	600
1 November 1996 - 30 April 1997 (£120 × 6)	720
Rent for year	1,320

PRACTICE CENTRAL ASSESSMENT 6: DREW INSTALLATIONS

SECTION 1

Task 1

DREW INSTALLATIONS	Trial balance		Adjustments		Accrued	Prepaid
Account	Debit	Credit	Debit	Credit		
	£	£	£	£	£	£
Purchases	339,500					
Sales		693,000				
Purchases returns		6,320				
Sales returns	1,780					
Carriage inwards	8,250					
Salaries and wages	106,200					
Bad debts	4,890					
Provision for bad debts		4,500	756			
Debtors control account	46,800					
Creditors control account		28,760				
Stock at 1 November 1996	113,450					
Motor vehicle expenses	5,780			260		
Motor vehicles (cost)	86,000					
Motor vehicles (prov for depreciation)		12,800		16,000		
Equipment (cost)	24,500					
Equipment (prov for depreciation)		6,700		1,780		
Rent	58,000				2,000	
Drawings	32,900		260			
Insurance	5,720					1,800
Bank	8,580					
Bank loan account		50,000				
Bank interest paid	2,400		2,000			
VAT (credit balance)		12,400				
Capital		32,750				
Suspense account	2,480					
Depreciation			17,780			
Closing stock (P&L)				106,800		
Closing stock (B/S)			106,800			
Provision for bad debts (adjustment)				756		
Loan interest owing				2,000		
SUBTOTAL	847,230	847,230	127,596	127,596	2,000	1,800
Profit for the year						
TOTAL	847,230	847,230	127,596	127,596	2,000	1,800

Task 2

	Dr £	Cr £
Suspense	200	
VAT		200
Motor Vehicle expenses	40	
Motor Vehicles		40
Sales returns	160	
Purchases returns	160	
Suspense		320
Suspense	90	
Purchases		90
Creditors control account	2,450	
Suspense		2,450

SECTION 2

1   £6,000

2   (a)   Dr   Purchases   £470
          Cr   Cash   £470

    (b)   Dr   Cash   £470
          Cr   Sales   £400
          Cr   VAT   £70

3   £10,000

4   (a)   No

    (b)   The trial balance only detects errors where the debit entry(ies) for a transaction are not the same as the credit entry(ies). In this case £5,514 would have been debited to the debtors control account, £4,800 credited to sales and £714 credited to VAT. Since the value of the debit is the same as the total value of the credits, the error would not have been detected.

5

MEMORANDUM

To: Colin Drew   Ref: Closing stock valuation
From: Date:

I refer to your recent note concerning the valuation of the closing stock. The suggestion you have made to include stock at selling price would increase the gross profit since the effect would be to include the profit from the stock of deluxe bathroom suites in this year's accounts rather than in the accounts for the period when the suites are sold. However, I do need to draw to your attention the requirements of SSAP 2 and SSAP 9. The prudence concept, which is covered in SSAP 2, states that profits should not be anticipated and should only be recognised once they are realised. This would take place when the suites are sold. SSAP 9 reinforces the point by stating that the value of stock should be taken at the lower of cost and net realisable value. Both standards therefore reject the idea of valuing stock at selling price and we are not therefore able to proceed on that basis.

I hope this fully covers the issue raised in your note.

SECTION 3

Task 1

	£
Opening stock	30,400
Purchases (120,750 + 16,850 – 15,600)	122,000
	152,400
Closing stock	32,700
Cost of goods sold	119,700

Task 2

Gross profit	£119,700

Task 3

	£
Cost of goods sold	119,700
Gross profit	119,700
Sales	239,400

Task 4

	£
Sales	239,400
Add opening debtors	22,800
	262,200
Less closing debtors	21,700
Receipts from debtors	240,500

Task 5

<table>
<tr><th></th><th colspan="2">Bank</th><th></th></tr>
<tr><td></td><td>£</td><td></td><td>£</td></tr>
<tr><td>Debtors</td><td>240,500</td><td>Balance b/d</td><td>4,300</td></tr>
<tr><td></td><td></td><td>Creditors</td><td>120,750</td></tr>
<tr><td></td><td></td><td>Expenses</td><td>52,800</td></tr>
<tr><td></td><td></td><td>Equipment</td><td>4,500</td></tr>
<tr><td></td><td></td><td>Drawings</td><td>42,300</td></tr>
<tr><td></td><td></td><td>Balance c/d</td><td>15,850</td></tr>
<tr><td></td><td>240,500</td><td></td><td>240,500</td></tr>
</table>

Task 6

Gross profit		119,700
Less		
Expenses (52,800 – 1,000 – 1,500)	50,300	
Depreciation Motor Vehicles	1,750	
Depreciation Equipment	661	
		52,711
Net profit		66,989

SUGGESTED ANSWERS TO THE SAMPLE CENTRAL ASSESSMENT

SECTION 1

Task 1

Extended Trial Balance at 30 April 1998

CREATIVE CATERING	Trial balance		Adjustments		Accrued	Prepaid
Account	Debit	Credit	Debit	Credit		
	£	£	£	£	£	£
Sales		620,700		860		
Purchases	410,650					
Purchases returns		390				
Salaries and wages	90,820					
Rent	16,300					1,300
Debtors control account	51,640					
Creditors control account		33,180				
Bad debts	6,650					
Provision for bad debts		3,100	518			
Motor vehicles (cost)	60,700					
Motor vehicles (prov for depreciation)		12,600		12,140		
Equipment (cost)	24,200					
Equipment (prov for depreciation)		6,300		1,790		
Drawings	28,500		5,000			
Cash	7,000			5,000		
Bank	6,250					
Lighting and heating	2,100					
Insurance	760					
Advertising	3,470				2,750	
VAT (credit balance)		8,400				
Stock at 1 May 1997	5,660					
Motor expenses	4,680					
Bank deposit account	20,000					
Bank interest received		700		700		
Capital		54,010				
Polar Insurance Company			860			
Depreciation			13,930			
Closing stock (P&L)				5,340		
Closing stock (B/S)			5,340			
Provision for bad debts (adjustment)				518		
Deposit account interest owing			700			
SUBTOTAL	739,380	739,380	26,348	26,348	2,750	1,300
Profit for the year						
TOTAL	739,380	739,380	26,348	26,348	2,750	1,300

Task 2

	£	£
Balance at bank as per cash book (15 May)		5,800
Add unpresented cheques		
606842	120	
606843	440	
606844	260	
		820
		6,620
Less Credit already in cash book		320
Balance at bank as per bank statement		6,300

Task 3

Creative Catering
Bank Reconciliation as at 29 May 1998

	£	£
Balance at bank as per cash book		7,365
Add unpresented cheques		
606845	620	
606847	490	
606850	260	
606851	320	
606852	1,400	
		3,090
		10,455
Less Tennis Club credit not yet banked		1,810
Balance as per bank statement		8,645

SECTION 2

1

(a)

	£
Depreciation 6 months to 30 April 1996	1,236
Depreciation 12 months to 30 April 1997	2,472
Depreciation 12 months to 30 April 1998	2,472
Depreciation 1 month to 31 May 1998	206
Total depreciation	6,386
Book value (£12,360 – £6,386)	5,974

(b) Profit on disposal (£6,500 – £5,974)   526

2

	£
Subscriptions received	98,000
Less owing from previous year	1,500
	96,500
Less prepaid for following year	2,500
	94,000
Income for year - 380 members at £250 each	95,000
Owing	1,000

£1,000/£250 = 4 members have not paid

3

(a)

			£
Dr	Debtors control account		329
Cr	Sales		280
Cr	VAT		49

(b)	Dr	Hospitality	329
	Cr	Creditors control account	329

4 When the equipment is acquired.

5   (a)   No.

   (b)   The debtors control account balance should, as a control, match the total of the balances in the sales ledger. Errors such as missing entries or entries for wrong amounts in the ledger will be detected. In this case the entry has been made for the correct amount in the ledger and the total of the balances will therefore be unaffected.

6

MEMORANDUM	
To: Jane Sutton	Ref: Closing stock valuation
From:	Date:

I refer to our recent conversation regarding the £500 invoice for soft drinks that had not been entered into the books of the business. I have considered the matter further and now conclude that the profits for the year ended 30 April 1998 would have been affected by this omission. Although the invoice was not entered into the purchases account, the drinks were included in the valuation of the closing stock. The cost of goods sold would therefore have been reduced by £500, inflating the gross profit by that amount. The current reported profit is thus incorrect, income from sales not having been matched against the correct cost of goods sold expenditure as required by the accruals concept. Please let me know if you require further information.

SECTION 3

1

	£
Opening stock of baking materials	1,000
Baking materials purchased	84,000
	85,000
Closing stock of baking materials	3,000
Baking materials used	82,000
Baking production wages	44,000
Prime cost	126,000

2

Prime cost	126,000
Baking supervisory wages	25,000
Baking overheads	22,000
Depreciation bakery premises	2,000
Depreciation bakery equipment	5,000
Production cost	180,000

3

Cost of goods to shop	60,000
Profit on sales (100% mark-up)	60,000
Cost of goods to caterers and retailers	120,000
Profit on sales (50% mark-up)	60,000
Total gross profit	120,000

4

Purchases	84,000
Add Creditors 1 January 1997	6,000
	90,000
Less Creditors 31 December 1997	7,000
Paid to creditors	83,000

5

Credit sales	180,000
Add Debtors at 1 January 1997	12,000
	192,000
Less Receipts from debtors	179,500
Debtors at 31 December 1997	12,500

Unit 5
Question Bank

RFB plc (December 1994)

Data

RFB plc was formed in the early nineteenth century producing wheels for horse-drawn vehicles. Today it is a successful, profitable company which still makes wheels, but for a variety of uses: wheelbarrows, carts, toys etc. The production operation consists of three departments: bending, cutting and assembly. The bending and cutting departments have general purpose machinery which is used to manufacture all the wheels it produces.

You have recently been appointed assistant to the management accountant and are performing a variety of routine cost accounting tasks to familiarise yourself with the running of the department. The following tasks represent today's work.

Task 1

Complete the form below by analysing the cost items into the appropriate columns and agreeing the balances.

	Total £	Prime cost £	Production expense £	Admin. expense £	Selling and distribution expense £
Wages of assembly employees	6,750	6750			
Wages of stores employees	3,250		3250		
Tyres for toy wheels	1,420	1420	810		
Safety goggles for operators	810			84	
Job advert for new employees	84				125
Depreciation of salesmen's cars	125		264		1,200
Depreciation of production machines	264				
Cost of trade exhibition	1,200			130	
Computer stationery	130			295	
Course fee for AAT training	295				
Royalty for the design of wheel 1477	240	240			
	14,568	8410	4324	509	1325

Task 2

There follow extracts from three purchase invoices which have been received for wire, code number 1471. The invoices have been passed by the purchase department and the standard price is £120 per coil.

(a) You are asked to :

(i) calculate the standard cost of the actual quantity purchased on each invoice;

(ii) name and calculate the variance, stating whether it is adverse or favourable, in each invoice.

Invoice number 3275	Your order number 57623
Date 1.11.94	
50 coils @ £132	£6,600
Standard cost of actual quantity	6000
............6 00............ variance	600 (A)

Invoice number 4517	Your order number 58127
Date 17.11.94	
150 coils @ £108	£16,200
Standard cost of actual quantity	18,000
............1800............ variance	1800 (F)

Invoice number 5178	Your order number 60173
Date 17.11.94	
100 coils @ £120	£12,000
Standard cost of actual quantity	12,000
.... variance	— (—)

(b) Enter the individual variances calculated in (a) in the variance account below. Do not calculate the balance on the account.

VARIANCE ACCOUNT

1.11.94	Material price Purchase	600	—	17.11.94	Material price Purchase.	1800	—	

(c) Suggest reasons for the variances in (a), and state what action, if any, needs to be taken. Who would be responsible for taking the action that you recommend?

Task 3

(a) Calculate the standard overhead absorption rates for the three departments below, selecting the appropriate data.

	Bending	Cutting	Assembly
Actual overheads £s	128,000	80,000	64,500
Budgeted overheads £s	120,000	90,000	60,000
Actual machine hours	11,800	2,750	-
Budgeted machine hours	10,000	3,000	-
Actual labour hours	-	-	15,900
Budgeted labour hours	-	-	15,000

(b) Using the information given below and the standard overhead rates calculated in (a), calculate the standard cost of producing 100 wheels for a toy car.

	Bending	Cutting	Assembly
Labour rates of pay per hour £	4	6	5
Labour hours per 100 wheels	0.8	0.5	1.2
Machine hours per 100 wheels	0.4	0.5	-

STANDARD COST CARD			
Toy car wheels	Part number 5917B		Date:
	Standard quantity 100 wheels		
	Performance standard	Standard rate/price	Standard cost £
Direct materials			
Tyres	100	10p each	10.00
Steel strip	50	£10.40 per 100	5.20
Wire	1000	2p each	20.00
			35.20
Direct labour	hours	£	
Bending	0.8|100	4	3.20
Cutting	0.5	6	3.00
Assembly	1.2	5	6.00
			12.20
Overheads	0.4	12	4.80
Bending	0.5	30	15.00
Cutting	1.2	4	4.80
Assembly			24.60
TOTAL COST			72.00 ✓

Task 4

RFB plc buys a chemical which it refines and then uses the refined product as a coating for the metal strip it uses in the manufacture of certain special products. You are asked to complete the following monthly cost statement. There is a normal loss of 5% of the input material (chemical) which has no sales value. Give your answer to the nearest £.

REFINING COST STATEMENT		
		November 1994
	Quantity (Kilos)	*Cost* (£)
Input material (chemical)	60	12,000
Labour		2,000
Overheads		8,000
	60	22,000
Output (refined product)	55	21228 ✓
Normal loss	3	
Abnormal loss	2	772. ✓
	60	22,000

A suggested answer to this exercise is given on page 199.

AMP plc (June 1994)

The four tasks below all relate to AMP plc.

Data

AMP plc, a printing company, specialises in producing accounting manuals for several accountancy training companies. The manuals are written by the training companies and passed to AMP. The company uses three main stages in producing the manuals:
(a) the preparation of the text;
(b) the printing of the text;
(c) the assembly and binding of the manuals.

The company is growing and you have recently been appointed assistant to the accountant with responsibility for the pricing of the materials issued and the calculation of the gross wages earned. AMP has plans to introduce standard costing and you will be involved in the routine work of establishing standard costs and analysing variances.

Task 1

There is no formal stores accounting system in operation at present.

You are asked, as a step towards improving this situation, to write up the following information on the stores record card given below using weighted average prices to value the issues.

Material: Paper - Code 1564A
Opening stock: 10,000 sheets - value £3,000

Purchases			Issues	
3 May	4,000 sheets	£1,600	6 May	7,000 sheets
12 May	10,000 sheets	£3,100	15 May	6,000 sheets
25 May	10,000 sheets	£3,200	22 May	7,200 sheets

(The calculation of the weighted average should be to two decimal places of a £ and that of the value of the issues to the nearest £.)

Stores Record Card									
Material: Paper								*Code:* 1564A	
		Receipts		Issues			Stock		
Date	*Details*	Sheets	£	Sheets	Price	£	Sheets	Price	£
	Opening Stock						10,000	30	3,000
3 MAY	Purchases	4000	1600				14,000	33	4600
6 MAY	Issues			7000	33	2310	7,000	33	2310
12 MAY	Purchase	10,000	3100				17,000	32	840
15 may	Issues			6000	32	1920	11,000	32	3520
22 MAY	Issues			7200	32	2304	3800	32	1216
25 May	Purchase	10,000	3,200				13800	32	4416

Task 2

(a) Calculate the gross wages earned for each of the following employees for week 32. The normal week is 38 hours and an individual production bonus of 10p per 100 sheets produced is paid.

	Singh	Smith
Basic rate per hour	£4.50	£4.00
Total hours worked	39½	41
Overtime hours paid:		
at time plus a third	1½	1
at time plus a half	-	2
Output (sheets)	10,500	10,900

(Calculations should be to two decimal places of a £.)

(b) There has been some pressure from the employees for a piecework system to be introduced.

What would the piecework price per 100 sheets have to be, to at least equal the gross wages earned by Singh in (a) above, assuming the same output level of 10,500 sheets?

(Calculations should be to two decimal places of a £.)

Task 3

The binding department has been chosen to illustrate the advantages that standard costing can offer to management. If management are convinced by this trial, standard costing will be introduced throughout the company. The binding department's output last period consisted of 1,200 copies of one manual 'AATA'. The standard cost of this manual is shown below.

Standard Cost Card			
Product: Manual AATA		**Date prepared:** June 1994	
Element	*Performance Standard*	*Standard Rate/Price*	*Std Cost*
Direct material	1 unit	90p per unit	0.90
Direct labour	¼ hour	£4 per hour	1.00
Variable overheads	¼ hour	£2 per hour	0.50
Fixed overheads	¼ hour	£6 per hour	1.50
		Cost per manual	£3.90

Complete the following departmental operating account, using the information from the standard cost card above to calculate the standard cost and the total variance for each element of cost. Each variance must be marked 'adverse' (A) or 'favourable' (F).

Departmental Operating Account

Month: May 1994
Date prepared: 10.6.94

Budget hours: 320
Actual hours: 290

Department: Binding
Manager: Mrs Jones

Actual Costs	£	Standard Costs			Total Variance £
		Output (Manuals)	Unit Cost £	Total Cost £	
Direct materials	1,200	1,200	90	1080	120 A
Direct labour:					
290 hours	1,300	1,200	1·00	1200	100 A
Variable overheads	580	1,200	50	600	20 F
Fixed overheads	1,920	1,200		1800	120 A
Total	5,000			4680	320 A

Task 4

(a) Analyse the direct labour cost variance in Task 3 above into the appropriate sub-variances.

(b) Suggest one reason for each of the sub-variances occurring and outline the corrective action that needs to be taken in each case.

(c) Who would be responsible for taking the corrective action in (b) above?

A suggested answer to this exercise is given on page 201.

Pears plc (December 1993)

The four tasks below should be answered in sequence. They all relate to the same company, Pears plc.

Data

Pears plc manufactures children's clothing. The general manager is concerned about how the costs of the various garments it produces are calculated. The material cost varies from one garment to another and the rates of pay in the various departments also vary to reflect the different skills offered. Both these prime costs are charged direct to individual garments so that any variation is taken into account. It is the overhead cost which has been concerning Pears for some time. The present overhead system uses one overhead rate for the whole company and is absorbed as a percentage of direct labour cost. The accounting department has been examining individual cost items and relating them as closely as possible to the department which incurs them. Some apportionment has also taken place and the forecasted overhead cost and other related information is as follows.

	Overhead cost £'000	Numbers employed	% of floor area	Material issued £'000	Machine hours
Production departments					
Cutting	187	10	40	200	15,000
Sewing	232	15	30	250	25,000
Finishing	106	8	15	100	
Service departments					
Stores	28	2	5	-	
Maintenance	50	3	10	50	

Task 1

Using the overhead analysis sheet below, apportion:

(a) the stores department's costs to the production and maintenance departments;
(b) the maintenance department's costs to the cutting and sewing departments only.

Select the most suitable base for each apportionment and state the bases used on the overhead analysis sheet. (Calculations should be to the nearest £.)

OVERHEAD ANALYSIS SHEET   DATE

	TOTAL	PRODUCTION			SERVICE	
		Cutting	Sewing	Finishing	Stores	Maintenance
	£	£	£	£	£	£
Overheads	603,000	187,000	232,000	106,000	28,000	50,000
Apportion Stores (Base: material value issued)	28000	9333	11667	41666	(28,000)	2334
Apportion Maintenance (Base: machine hrs)	52334	19625	32709	/	/	/
		215958	276376	110666		

Task 2

(a) Given that 12,000 labour hours will be worked in the finishing department calculate overhead absorption rates for the three production departments using machine hour rates for the cutting and sewing departments, and a labour hour rate for the finishing department.

(Calculations should be to two decimal places of the £.)

(b) Explain briefly why it is appropriate to use machine hour rates in the cutting and sewing departments.

Task 3

Using the form provided below, calculate the standard cost of a new garment 'XL'. It is established that direct material cost will be £4.32. Direct labour cost is to be based on $1/4$ hour in the cutting department, 1 hour in the sewing department and $1/2$ hour in the finishing department. The standard hourly rates of pay are £4.00 in cutting, £3.00 in sewing and £5.00 in finishing. Overheads are to be included using the hourly rates calculated in Task 2(a) above and the same hours as used in the labour cost above.

```
┌─────────────────────────────────────────────────────────────────────────────┐
│                        STANDARD PRODUCT COST SHEET                            │
│                           PRODUCT : 'XL'              Date:                    │
├─────────────────────────────────────────────────────────┬─────────┬──────────┤
│                                                          │    £    │    £     │
├─────────────────────────────────────────────────────────┼─────────┼──────────┤
│ Direct Material Cost                                     │  4·32   │          │
```

	Hours	Rate £	£	£
Direct Material Cost			4·32	
Direct Labour Cost				
- cutting	1/4	4·00	1·00	
- sewing	1	3·00	3·00	
- finishing	1/2	5·00	2·50	
Total Labour Cost			6·50	

	Hours	Rate £	£	£
Overhead Cost				
- cutting	1/4	14·40	3·60	
- sewing	1	11·06	11·06	
- finishing	1/2	9·22	4·61	
Total Overhead Cost			19·27	
TOTAL COST				30·09 ✓

Task 4

Pears plc has obtained 50 metres of a material at a special price of £2.00 per metre as it is slightly substandard. The standard price for this material is £3.00 per metre. From this material 20 garments have been made for which the standard quantity is 2 metres per garment.

(a) Calculate the following.

   (i)   Material price variance
   (ii)   Material usage variance
   (iii) Total material cost variance

(b) List the responsible managers who should be informed of each of these variances as part of the routine reporting procedures.

(c) Explain whether the decision to buy this material was correct.

A suggested answer to this exercise is given on page 203.

McHugh Ltd

The eight tasks below should be answered in sequence as the answers to earlier tasks may need to be used later.

Data

Your organisation, McHugh Ltd, produces a single product, the N-17T, which passes through three production processes (forming, colouring and assembly). The output of the forming process becomes the input of the colouring process and the input of the assembly process is the output of the colouring process. There are also two service departments, maintenance and general.

The budgeted overheads for the 12 months to 31 December 19X3 are as follows.

	£	£
Rent and rates		8,000 ✗
Power		750 ✗
Light, heat		5,000 ✗
Repairs, maintenance:		
Forming	800	
Colouring	1,800	
Assembly	300	
Maintenance	200	
General	100	
		3,200
Departmental expenses:		
Forming	1,500	
Colouring	2,300	
Assembly	1,100	
Maintenance	900	
General	1,500	
		7,300
Depreciation:		
Plant		10,000 ✗
Fixtures and fittings		250 ✗
Insurance:		
Plant		2,000 ✗
Buildings		500 ✗
Indirect labour:		
Forming	3,000	
Colouring	5,000	
Assembly	1,500	
Maintenance	4,000	
General	2,000	
		15,500
		52,500

Other data are available as follows.

	Floor area sq. ft	Plant value £	Fixtures & fittings £	Effective horse-power		Budget Labour hours	Machine hours
Forming	2,000	25,000	1,000	40	27	27,400	5,000
Colouring	4,000	60,000	500	90	60	3,000	14,400
Assembly	3,000	7,500	2,000	15	10	20,000	2,600
Maintenance	500	7,500	1,000	5	3	-	-
General	500	-	500	-		-	-
	10,000	100,000	5,000	150		50,400	22,000

	Budget Maintenance work to be provided by maintenance department Hours		General work to be provided by general service department Hours	
Forming	2,000	20	1,200	20
Colouring	5,000	50	3,600	60
Assembly	2,000	20	600	16
Maintenance	-		600	10
General	1,000	10	-	
	10,000		6,000	

Task 1

Prepare a table which shows the overheads which can be directly allocated to the five departments. ✓

Task 2

Complete the table you started in Task 1 by apportioning the remaining overheads to the five departments, clearly indicating the basis of apportionment that you have used.

Task 3

Apportion the service department overheads to the production departments using the repeated distribution method.

Task 4

Calculate suitable overhead absorption rates for the three production departments.

Task 5

During the year to 31 December 19X3, 30,000 labour hours were worked in the forming department, 3,150 in the colouring department and 18,500 in the assembly department. Machines ran for 4,900 hours in the forming department, 16,000 hours in the colouring department and 3,297 in the assembly department. The overheads actually incurred in the three production departments (after allocation and apportionment) were as follows.

	£
Forming	14,580
Colouring	30,050
Assembly	9,840

Calculate any under- or over-absorbed overhead for the twelve months to 31 December 19X3.

Task 6

The production manager of McHugh Ltd, Jenny Chang, returns from a conference and telephones you. She explains that a lot of the other delegates at the conference were talking about job costing but she thinks your predecessor had mentioned that McHugh Ltd uses processing costing (she can't quite remember the correct term). She wonders why McHugh Ltd doesn't use job costing since all the workers are doing jobs. She asks for your comments in writing.

Draft a short memorandum to Jenny Chang which explains why job costing is not appropriate for McHugh Ltd and why the company uses the costing method that it does.

Task 7

The engineering department of McHugh Ltd have realised that the metal shavings produced during the forming process and previously treated as wastage can, in fact, be sold as a commercially viable product - KJ53.

Set out the factors which will determine whether product KJ53 will be classified as a joint product or a by-product.

Task 8

The selling price of the KJ53 is set at £100 per unit whereas that of the N-17T is set at £120 per unit.

During the twelve months to 31 December 19X3 the common processing costs of the two products are £3,725,000, 10,000 units of KJ53 are produced and sold and 30,000 units of N-17T are produced and sold.

KJ53 needs no further processing after the point of separation. The units of N-17T incurred £1,750,000 in further processing costs.

Calculate two different allocations of the common processing costs to the two products.

A suggested answer to this exercise is given on page 204.

Jasperino Ltd

The eight tasks below should be answered in sequence as the answers to earlier tasks may need to be used later.

Data

You work for an engineering company called Jasperino Ltd which operates a job costing system which is fully integrated with the financial accounts. The following data relate to May 19X2.

	£
Balances at the beginning of the month	
Stores ledger control account	8,000
Work in progress control account	15,000
Finished goods control account	22,000
Prepayments of production overheads, brought forward from April 19X2	1,000
Transactions during the month	
Materials purchased	75,000
Materials issued to production	34,000
Materials issued to factory maintenance	4,000
Materials transferred between jobs	3,500
Total wages of direct workers	18,000
Recorded non-productive time of direct workers	2,500
Wages of indirect production workers (total)	11,000
Other production overheads incurred	16,000
Selling and distribution overheads incurred	12,000
Sales	110,000
Cost of finished goods sold	65,000
Cost of finished goods damaged and scrapped in the month	2,000
Value of work in progress at 31 May 19X2	18,000

Production overhead absorption rate is 200% of direct wages.

Task 1

Prepare the stores ledger control account.

Task 2

Prepare the work in progress control account.

Task 3

Calculate the under- or over-absorbed overhead in the month.

Task 4

Prepare the finished goods control account.

Task 5

Calculate the profit for May.

Task 6

The ten machines used by Jasperino Ltd are eight years old. They have been depreciated on a straight line basis over 5 years and so depreciation is no longer charged to the production overhead control account.

At the beginning of June 19X2 the company decides to buy a new machine for £17,580. It has not yet been established whether the machine is to be depreciated on a straight line basis over five years or on a 25% reducing balance basis.

Calculate the annual depreciation which would be charged over the next five years under the two methods.

Task 7

On 1 May 19X2, there was only one uncompleted job in Jasperino Ltd's factory. The job card for this work is summarised below.

JOB CARD
Job 212/A

Costs to date	£
Direct materials	7,080
Direct labour	1,314
Production overhead	2,628
Factory cost to date	11,022

During May a number of new jobs were started. The chief cost accountant is exceptionally busy and so you have been asked to prepare job accounts for jobs 212/A and one of the new jobs, 219/C. You have gathered together the following information.

Direct materials		£
Issued to	212/A	3,122
	219/C	4,003
Transfers from	212/A to 219/C	3,500

Direct labour		
	212/A	1,922
	219/C	7,255

Prepare job accounts for 212/A and 219/C

Task 8

If administration and marketing overheads are added to cost of sales at a rate of 15% of factory cost and invoiced amounts are £20,500 for job 212/A and £28,750 for job 219/C, calculate the profit or loss on the two jobs.

A suggested answer to this exercise is given on page 207.

Group A (December 1994)

Questions 1-5 inclusive are based on the scenario in the short problem RFB plc (page 141). You may have to refer back to the information in that problem in order to answer the questions.

1　Using the standard cost card from Task 3(b), calculate the target selling price per 100 wheels if the company expects a profit of 10% of the target selling price.

2　How would the standard labour hours for producing 100 wheels be determined?

3　The cost of both the stores and the personnel departments has to be apportioned across the other cost centres. What bases would you recommend?

4　How would you deal with the cost of the abnormal loss (from Task 4) in the cost accounts?

5　Protective gloves are used in the production departments and are drawn from stores at regular intervals. Records show the following for November:

1.11.94	Opening stock	100 pairs @ £2 each
7.11.94	Purchases	200 pairs @ £1.90 each
18.11.94	Issues	150 pairs

Calculate the value of the closing stock of gloves given that the FIFO system of valuing issues is used.

6　An employee makes 200 units of product A, 350 units of product B and 300 units of product C. The standard time allowed per unit was:

A　4 minutes,　B　2 minutes　C　3 minutes

Calculate the standard hours produced by the employee.

7　A company has established reorder levels for each of the major materials it holds. Give *two* factors which influence a reorder level.

8　Give *two* significant overhead costs likely to be incurred by an international firm of management consultants.

9　For a mixed farm, growing crops and raising cattle, suggest *one* cost unit and *two* cost centres.

10　The overheads of a cost centre were substantially over absorbed last period.

(a)　What is the costing treatment for this?
(b)　Will it increase or decrease the costing profit for the period?

11　What is differential piecework?

12　A standard cost is only a guess at what the cost of something should be. It is of little relevance once the actual cost is known. True or false?

A suggested answer to this exercise is given on page 210.

Group B (June 1994)

Questions 1 - 4 inclusive are based on the scenario in the short problem AMP plc (page 144). You may have to refer back to the information in that problem in order to answer the questions.

1　AMP has always held large quantities of paper in stock in case it should become difficult to obtain. Suggest two problems that this could create.

2　The overtime premium paid to Singh and Smith in Task 2(a) could be analysed to direct wages or to departmental overheads. Detail the circumstances which would give rise to these differing treatments.

3　Name one overhead variance from Task 3 that you would expect to find in the binding department. Explain whether it would be adverse or favourable.

Calculations are not required.

4   When setting the standard cost of the various manuals it produces, the company had to decide whether to use ideal standards or current/expected standards. State which of the two standards you would use and explain why.

5   The actual overheads for a department were £6,500 last period and the actual output was 540 machine hours. The budgeted overheads were £5,995 and the budgeted output was 550 machine hours. Calculate the under- or over-absorbed overhead and state whether it would increase or reduce the profit for the period.

6   With activity-based costing, 'cost drivers' are used.

   (a)   Are cost drivers a means of:

           (i)   establishing the overhead cost of activities; or
           (ii)   calculating the value of the direct materials used; or
           (iii) determining the most suitable cost centres.

   (b)   Suggest a suitable cost driver for the purchasing department of a large manufacturing company.

7   The operation of a joint process produces the following output.

Product	Output	Sales price per kg
	kg	£
A	100	5
B	50	12
C	20	1
D	20	18

   (a)   Identify the joint products of the process.

   (b)   Explain how you would treat the sales value of any remaining product(s) in the cost accounts.

8   Which of the following organisation(s) would you expect to use process costing.

   (a)   A paint manufacturer
   (b)   A light engineering company
   (c)   A supermarket
   (d)   The chemical industry

9   A personal computer costing £3,000 was expected to last for four years and to have a resale value of £200. The company policy is to depreciate assets using the straight-line method of depreciation.

   (a)   What is the annual depreciation charge to the administration cost centre?

   (b)   The computer was replaced after three years with no resale value. Calculate the obsolescence charge and state where this charge should be shown in the cost accounts.

10   Suggest suitable cost drivers for the following cost pools.

   Production scheduling costs
   Despatch costs

11   A direct materials price variance may be calculated and entered in the accounts of a business at either the time of receipt of the stock, or the time of issue from stores to production. Which of the methods is usually regarded as the better, and why?

12   Fill in the missing words

   Batch costing is a form of costing that is similar to_____costing except that costs are collected for_____. The cost unit is the_____. A cost per unit is calculated by_____.

A suggested answer to this exercise is given on page 211.

Group C (December 1993)

1   Explain briefly the purpose of establishing stock levels for each type of material in a stock control system.

2   What is the purpose of:

   (a)   a stores requisition?
   (b)   a purchase requisition?

3   In a period of rising prices which of the following methods of pricing issues would place the lowest value on the closing stocks?

   (a)   Weighted average
   (b)   FIFO
   (c)   LIFO

4   List two advantages of paying employees by the results achieved.

5   Give two reasons why the majority of employees are paid on the basis of time, eg hourly rates of pay.

6   A joint process cost of £14,400 produces the following output in kilos: product A 1,000, product B 2,000 and product C 6,000. Complete the following profit statement.

	Total	*A*	*B*	*C*
	£	*£*	*£*	*£*
Sales	16,000	4,000	6,000	6,000
Joint cost	14,400			
Profit	1,600			

7   Complete the following process centre report:

Input (kilos)	100
Output (kilos)	89
Normal loss (10% of input)	
Abnormal loss	
Total (kilos)	100

8   Indirect materials costs can also be called indirect expenses. True or false?

9   Choose the appropriate words.

The workforce of Casios Ltd have been working at a less efficient rate than standard to produce a given output. The result is a *favourable/adverse* fixed overhead *usage/capacity* variance.

The total number of hours worked was, however, more than was originally budgeted. The effect is measured by a *favourable/adverse* fixed overhead *usage/capacity* variance.

10   Annual demand for a material is 200,000 units. It costs £3.20 to hold one unit in stock for one year. Ordering costs are £18 per order. What should the reorder quantity be in order to minimise stock administration costs?

11   The overhead absorption rate for the machining department at Jefferson Ltd is £5 per direct labour hour. During the year to 31 December 1,753 direct labour hours were worked and overheads incurred were £9,322. During the twelve-month period overheads were therefore over absorbed. True or false?

12   Prime cost is

   A   all costs incurred in manufacturing a product
   B   the total of direct costs
   C   the material cost of a product
   D   the cost of operating a department

A suggested answer to this exercise is given on page 212.

Group D

1   What is the advantage of charging as many costs as possible to cost units rather than treating them as overheads?

2   At a time of rapidly rising prices a manufacturing company decides to change from a FIFO to a LIFO system of pricing material issues. What would be the effect on the following?

(a) Stock valuation
(b) Cost of materials charged to production

3 How would additional payments to production workers for weekend working be treated in the cost accounts?

4 Suggest the cost units which would be appropriate for management information systems in the following industries.

(a) A building contractor
(b) An airline

5 In a particular month production overheads were under absorbed because Excelsior plc had to cut back production due to a lack of orders.

(a) Which variance account would be affected by this situation?
(b) What would be the effect on unit costs of production?

6 Give four factors which should be considered in deciding the optimum level of stocks of component parts to be held in a stores which serves a mass production assembly line.

7 Suggest an appropriate basis for apportioning each of the following overhead costs to production cost centres in a manufacturing company.

(a) Canteen costs
(b) Heating and lighting
(c) Building maintenance

8 Explain briefly the machine hour rate method of absorbing overhead costs into cost units in a manufacturing organisation.

9 Explain briefly the function of cost drivers in an activity based costing system, giving an example.

10 Explain how the term 'reorder level' differs from 'minimum level' and 'maximum level'.

11 Name one advantage and one disadvantage of using an ideal standard.

12 Suggest appropriate costing methods for the following organisations.

(a) A manufacturer of tinned baby foods
(b) A plumbing business
(c) A clothing manufacturer
(d) A drug manufacturer
(e) A brewer
(f) A caterer

A suggested answer to this exercise is given on page 213.

Group E

1 Explain the meaning of the term 'interdependence of variances'.

2 When using absorption costing, explain why the use of an overhead absorption rate based on direct labour hours is generally favoured over a direct wages percentage rate for a labour intensive operation.

3 Which one of the following statements is *incorrect*?

A Job costs are collected separately, whereas process costs are averages.

B In job costing, the progress of a job can be ascertained from materials requisition notes and job tickets or time sheets.

C In process costing, information is needed about work passing through a process and work remaining in each process.

D In process costing, but not job costing, the cost of normal loss will be incorporated into normal product costs.

4 Jemima Ltd uses a standard costing system and values all of its stocks of raw materials at standard price. Stocks are issued to work in progress at standard price. There is an adverse material price variance during an accounting period. What is the cost accounting entry for the material price variance?

5   In what circumstances is it necessary to calculate the equivalent units of production in a process for a given period?

6   4,000 units were input to a process and 3,200 were completed. Closing WIP was only 60% complete as to materials and labour. The cost of materials in the period was £5,520 and the cost of labour £1,840.

What is the value of closing WIP?

7   How is a usage or efficiency variance calculated?

8   Bryan Limited budgets to produce 500 units of ferginude during August 19X2. The expected time to produce one unit of ferginude is 2.5 hours and the budgeted fixed production overhead is £10,000. Actual fixed production overhead expenditure in August 19X2 turns out to be £10,500 and the labour force manages to produce 600 units in 1,350 hours of work.

Comment on the above information, performing whatever calculations you think are most appropriate.

9   (a)   Suggest two suitable cost centres for a hospital.
      (b)   Suggest two suitable cost units for a hospital.

10   On what factors does a maximum stock level depend?

11   What are the main advantages of using a system of numbers to identify stock held?

12   (a)   Who is likely to be responsible for an adverse materials usage variance?
      (b)   Who is likely to be responsible for an adverse labour rate variance?

A suggested answer to this exercise is given on page 215.

PRACTICE CENTRAL ASSESSMENT 1: DOWRA LTD (JUNE 1995)

SECTION 1

The suggested time allocation for this exercise is 75 minutes.

Data

Dowra Ltd manufactures high quality wooden toys. Production varies from long runs of popular models to short runs of specially designed expensive toys.

The factory is divided into five cost centres for analysis purposes.

Production

The **cutting department** cuts the timber to shape.

The **assembly department** assembles the parts of the toy which have been pre-cut by the cutting department.

The **finishing department** paints, varnishes and packs the completed wooden toys.

Service

The **design department** prepares drawings and product specifications for the individual wooden toys.

The **stores department** stores and handles the following.

(a) The materials used in production, including timber, paint, glue, screws, nails and packing materials

(b) The work-in-progress

(d) The finished goods

The company's system for dealing with budgeted factory overheads is as follows.

(a) Where possible, budgeted overheads are allocated to the five cost centres as shown in the data below. Any overheads which cannot be directly allocated to cost centres are allocated to an overall factory cost centre and apportioned to the five cost centres according to floor area.

(b) Budgeted stores overheads are apportioned to the other four cost centres according to the value of materials requisitions

(c) Budgeted design overheads are apportioned to the production cost centres in equal proportions.

(d) Production overheads are charged to production runs on the basis of machine hours in each of the three production cost centres.

Budgeted data for the year ending 30 June 1996 is as follows.

Allocated overheads	Cutting	Assembly	Finishing	Design	Stores
Indirect labour (£)	72,400	83,900	108,600	126,100	18,500
Indirect materials (£)	1,850	780	12,640	4,650	600
Machine costs (£)	64,000	56,400	48,900	63,400	2,900
Total allocated overhead(£)	138,250	141,080	170,140	194,150	22,000

Unallocated budgeted factory overheads amount to £184,000. — *flow space*

Other data:

	Cutting	Assembly	Finishing	Design	Stores
Floor area (sq metres)	770	1,310	1,080	480	360
Material requisitions (£)	97,760	109,400	45,000	4,640	-
Material requisitions (No.)	800	750	1,200	550	-
Machine hours	180,000	85,000	240,000	-	-

Task 1

Using the overhead analysis sheet below, calculate a machine hour overhead absorption rate for each of the three production cost centres.

Department	Cutting £	Assembly £	Finishing £	Design £	Stores £
DOWRA LTD Overhead analysis sheet					
Allocated overheads	138250	141080	170140	194150	22,000
Factory overheads	35420	60260	49680	22080	16560
Stores	14691	16426	6748	695	(38560)
Design	72308	72308	72309	(216925)	—
Total	260669	290074	298877	—	—
Machine hours	180,000	85,000	240,000		
Absorption rate per machine hour	1·45	3·41	1·25		

Data

One of the products manufactured by Dowra Ltd is a small wooden duck on wheels, pulled by a string.

The product materials specification is as follows.

Materials Specification Wooden Duck on Wheels		
Materials	*Quantity*	*Treatment*
5 mm board	0.2 sq metres	Direct
4 cm diameter wheels	4	Direct
String	30cm	Indirect
Wire	20cm	Indirect
White paint		Indirect
Brown paint		Indirect
Red paint		Indirect
Varnish		Indirect
Glue		Indirect
Box	1	Direct

The standard time for manufacture is as follows.

Wooden Duck on Wheels	
Process	*Time*
Cutting head	20 seconds
Cutting body	40 seconds
Cutting base	30 seconds
Assembly	3 minutes
Painting	4 minutes
Packing	30 seconds

Note: All the above times are both direct labour hours and machine hours.

Additional information is as follows.

Materials Price List (extract)		
Board:	5 mm	£4.60 per sq. metre
Wheels:	4cm diameter	£18.20 per 100
Boxes:	Wooden duck	£16.00 per 100

Current Wage Rates	
Grade	*Rate per hour*
Cutter	£7.50
Assembler	£6.80
Painter	£8.20
Packer	£5.00

Task 2

Complete the Standard Cost Card below for the wooden duck on wheels. Use the overhead absorption rates you calculated in task 1.

Standard Cost Card Wooden Duck on Wheels			
Materials	*Quantity*	*Price* £	*Value* £
5 mm board	0.2 metre	4.60 per metre	0.92
4 cm diameter wheels	4	18.2	0.728
Box	1	16	0.16
Subtotal:			1.808
Labour	*Time*	*Rate* £	*Value* £
Cutter	1½ mins	7.50	0.1875
Assembler	3 mins	6.80	0.34
Painter	4 mins	8.20	0.547
Packer	½ mins	5.00	0.042
Subtotal:			1.117
Production overheads	*Time*	*Rate* £	*Value* £
Cutting	1½ m	1.45	0.036
Assembly	3	3.41	0.171
Finishing	4½	1.25	0.094
Subtotal:			0.301
GRAND TOTAL			3.226

Data

The sales manager was concerned that demand for many of the popular products was falling. Quotations were being sent out to potential customers, but were being rejected in favour of lower quotations from other suppliers. On the other hand, quotations for one-off expensive items were being accepted.

The production manager was certain that materials being used were similar to those used by other manufacturers and that wage rates were no higher than elsewhere in the industry. He thought that the answer might lie in the way the production overheads were apportioned to the different products.

Task 3

Write a short memorandum to the sales manager and production manager suggesting ways in which the apportionment of the production overheads might be improved to give more accurate product costs.

The memorandum should consider the apportionment of each of the following production overheads in separate paragraphs.

(a)   Unallocated factory costs
(b)   Stores overheads
(c)   Design overheads

In each case the present method of apportionment should be criticised and a fairer alternative suggested.

Data

The standard costs of wooden ducks on wheels, for the **CURRENT** year, for 5 mm board and for cutting are as follows.

5 mm board: 0.2 sq metres at £4.50 per sq metre
Cutters: 1.5 minutes at £7.20 per hour.
In the most recent period, 120 wooden ducks on wheels were produced.
25 sq metres of 5 mm board were requisitioned from Stores at a total cost of £110.
2.75 hours were recorded for cutters at a total cost of £22.

Task 4

(a)   (i)   Calculate the material price variance and material usage variance for 5 mm board.

      (ii)   Calculate the wage rate variance and labour efficiency variance for cutters.

(b)   Suggest possible reasons for the variances calculated.

SECTION 2

All the questions in this exercise relate to the data concerning Dowra Ltd provided in Section 1.

The suggested time allocation for this exercise is 45 minutes.

1   Give TWO examples of work in progress that would apply to Dowra Ltd.

2   Give TWO examples of indirect materials used by the design department.

3   Suggest why string and wire are treated as indirect materials.

4   How would the standard labour times for manufacture in Section 1, Task 2 have been calculated?

5   Which method of stock valuation should be used in the preparation of quotations in order to cost at the most realistic valuation? Give reasons for your answer.

6   Explain why it has been possible to allocate some production overheads directly to cost centres. Give an example of such an allocation.

7   The management accountant is considering introducing an idle time variance in the labour variance calculations.

    What is the purpose of an idle time variance?

8   The factory manager has been considering the possibility of introducing a system of bonus payments.

What should a good bonus payments system achieve for both the company and the employees?

9   In the company's stock control system, explain the terms 'reorder level' and 'minimum level'.

10   The formula to calculate the economic ordering quantity depends upon stockholding costs and ordering costs.

    (a)   Give TWO examples of stockholding costs.

    (b)   Give TWO examples of ordering costs.

11   The warehouse is concerned with the time taken up with stocktaking. The warehouse manager has heard that computerised stock control systems hold records on stock levels at all times and that, therefore, stocktaking will not be necessary.

    Is the warehouse manager correct? Give reasons for your answer.

12   The company is planning to produce a wooden model based on a cartoon character. To do this, it will have to pay the copyright holder a copyright fee of £1 per model produced. The company is not sure how to treat the £1 copyright fee: it might be a production overhead, a direct expense or a selling and distribution overhead.

    Explain which classification of cost it should be, giving reasons for your answer.

A SUGGESTED ANSWER TO THIS PRACTICE CENTRAL ASSESSMENT IS GIVEN ON PAGE 217.

PRACTICE CENTRAL ASSESSMENT 2: SOUTHWOOD COLLEGE (DECEMBER 1995)

SECTION 1

The suggested time allocation for this exercise is 80 minutes.

Data

Southwood College is a small private college in the south of England. It runs courses in accountancy and banking, largely for groups of employees from large and medium-sized companies.

The college consists of three classrooms, one of which is a computer room, an administrative office, a dining room and a kitchen.

You are employed by the college and you have been given a number of tasks by the chief accountant to help introduce more rigorous cost controls and develop a new pricing system.

There is some uncertainty about how to value the stock of paper used to photocopy teaching materials.

At present a system of standard costing is in operation.

The following data applies to October 1995:

Standard cost of photocopy paper: £24 per ream*

| 2 October | Opening stock | 84 reams (all bought at £23 per ream) |

Purchases were as follows.

| 5 October | 100 reams | £2,400 less 10% quantity discount |
| 12 October | 80 reams | £2,100 |

Issues:

2 October	Acdo Ltd AAT course	70 reams
9 October	Barco Ltd Introductory Banking	80 reams
26 October	Casco Ltd Introductory Costing	70 reams

*NB. A ream is a unit used to express quantities of paper.

Task 1

Complete the stores ledger record card below for October, assuming that issues are priced on a FIFO basis.

STORES LEDGER RECORD										
PHOTOCOPY PAPER										
Date	Receipts			Issues			Balance			
	Qty	Price £	Value £	Qty	Price £	Value £	Qty	Price £	Value £	
Oct 2							84	23.00	1,932	

Task 2

Calculate the value of closing stock using the following methods.

(i) FIFO;
(ii) LIFO;
(iii) standard cost.

Give your answer in the table below.

Method	Closing stock valuation		
	Quantity	Price £	Value £
FIFO	44	26.25	1155
LIFO	44	23.00 26.25 21.60	1016.50
Standard cost	44	24.00	1056

Task 3

Write a short memorandum to the chief accountant which explains the difference between the FIFO, LIFO and standard cost methods of stock valuation. Recommend which method should be used when charging for photocopies on courses, giving your reasons.

Task 4

Write a short memorandum to the administration manager which includes a calculation of the total material price variance for all purchases of photocopy paper for October. Explain the variance.

Task 5

10% discount is available on purchases of photocopy paper when 100 or more reams are purchased and 15% when 200 or more reams are purchased. The administration manager is keen to take advantage of this discount. Write a short report to the administration manager outlining the advantages and disadvantages of buying in bulk and outlining the information you would require in order to calculate the optimum purchase quantity.

Data

You have been given the following budget data for the five cost centres within Southwood college for the forthcoming year.

	Classroom A	Classroom B	Classroom C	Admin	Catering
Wages (£)	-	-	-	76,000	48,000
Student days	3,800	2,600	1,600	-	-
Book value of equipment (£)	4,000	6,000	60,000	20,000	10,000
Areas (m²)	250	200	150	200	200

The following costs are common to all cost centres in the college:

Heating and lighting	£40,000	~ area
Depreciation of equipment	£60,000	~ Book value of Eq.

The following is an example of a costing document used to calculate the cost of a course:

Course:	AAT Recording Cost Information	
Duration:	10 days @ 7 hours per day	
Estimated students	20	
		£
Direct costs:		
Teaching time		2100
Photocopy costs		60
Food and drink		600
Indirect costs		
Catering		1550
Administration		800
Other overhead costs		892
Total cost		6002

NB. All figures to the nearest £

Task 6

Complete the costing document above, according to the following instructions.

1. Teaching time is costed at the current standard hourly rate, which is £30 per hour.

2. Standard photocopy costs are £30 per ream. Each student will use 0.1 reams.

3   The cost of food and drink has been estimated at £3 per student day.

4   Heating and lighting is apportioned between the five cost centres according to area and depreciation of equipment is apportioned between the five cost centres according to the book value of equipment.

5   Catering costs

     The three elements of catering (wages, heating and lighting and depreciation of equipment) are totalled and divided by the budgeted total student days to give an absorption rate per student day.

6   Administration costs

     The three elements of administration cost (wages, heating and lighting and depreciation of equipment) are totalled and divided by the estimated number of courses to give an absorption rate per course. The estimated number of courses for the forthcoming year is 120.

7   Other overhead costs

     These relate to classroom overheads and consist of the heating and lighting and depreciation of equipment apportioned to each classroom. The total of these overheads for each classroom is divided by the estimated student days, to arrive at an absorption rate per student day. The AAT Recording Cost Information course will take place in Classroom B.

8   The three absorption rates calculated in 5, 6 and 7 above, are used to calculate the indirect costs for the course.

Notes

(1)   All absorption rates are calculated to two decimal places.

(2)   Use the table below to help calculate the absorption rates.

	Classroom A	Classroom B	Classroom C	Admin	Catering	Total
	£	£	£	£	£	£
Wages	-	-	-	76,000	48,000	
Heating and lighting						40,000
Depreciation of equipment						60,000
Total						

SECTION 2

The suggested time allocation for this exercise is 40 minutes.

The first five questions are based on the following information.

J Thompson Ltd is a small engineering company making specialist components for use in the oil industry. Shown below is a job card for the manufacture of a batch of machine tool components for R Patel & Co.

Note: The company uses a labour hour rate for absorbing production overheads.

			Materials	Labour		Other direct costs	Overheads

JOB CARD

Customer: R Patel & Co   **Job No:** 172467

1995	Materials £	Labour hours	£	Other direct costs £	Overheads £
13 October MR 648	642				
16 October MR 652	192				
17 October Consultant's fee				700	
20 October Wages analysis (w/e 20.10.95)		80	960		880
23 October MRN 214	(68)				

1. Describe what the entry for 13 October means.

2. Explain why the consultant's fee of £700, charged on 17 October, was judged to be a direct cost.

3. Where would the information about the 80 labour hours worked on the job on w/e 20.10.95 have come from?

4. Calculate the overhead absorption rate.

5. Explain the entry for 23 October.

The following questions do not refer to the job card above and are general questions

6. Should overtime premium paid to a direct labour force be classified as a direct or an indirect cost? Give reasons for your answer.

7. If a member of the direct labour force of a building company spends one week building a new extension to the company premises, how should the pay for that week be dealt with in the accounts? Give reasons for your answer.

8. A company's wages control account for last week had two credit entries:

    (a) Work-in-progress control account   £8,200
    (b) Production overhead control account   £3,800

    Explain the purpose of the two entries.

9. Explain what is meant by 'lead time' and why it is important in the calculation of stock re-order levels.

10. For one of its materials for last month, a company has a favourable material price variance and an adverse material usage variance. Explain how these two variances might be connected.

11. A company's management should take action on reported variances that are both significant and controllable. Explain the terms 'significant' and 'controllable', giving examples.

12. The workers in a factory which makes jeans are paid a piecework rate of £1.19 per pair produced. Would this be a fixed cost or a variable cost?

A SUGGESTED ANSWER TO THIS PRACTICE CENTRAL ASSESSMENT IS GIVEN ON PAGE 222.

PRACTICE CENTRAL ASSESSMENT 3: WHITEWALL LIMITED (JUNE 1996)

SECTION 1

The suggested time allocation for this exercise is 80 minutes.

Data

You are employed as an Accounting Technician in the cost office of Whitewall Limited, an engineering company. You report to the Cost Accountant and have been given a number of tasks concerned with the cost data on a job for a client. The job is coded 'Wheelbase' and was undertaken during the month of May.

Job Wheelbase used two materials during May, Exon and Delton. Company policy is to issue material Exon on a FIFO basis and material Delton on a LIFO basis. You are given the following movements for May for both materials by a cost clerk within the costing office. The issues on May 18 and May 19 were to Job Wheelbase and there were no issues of Exon or Delton for any other job during May.

MATERIAL EXON - FIFO BASIS

		Kilos	£ price
May 1	Opening balance	30,000	2.00
May 7	Receipts	10,000	2.25
May 14	Receipts	12,000	2.50
May 18	Issue	35,000	

MATERIAL DELTON - LIFO BASIS

		Kilos	£ price
May 1	Opening balance	25,000	3.00
May 8	Receipts	9,000	3.20
May 15	Receipts	8,000	3.40
May 19	Issue	20,000	

Task 1

(a) Complete the stores ledger for May for Exon and Delton below.

STORES LEDGER RECORD
MATERIAL: EXON ~ *FIFO*

Date	Receipts			Issues			Balance		
	Kilos	Price £	Value £	Kilos	Price £	Value £	Kilos	Price £	Balance £
May 1							30,000	2.00	60,000
May 7	10,000	2.25	22,500						
May 14	12,000	2.50	30,000						
May 18				35,000	30,000 ×2 / 5,000 ×2	60,000 / 11250	8,000 / 12,000	2 25 / 250	18000 / 30000

STORES LEDGER RECORD
MATERIAL: DELTON   LIFO

Date	Receipts			Issues			Balance		
	Kilos	Price £	Value £	Kilos	Price £	Value £	Kilos	Price £	Balance £
May 1							25,000	3.00	75,000
May 8	9,000	3.20	28,800						
May 15	8,000	3.40	27,200		3,000 x 3	9 000			
May 19				20,000	9,000 3.20 8,000 x340	28,8000 27200	22,000	3 00	66,000

(b) One of your assistants in the Cost Office has had a telephone conversation with the stores supervisor who acknowledge that FIFO stands for 'first in first out' and LIFO stands for 'last in first out' but understands this to relate to the physical movement of stock.

Set out for your assistant notes for a telephone call in reply to the stores supervisor.

The reply should cover:

(i)   why FIFO and LIFO are used as methods of pricing issues;
(ii)   whether the stores supervisor is correct in his understanding of FIFO and LIFO.

Data

Job Wheelbase used labour from the assembly, moulding and finishing departments. Data relating to labour is given on the labour cost card below.

The Company has negotiated with the workforce a bonus scheme whereby the workers receive 50% of standard hours saved in each department paid at the *actual* labour rate paid per hour. This is not included in the actual wage cost given below, which shows actual hours paid at the basic actual wage rate per hour. There have been no overtime payments.

Task 2

Cost the labour requirements for Job Wheelbase using the labour cost card below.

LABOUR COST CARD			
JOB: WHEELBASE Date: May 1996			
	Assembly	Moulding	Finishing
Actual wage cost £	26,970	34,020	36,540
Standard hours produced	6,000	7,500	7,600
Actual hours worked	6,200	7,000	7,000
Standard hours saved	—	500	600
Actual wage rate per hour £	4.35	4.86	5.22
Bonus £	—	1215	1566
Total labour cost £	26970	35235	38106

Data

Whitewall Ltd charges overheads on the basis of machine hours. Budgeted data for the company available to you within the cost office is shown on the overhead analysis sheet below.

The totalled amounts are after service departments' overheads have been apportioned to the production departments.

OVERHEAD ANALYSIS SHEET

	Assembly	*Moulding*	*Finishing*
Budgeted total overheads	£3,249,000	£3,950,400	£3,419,900
Budgeted machine hours	90,000	120,000	110,000
Budgeted overhead absorption rate	36·10	32.92	31·09

The details relevant to Job Wheelbase are given in the job overhead analysis card below.

JOB OVERHEAD ANALYSIS CARD

		Assembly	*Moulding*	*Finishing*
Job machine hours		6,000	6,800	6,600
Budgeted overhead absorption rate	£	36.10	32.92	31·09
Overhead absorbed by job	£	216600	223856	205194

Task 3

(a) Calculate the overhead absorption rates for each department and insert them in the overhead analysis sheet above.

(b) Calculate the overhead absorbed by the job and insert it in the job overhead analysis card above.

(c) The supervisor for Job Wheelbase is questioning the use of budgeted machine hours as a basis to absorb overheads. He feels that a simpler approach would be to divide the budgeted total overheads for the company by the number of jobs for that year.

Reply to the Job Wheelbase supervisor in a memorandum. Your reply should:

(i) outline the purpose of overhead absorption;
(ii) give reasons why machine hours have been used as a basis of absorption;
(iii) state whether you agree or disagree with the supervisor's suggested approach.

Data

Below is the job cost card for Job Wheelbase. Whitewall's pricing policy is to charge a profit of 25% of the job price.

Task 4

Using the data you have prepared in tasks 1, 2 and 3, complete the job card for Job Wheelbase to the nearest pound.

JOB COST CARD

Job: Wheelbase   Date: May 1996

	Total
Material	
Exon	71250
Delton	65000
	136250
Labour	
Assembly	26970
Moulding	35235
Finishing	38106
	100311
Overhead	
Assembly	216600
Moulding	223855
Finishing	205194
	645649
Total cost	882210
Profit	2205525.0
Job price	1102762.50

÷75×100

1176281

Data

You have been asked by the Production Manager to review the labour cost associated with the assembly department on Job Wheelbase, a summary of which is given below.

SUMMARY OF ASSEMBLY WAGE COSTS ON JOB WHEELBASE

Budgeted wage rate	£4.50
Standard hours produced	6,000
Actual hours worked	6,200
Actual wage costs	£26,970

Task 5

(a) Calculate the following for the assembly department labour costs only:

    (i)   total labour cost variance;
    (ii)   labour efficiency variance;
    (iii)   labour wage rate variance.

(b) Write a short memo to the Production Manager explaining the variances for the assembly department and offering explanations.

Data

You have been asked to review the overhead expenditure for the finishing department for the period under review. You are given the following data for the period.

Finishing department		Data
Budgeted total overheads		£3,419,900
Budgeted machine hours		110,000
Budgeted overhead absorption rate	£	31·09·
Actual machine hours		108,000
Overhead absorbed	£	3,357,720
Actual overheads		£3,572,000
Over/(under) absorption of overheads	£	(2142·80)

Task 6

Complete the above table and write a short report to the Cost Accountant explaining:

(i)   the consequences of these results;
(ii) the possible causes;
(iii) the effect on costing such jobs as Wheelbase;
(iv) possible remedial action for the future.

SECTION 2

All the questions in this exercise relate to the data concerning Whitewall Limited provided in Section 1.

The suggested time allocation for this exercise is 40 minutes.

1   Materials Exon and Delton were costed on a FIFO and LIFO basis respectively. Briefly explain the difference between these two methods.

2   Give *two* examples of:

(i)   stock holding costs and
(ii)   stock ordering costs

that Whitewall Limited is likely to incur.

3   Explain the nature and purpose of a stocktake.

4   Give *two* different methods of a stocktake that Whitewall Limited might use.

5   Whitewall Limited uses standard hours produced to measure its labour output. Explain what a standard hour produced is.

6   State *two* ways in which information on actual labour hours worked on Job Wheelbase could have been collected.

7   Give a ratio that would measure the efficiency of the direct workers on Job Wheelbase and explain how it would be calculated.

8   Provide the double entry for the under/over absorbed overheads in the finishing department that will appear in the cost accounts for Whitewall Limited.

9   Task 3 in Section 1 gives the budgeted overheads for each production department after service department overheads (eg catering, stores etc) have been apportioned. *Briefly* explain the purpose for apportioning overheads of service cost centres to production cost centres, giving *one* example of a basis of apportionment for a service cost centre.

10 Job Wheelbase has incurred overheads but not direct expenses. *Briefly* explain the difference between these two costs.

11 Give *two* examples of overhead costs that might have been incurred on Job Wheelbase.

12 Whitewall Limited is considering an activity-based costing system to replace its current system of overhead absorption. Such a system uses cost drivers.

(a)   Explain what a cost driver is.
(b)   Give an example of a possible cost driver on Job Wheelbase.

A SUGGESTED ANSWER TO THIS PRACTICE CENTRAL ASSESSMENT IS GIVEN ON PAGE 226.

PRACTICE CENTRAL ASSESSMENT 4: TAMWORTH LTD (DECEMBER 1996)

SECTION 1

The suggested time allocation for this exercise is 75 minutes.

Data

You are employed as an accounting technician by Tamworth Limited and you report to the management accountant. Tamworth is a medium-sized company employing 760 people at a factory in northern England and it is primarily engaged in the manufacture of a bathroom accessory. You have been given a number of tasks concerned with the performance of the cutting, moulding, finishing and packaging departments for the year ended 30 November 1996.

Tamworth Ltd has a budgetary control system and uses standard costing. You have been given the following budget and actual performance data.

Year ended 30 November 1996

Department	Cutting	Moulding	Finishing	Packaging
Budgeted production (units)	379,000	356,000	362,100	375,000
Standard time per unit	6 mins	7.5 mins	8 mins	4 mins
Budgeted wage rate per hour	£5.25	£4.60	£5.10	£5.05
Actual production (units)	376,400	353,200	364,125	372,825
Actual wages	£200,956	£197,823	£247,720	£124,000
Actual labour hours worked	37,214	41,213	45,874	24,315
Average number of workers	164	173	162	195
Workers leaving during the year	35	14	11	13

Task 1

The production manager, who has responsibility for all four departments, is concerned about staff retention rates.

(a) Complete the following table using data from the table above.

(*Note.* Round off your workings to one decimal place.)

Department	Cutting	Moulding	Finishing	Packaging
Average number of workers	164	173	162	195
Workers leaving during the year	35	14	11	13
% of staff leaving 1996	21.3	8.1	6.8	6.7
% of staff leaving 1995	12.1%	7.8%	7.3%	7.4%

(b) Write a memo to the production manager

    (i)   analysing your results from Task 1 (a);
    (ii)   highlighting areas of concern and possible causes;
    (iii)   explaining the potential costs and consequences for the company.

Task 2

The management accountant is keen to inform the packaging department of its efficiency and capacity performance in relation to other departments.

(a) Using the data above you have been asked by the management accountant to complete the following table for the packaging department.

    (*Note.* Round off your ratio workings to one decimal place.)

Department	Cutting	Moulding	Finishing	Packaging
Budgeted production (hours)	37,900	44,500	48,280	25000 ✓
Actual labour hours worked	37,214	41,213	45,874	24135 ✓
Standard hours produced	37,640	44,150	48,550	24855 ✓
Capacity ratio	98.2%	92.6%	95.0%	99.4 ✗ 96.5 ✓
Efficiency ratio	101.1%	107.1%	105.8%	103 ✗ 10.29

Note: Capacity ratio $=$ $\dfrac{\text{Actual labour hours worked}}{\text{Budgeted hours}}$

Efficiency ratio $=$ $\dfrac{\text{Standard hours produced}}{\text{Actual labour hours worked}}$

(b) Write a note to the packaging department supervisor explaining the results of his department and giving possible reasons.

Task 3

The production manager is considering purchasing a new cutting machine for the cutting department. The cost of the machine is likely to be £180,000 and it will have a life of approximately five years and scrap value of between £10,000 and £15,000. Past experience has shown that such machinery will lose value and have most usage in the early part of its life.

Write a report to the production manager detailing:

(i) the method of depreciation that should be used;

(ii) an approximate rate that could be applied, showing any workings that allow you to arrive at that rate;

(iii) reasons for the choice of depreciation method.

Task 4

Tamworth Limited uses a budgeted overhead absorption rate based on labour hours. Data relating to the year ended 30 November 1996 is given in the table below and on page 173.

Complete the table below for the four production departments in the factory.

Note. Round off your figures to the nearest £.

Department	Cutting	Moulding	Finishing	Packaging
Actual overheads incurred	£1,234,736	£1,156,347	£938,463	£834,674
Budgeted absorption rate per labour hour	£33.82	£26.80	£20.25	£29.62
Actual labour hours worked	37214	41213	45874	24135
Overheads absorbed	1,258,577	1,104,508	928,949	720210
(Under) / over absorbed overheads	23841	(51839)	(9514)	(114464)

Task 5

Your assistant has taken a telephone call from the production manager, who has asked about effectiveness of standard cost as a method of pricing material issues and valuing stock.

List some points that will form the basis of a reply to the production manager. You should explain:

(i) what a standard material price represents;

(ii) how standard prices for materials will be ascertained;

(iii) the benefits and weaknesses of such a system.

SECTION 2

The suggested time allocation for this exercise is 45 minutes.

1 Where would the information about workers leaving the company in Task 1 of Section 1 have come from?

2 The budgeted wage rate per hour for the finishing department is £5.10. Explain how this might have been arrived at.

3 List *three* indirect wage costs that might have been incurred in the packaging department. *Pension O/T Bonus*

4 The material used by the production departments of Tamworth Ltd would have come from the stores department, a service cost centre. Suggest how the costs for the stores department would be incorporated into product cost.

5 Activity-based costing has been put forward as a realistic alternative to more traditional methods of overhead absorption. Explain one way in which an activity-based costing (ABC) system differs from the more traditional methods of overhead absorption.

6 An order has been placed for a particular material that is used in the cutting department. The order delivery time could take from 2 to 4 weeks and the usage of the material fluctuates from a minimum of 3,000 units to a maximum of 5,000 units per week. Calculate the re-order level. *5000 × 4 = 20000*

7 The output of a process cost system will usually be reduced by normal loss and abnormal loss. Briefly explain the difference between the two and state how they will be treated in the accounts.

8 Give an example of a cost centre from the data provided in Section 1 for Tamworth Ltd.

9 Overhead costs will either be allocated to a cost centre or apportioned to a cost centre.

   (a) Briefly explain the difference between the processes of allocation and apportionment.

   (b) Give *one* example of:
      (i) an allocated overhead for the packaging department; *– Direct Labour*
      (ii) an apportioned overhead for the moulding department. *Rent + rates*

10 The overheads for four production departments were under-absorbed by £151,977.

   (a) Does this mean actual overheads are less than absorbed overheads? *No*

   (b) What effect will this under-absorption have on budgeted profit? *Profit*

11 Explain the purpose of coding costs. *– reference. Key characteristics*

12 A company has the following details for the movement of an item of stock for November.

		Units	Cost per unit £	Cost £
1 Nov	Opening balance	1,000	3	3,000
10 Nov	Receipts	1,200	3.5	4,200
25 Nov	Issues	1,800		

Complete the following table for FIFO and LIFO.

Date	Description	FIFO £	LIFO £
25 Nov	Total issue value	5800	6000
30 Nov	Total closing stock value	1400	1200

A SUGGESTED ANSWER TO THIS PRACTICE CENTRAL ASSESSMENT IS GIVEN ON PAGE 231.

PRACTICE CENTRAL ASSESSMENT 5: BRAMWELL LTD (JUNE 1997)

SECTION 1

The suggested time allocation for this exercise is 75 minutes.

Data

You are an accounting technician working in the cost office of Bramwell Ltd, a company specialising in the production of confectionery. You report to the cost accountant who in turn reports to the production manager. The company's operations consist of the following production departments.

> Processing
> Quality assurance
> Packing

These production departments are supported by the following service departments.

> Stores
> Factory maintenance

Bramwell Ltd operates a budgetary control system and uses standard costing.

You have been given a number of tasks to do in your office.

Task 1

The following budgeted figures for next year are given to you for a new chocolate bar called 'Snick-Snack' at a full level of production of 6,000,000 bars.

	£
Direct material	300,000
Direct labour	250,000
Direct expenses	200,000
Prime cost	750,000
Variable overheads	150,000
Fixed overheads	300,000
Total cost	1,200,000

(a) Demand for the product is uncertain so the cost accountant has asked you to complete the table below for the account manager of Snick-Snack, detailing total costs per bar at the different levels of production.

Costs	Production (bars) % of capacity	5,400,000 90% £	5,700,000 95% £	6,000,000 100% £
Direct material		270,000	285,000	300,000
Direct labour		225,000	237500	250,000
Direct expenses		180,000	190,000	200,000
Prime cost		675,000	712,500	750,000
Variable overheads		135000	142500	150,000
Fixed overheads		300,000	300,000	300,000
Total cost		1,110,000	1,155,000	1,200,000
Total cost per bar (to 4 decimal places)		0.2056	0.2026	0.2000

(b) The account manager is surprised at the movement in the cost per bar.

Write a short memo:

(i) outlining the trend in cost per bar over the range of production;
(ii) explaining the reason for this trend.

Task 2

The cost accountant is concerned about the cost of biscuit used in the manufacture of a long established product by the name of 'Nutbite' for period 11. He has arranged a meeting with the production manager to discuss this and has asked you to review the results for period 11.

Results for period 11 are:

Actual production	850,000 bars
Actual biscuit usage	93,500 kgs
Actual cost of biscuit usage	£40,205

The budget set out the following data.

Standard price per kilo of biscuit	£0.415
Standard usage at production level of 850,000 bars	89,250 kgs

You are required to:

(a) detail the variances for period 11; and
(b) offer possible reasons for the causes of these variances.

Note. Provide your answers to the nearest £.

Task 3

At a meeting between you, the cost accountant and the production manager, doubts were raised about the efficiency of labour and the increased cost implications. A general discussion followed about the introduction of a bonus scheme, whereby direct labour personnel would be given a bonus of 50% of standard hours saved, paid at the basic rate of pay. However, the production manager has a number of reservations about how such a bonus scheme could:

(a) encourage direct labour to work more efficiently;
(b) save money for the company.

At the end of the meeting you have been asked to write a report which:

(a) outlines the characteristics of a bonus scheme that operates as a percentage of standard hours saved;

(b) explains the incentives that will be given to direct labour to work more efficiently using the figures given below;

(c) indicates how such a bonus scheme would increase profitability for the company;

(d) highlights any concerns that you may want addressed for the effective implementation of such a bonus scheme.

For the basis of the report you may assume that an average member of the direct labour personnel working 35 hours a week at a basic rate of £6.00 per hour would produce 168 units. Each unit has a standard production time allowance of 15 minutes.

Task 4

The cost accountant has given you the task of preparing a budgeted production overhead schedule for the company. You are given the following data to assist you.

	Total	Processing	Quality assurance	Packing	Stores	Factory maintenance
Number of personnel	650	440	40	100	40	30
Area (sq ft)	100,000	52,000	16,000	10,000	10,000	12,000
Machine usage (hours)	65,000	45,000	2,000	18,000		
Number of material requisitions	11,000	6,260	2,450	1,290		1,000
Number of maintenance hours	50,000	32,000	4,000	14,000		

You are required to complete the following overhead analysis schedule using appropriate bases of apportionment from the data given above.

	Basis	Total £	Processing £	Quality assurance £	Packing £	Stores £	Factory maintenance £
Rent and rates	Area	320,000	166400	51200	32000	32000	38400
Canteen costs	No of person	169,000					
Depreciation of machinery	Machine usage	273,000					
Total		762,000					

SECTION 2

The suggested time allocation for this exercise is 45 minutes.

1. Bramwell Ltd has a policy of holding a buffer stock for most of the stock that it purchases. Explain what a 'buffer stock' is.

2. Bramwell Ltd uses standard costing. Explain what this means for stock issues and stock valuation.

3. The production manager is considering using FIFO and LIFO for pricing issues and stock valuation. Explain the costing differences between these two methods.

4. For Section 1, Task 3 you wrote a report about the implementation of a bonus scheme for Bramwell Ltd.

   (a) In a bonus scheme is it budgeted labour hours or standard labour hours produced which are used to help calculate a bonus?

   (b) Explain the difference between budgeted labour hours and standard labour hours produced.

5. In Section 1, Task 1 you were given a task concerning fixed costs and variable costs in Bramwell Ltd. Sketch in the graphs below how fixed costs and variable costs behave with changes in the level of activity.

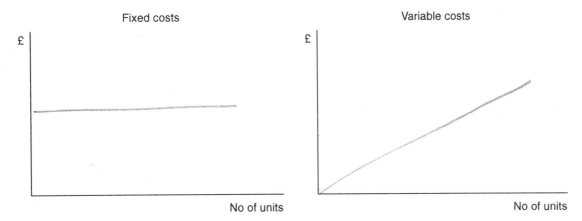

Fixed costs

£

No of units

Variable costs

£

No of units

6   In Section 1, Task 4 you were given a task on apportionment of overheads in Bramwell Ltd. Explain the difference between the apportionment and absorption of overheads.

7   In Section 1, Task 4 you were asked to calculate a budgeted production overhead schedule for Bramwell Ltd.

(a) Outline what now needs to be done with the budgeted costs of the service departments in order to arrive at overhead absorption rates for the production departments.

(b) Explain the reasons for your recommended action in (a) above.

8   Last year the Quality Assurance Department under-absorbed £15,000 of overheads. Explain what this means.

9   Bramwell Ltd uses a process costing system rather than a job costing system. Explain why this is the case.

10   During period 11, for one of the products made by Bramwell Ltd, 4,000 kgs of biscuit were input into the process and the output from the process was 3,700 kgs. Budgeted normal loss is 5%.

(a) Identify the normal and abnormal loss of this process by kg.

(b) Give the bookkeeping entry for any abnormal loss.

11   Identify the double entry for the material usage variance that you calculated in Section 1, Task 2.

Description	DR	CR

A SUGGESTED ANSWER TO THIS PRACTICE CENTRAL ASSESSMENT IS GIVEN ON PAGE 235.

PRACTICE CENTRAL ASSESSMENT 6: EDWARDS LTD (DECEMBER 1997)

SECTION 1

The suggested time allocation for this exercise is 75 minutes.

Please note that the tasks should be attempted in numerical order.

Data

You are an accounting technician working in the cost office of Edwards Ltd, a company that uses a job costing system. You are reviewing the work of a cost clerk who has completed a number of tasks on Job 548, which has been undertaken at a small subsidiary factory of the company. The factory is a separate cost centre and cost accounts are prepared at each month end. Job 548 was the only job undertaken during the month of November 1997 at the factory and it was both started and finished within the month.

Task 1

The cost clerk has provided you with the following table showing the issues of material Bitcom to Job 548 for the month of November 1997. Material Bitcom was used only on Job 548 during this period and the first-in-first-out method has been used for costing the issues and valuing stock.

		MATERIAL BITCOM							
JOB: 548									MONTH: NOV 97
Date	Receipts			Issues			Stock		
	Qty (Units)	Unit Price £	Value £	Qty (Units)	Unit Price £	Value £	Qty (Units)	Unit Price £	Value £
Bal 1 Nov							50	40	2,000
2 Nov	450	50	22,500				500	(50 × 40) (450 × 50)	24,500
6 Nov				240	(50 × 40) (190 × 50)	11,500	260	50	13,000
12 Nov	360	60	21,600				620	(260 × 50) (360 × 60)	34,600
14 Nov				290	(260 × 50) (30 × 60)	14,800	330	60	19,800
20 Nov	300	90	27,000				630	(330 × 60) (300 × 90)	46,800
23 Nov				320	60	19,200	310	(10 × 60) (300 × 90)	27,600
30 Nov				280	(10 × 60) (270 × 90)	24,900	30	90	2,700

You have decided that last-in-first-out is the most appropriate method for costing the issues of material Bitcom to Job 548.

(a) Using the table below, cost the issues and value the stock of material Bitcom on a last-in-first-out basis.

	Receipts			Issues			Stock		
JOB: 548								**MONTH: NOV 97**	
Date	Receipts			Issues			Stock		
	Qty (Units)	Unit Price £	Value £	Qty (Units)	Unit Price £	Value £	Qty (Units)	Unit Price £	Value £
Bal 1 Nov							50	40	2,000
2 Nov	450	50	22,500				500	50×40 450×50	24,500
6 Nov				240	50	12,000	260	50×40 210×50	12,500
12 Nov	360	60	21,600				620	50×40 210×50 360×60	34,100
14 Nov				290	60	17,400	330	50×40 210×50 70×60	16,700
20 Nov	300	90	27,000				630	AS Above 300×90	43,700
23 Nov				320	20×60 300×90	28,200	310	50×40 210×50 50×60	15,500
30 Nov				280	210×50 50×60 20×40	14,300	30	40	1,200

(b) Write a short memo to the cost clerk explaining:

    (i)   the main differences between FIFO and LIFO costing methods;

    (ii)   the consequences of the change in policy for Job 548 and the stock of material Bitcom.

Task 2

The cost clerk has collected the following data about direct labour costs for Job 548 for November 1997.

Standard wage rate per direct labour hour	Standard labour cost	Actual direct labour hours worked	Actual direct labour cost
£8.50	£35,700	4,160 hrs	£38,480

One category of labour was used and one standard wage rate payment was budgeted for.

(a) Calculate the labour variances for November 1997;

(b) Briefly offer possible causes of the labour efficiency variance and the labour wage rate variance.

Task 3

The cost clerk has asked for your assistance in completing a job cost card for Job 548.

You are told that:

- Bitcom was the only material used on Job 548 and it is to be costed on a LIFO basis as calculated in Task 1

- direct labour costs are as reported in Task 2

- direct expenses comprise of 195 hours of machine hire which cost £15 per hour

- production overheads are absorbed on the basis of direct labour hours

- administration overheads are absorbed on the basis of 1/3 of total production cost

- total budgeted production overheads for the year for the factory are £1,324,925

- total budgeted direct labour hours for the year for the factory are 58,625

Complete the job cost card below.

JOB COST CARD	
JOB:	**MONTH:**
	£
Direct material	71900
Direct labour	38480
Direct expenses	2925
Production overhead	94016
Production cost	207321
Administration overhead	69107
Total cost	276428
Profit (33 1/3% of job price)	138214
Job price	414642

Task 4

The cost clerk has identified overheads incurred for the factory at which Job 548 was completed.

(a) Complete the following table using the information you have compiled in Task 3.

(b) Write brief notes that explain your results and the effect on the profitability of Job 548.

OVERHEAD SUMMARY			
MONTH: NOVEMBER 1997		**COST CENTRE: JOB 548**	
	Overhead absorbed	Overhead incurred	(Under)/Over absorption of overhead
	£	£	£
Production overhead	94016	99,328	(5312)
Administration overhead	69107	74,269	(5162)

SECTION 2

The suggested time allocation for this exercise is 45 minutes.

1   Edwards Ltd uses a job costing system for Job 548. Identify one reason why job costing would be used.

2   Two of the costs outlined in the job cost card in Section 1, Task 3 are direct expenses and production overheads. Give *two* examples of direct expenses and production overhead that might relate to Job 548.

3   In Section 1, Task 3 production overheads were absorbed on a direct labour hour basis. State another method of overhead absorption which is based upon time.

4   Explain why a method of overhead absorption based on time is considered more appropriate than a method based upon monetary value, eg percentage of labour cost.

5   Explain the difference between a material requisition and a purchase requisition with particular reference to the material Bitcom used in Job 548.

6   You are told that the lead time for material Bitcom is 10 days and the buffer stock is 25 units. Explain what this means.

7   The stores department is responsible for a stocktake. Explain what a stocktake is, and state two timeframes within which the process of stocktaking can be carried out.

8   (a)   Calculate the standard hours saved on Job 548 using the data from Section 1, Task 2.

(b) Assume that the direct workers on Job 548 were paid a bonus equal to 75% of standard hours saved at actual basic wage rate. Calculate the total labour bonus payment on Job 548 for November 1997.

9 Section 1, Task 2 used a standard wage rate of £8.50 per labour hour. List *two* factors that might have been taken into account in arriving at a standard wage rate.

10 Explain what idle time is, and give *two* causes of idle time.

11 Complete the account below using your figures from Section 1, Task 4 as at the end of November 1997.

Under/Overabsorbed Overheads A/C

A SUGGESTED ANSWER TO THIS PRACTICE CENTRAL ASSESSMENT IS GIVEN ON PAGE 240.

SAMPLE CENTRAL ASSESSMENT

INTERMEDIATE STAGE - NVQ/SVQ3

Unit 5

Recording cost information
(AAT Specimen)

This Sample Central Assessment is the AAT's Specimen Central Assessment for Unit 5. Its purpose is to give you an idea of what an AAT central assessment looks like. It is not intended as a definitive guide to the tasks you may be required to perform.

The suggested time allowance for this Assessment is three hours. You are advised to spend approximately 75 minutes on Section 1, 45 minutes on Section 2 and 60 minutes on Section 3.

Calculators may be used but no reference material is permitted.

**DO NOT OPEN THIS PAPER UNTIL YOU ARE READY TO START
UNDER TIMED CONDITIONS**

INSTRUCTIONS

This Central Assessment is designed to test your ability to record cost information.

The Central Assessment is in **three** sections.

You are provided with data which you must use to complete the tasks, and space to set out your answers.

You are allowed **three hours** to complete your work. You are reminded that competence must be achieved in each section. You should therefore attempt and aim to complete **every** task in **each** section. All essential workings should be included in your answer where appropriate.

A high level of accuracy is required. Check your work carefully.

Correcting fluid may be used in moderation. Errors should be crossed out neatly and clearly. You should write in black ink, not pencil.

A suggested answer to this Assessment is given on page 244.

WICKFORD LIMITED

SECTION 1

You are advised to spend approximately 75 minutes on this section.

Please note that the tasks should be attempted in numerical order.

Data

Wickford Limited is a company that specialises in the manufacture of crystal glass. It makes a number of standard products, for which there is a buoyant demand, and also makes one-off products. One such one-off product is a commemorative vase to celebrate one hundred and fifty years of glass-making within the factory.

The manufacturing process within the factory is organised into three production cost centres, which are:

- Blowing
- Cutting
- Engraving

These production cost centres are serviced by three service cost centres, which are:

- Quality control
- Stores
- Maintenance

You are an accounting technician working in the cost department and you report to the cost accountant. You have been given a number of tasks concerned with the factory's activities for 1997 and its plans for 1998.

Task 1

Your office has been given the responsibility of compiling the budgeted costs for the commemorative vase. Initially, production was forecast at 750,000 units; however, overseas interest now means that demand could be as high as 1,000,000 or 1,250,000 units.

Complete the budgeted cost schedule below for 1,000,000 and 1,250,000 units.

		1998 BUDGETED PRODUCTION COSTS		
Costs	Units	750,000	1,000,000	1,250,000
Variable costs		£	£	£
Material		2,250,000	3,600,000	3,75,0000
Labour		2,437,500	3,250,000	4,062,500
Overhead		2,062,500	2,750,000	3,437,500
Total		6,750,000	9,000,000	11,240,000
Fixed costs				
Labour		1,100,000	1,100,000	1,100,000
Overhead		1,750,000	1,750,000	1,750,000
Total		2,850,000	2850 000	2,850,000
Total production cost		9,600,000	11,850,000	14,090000
Cost per unit		12.80	11.85	11.272

Task 2

Labour in the blowing department is organised into teams of three. For the manufacturing of the commemorative vase there will be a master blower, blower and a general assistant in each team.

You are told that the following rates of pay apply in the blowing department:

Master blower   £8.60 per hour
Blower   £6.40 per hour
General assistant £4.20 per hour

Standards set for the production of the commemorative vase are that each team should produce 30 vases per hour. In order to encourage production, it has been agreed that each member of the team should receive a bonus of 50% of any time saved, paid at the standard rate.

During January 1998, Team Alpha in the blowing department produced 5,370 vases. Team Alpha worked four five-day weeks in January 1998 and each working day was seven and three-quarters hours.

Complete the wage schedule below to determine the total pay for each member of Team Alpha for January 1998.

WAGE SCHEDULE				
Blowing dept: Team Alpha			Month: January 1998	
	Team	*Master Blower*	*Blower*	*Gen Assistant*
Wage rate (£)		8.60	6.40	4.20
Hrs worked	465	155	155	155
Total wage (£)		1333.00	992.00	651.00
Standard hours produced	537			
Standard hours saved	72			
Bonus (£)		103.20	76.80	50.40
Total wage + bonus (£)		1436.20	1068.80	701.40

Task 3

The raw materials that are used in the manufacture of the commemorative crystal vase are silica sand, potash and lead monoxide. The company has noted that the cost of silica sand from suppliers fluctuates and it needs to ensure that it issues the sand to production at a cost that reflects the most recent price.

Complete the store card below using the last-in-first-out costing method to cost issues of silica sand and value stock for the month of November 1997.

STORE CARD											
Material: Silica Sand									MONTH: NOV 97		
Date	Receipts			Issues			Stock				
Nov	Qty '000 kg	Cost per kg £	Value £'000	Qty '000 kg	Cost per kg £	Value £'000	Qty '000 kg	Cost per kg £	Value £'000		
Bal 1							1,470	2.00	2,940		
5	860	2.15	1849				1470 / 860	2.00 / 2.15	2940 / 1849		
9				1,060	200 200 2.15×860	400 1849	1270	2.00	2540		
14	1,100	2.25	2475				1270 / 1100	2.00 / 2.25	2540 / 2475		
18	1,050	2.20	2310		15×2	300	1270 / 80	2.00 / 2.20	2540 / 2475	2310
21				2,300	1100×2.25 1050×2.20	2475 2310	1120	2.00	2240		
23	1,430	2.40	3432				1120 / 1430	2.00 / 2.40	2240 / 3432		
25				1,540	1430×2.40 110×2.00	3432 220					
28				820	820×2	1640	190	2.00	380		

Task 4

It has been decided that production overheads will be charged to the commemorative vases on the basis of the pre-determined production overhead rates for each of the production cost centres.

You are given the following budgeted information for 1998:

- The production departments (blowing, cutting and engraving) are serviced by the quality control, stores and maintenance departments.

- The maintenance department will provide the following service hours to the other departments for 1998:

Blowing	1,400	3080	45.5
Cutting	725		23.5
Engraving	475		15.4
Quality control	240		7.8
Stores	240		7.8

- The stores department is budgeted to receive the following requisitions orders from the other cost centres:

Blowing	1,944		58
Cutting	712	3352	21.2
Engraving	524		15.6
Quality control	172		5.2

- The quality control department is budgeted to provide the following hours of service to the production cost centres:

Blowing	6,300		61.8
Cutting	2,100	10200	20.6
Engraving	1,800		17.6

- Production overheads will be absorbed on a labour hour basis.

(a) **Complete the budgeted production overhead schedule below to reapportion the service department overheads and calculate the total budgeted overheads for the three production departments. Ignore variable overheads.**

Year: 1998	Budgeted Production Overhead Schedule						
Cost	Cost centre Blowing £'000	Cutting £'000	Engraving £'000	Quality control £'000	Stores £'000	Maintenance £'000	Total £'000
Allocated overhead	876	534	413	278	374	292	2,767
Apportioned overhead	1,138	793	541	311	416	324	3,523
Sub-total	**2,014**	**1,327**	**954**	**589**	**790**	**616**	**6,290**
Maintenance	280	145	95	48	48	(616)	—
Stores	486	178	131	43	(838)	—	—
Quality control	420	140	120	(680)	—	—	—
Total budgeted overheads	3 200	1790	1300	—	—	—	6290

(b) **Complete the following table when you have completed part (a).**

	Blowing	Cutting	Engraving
Total budgeted overheads (£)	3200 000	1790 000	1300 000
Budgeted labour hours	48,000	35,800	32,500
Budgeted overhead absorption rate £ per labour hour	66.67	50.00	40.00

Note. Show the budgeted overhead absorption rate to two decimal places.

It is envisaged that each commemorative vase will spend the following times in the production cost centres.

	Blowing	Cutting	Engraving
Labour time (mins)	9	7½	12

(c) **Complete the following table to show the production overhead to be absorbed by each vase.**

Department	Time	Budgeted overhead absorption rate per labour hour	Overhead absorbed
	Minutes	£	£
Blowing	9	66.67	10.00
Cutting	7½	50.00	6.25
Engraving	12	40.00	8.00
Total			24.25

SECTION 2

You are advised to spent 45 minutes on this section.

Task 1

Briefly describe and explain the trend in costs per unit for the three budgeted levels of production in Task 1, Section 1.

The trend is for the costs to reduce, the
fixed costs will remain the same - whatever
the production, the variable costs will
increase according to production.
Ecominic of scale - more producte it
will get Cheaper

Task 2

Sketch in the graphs below to show how fixed and variable costs behave in general with changes in the level of production.

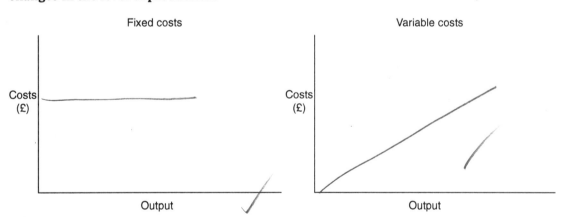

Task 3

The cost schedule in Task 1 of Section 1 defined overhead costs as being either fixed or variable with changes in the level of activity.

Give ONE other classification of behaviour of overhead cost and an example of an overhead cost that matches this classification. Then sketch a graph to show how the cost behaves with changes in the level of activity.

Classification ...... Stepped

Example ...... Bonus increase on certain
turnover
discentary

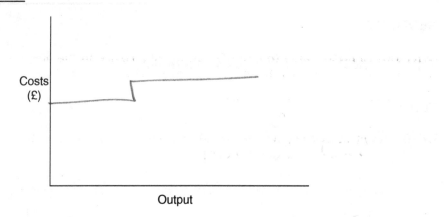

Costs
(£)

Output

Task 4

Briefly explain the benefits of a bonus scheme to workers and employers.

(a) **Benefits to workers**

Increase wages, can be motivating
can extra   The benefit to it
                 is increased product. Fu
Staff   more motivated

(b) **Benefits to employers**

Increase productivity, more motivated
staff

Task 5

In order to introduce a bonus in Task 2 of Section 1, it was necessary to establish standard times of production. Briefly explain how these standard times for the blowing team will have been established.

- Observed - time in motion study
- Each part of the job breandown and
  timed

Task 6

Wickford Limited wants to identify periods of absence in the blowing department during 1998. Identify TWO documents that will provide this information.

(i) Time sheets. - staff sign in when working and out when not

(ii) Job Cards - time is allocated to the job that the person is working on

Task 7

Explain why LIFO was chosen as the method to cost issues of silica sand in Task 3 of Section 1.

To ensure pricing on material is always up to date ✓

Task 8

Briefly highlight the weaknesses of the LIFO method of costing issues and valuing stock.

Weakness - Stock is valuated at the lowest cost

— Not recognised by Inland Revenue

— Considered appreciate for external report purpose.

Task 9

The company carries a large volume of silica sand, potash and lead monoxide and is concerned about the costs of holding and ordering stock.

List TWO costs of holding stock and TWO costs of ordering stock.

Holding cost

(i) Insurance

(ii) Rent+ Rates

financing costs

Ordering cost *Purchase*

(i) Ordering dept

(ii) Telephones

Overheads

Task 10

(a) **Identify a method that the company could use to minimise the costs listed in Task 9 above.**

Had a mininum + maximum stockholding and ensure there is an re-order quality in base. Also an agreed buffer stock level to avoid stock out

✓ EOQ - Encomic Order quality

(b) **Briefly explain what this method sets out to achieve.**

It aims to ensure that there is alway stock available to avoid over stock or running out

- Minimise cost of ordering and holding stock - given level of demand.

Task 11

Task 4 in Section 1 shows allocated overheads and apportioned overheads for each cost centre. Give one example of each type for the flowing department.

Blowing department allocated overhead ✓ Supervisor Salary

Blowing department apportioned overhead Lighting + Heating

Task 12

Briefly explain the reasons for your choice of allocated and apportioned overheads for the blowing department in task 11 above.

? Lighting + Heating - depends on Space taken up with factory

SECTION 3

You are advised to spend approximately 60 minutes on this section.

Task 1

You have been given the task of reviewing the performance of the blowing department for the month of January 1998. Variances for material and labour have been calculated by a cost clerk in your office and are shown in the table on page 196.

The fixed overhead variances have not been calculated but you have ascertained the following information for the blowing department for January 1998.

Budgeted overheads (£)	217,750
Budgeted hours	3,250
Budgeted overhead absorption rate (£)	£67 per labour hour
Actual overheads (£)	234,270
Actual hours worked	3,100
Standard hour produced	3,180

You have been told that the material used in the blowing department has been acquired from new suppliers as the company is concerned to keep costs under control and the new supplier's prices were cheaper.

The company had budgeted for a small cost-of-living wage increase to be implemented in January 1998; however, this had been renegotiated to a figure that was almost double the original rise.

Complete the table of variances and prepare a report, using the proforma on page 196 that:

- Summarises the variances for material, labour and overheads and notes any significant sub-variance in excess of £4,000.

- Highlights the causes of all material and labour variances from information given.

- Derives the under/over-absorption of overheads from the variances calculated and explains how the under/over-absorption has come about.

VARIANCE SCHEDULE

Blowing dept			January 1998
		£	£
Material variance			
Material usage			4,236 (A)
Material price			1,125 (F)
Total			**3,111 (A)**
Labour variance			
Labour efficiency			1,750 (F)
Labour wage-rate			5,865 (A)
Total			**4,115 (A)**
Fixed overhead variance			
Expenditure			✓ 16 520 A
	Capacity	10050 A	10050 A
	Efficiency	5360 F	5360 F
Volume			4690 A
Total			

REPORT

Summary:

Whilst the price has decrease on Material, there has been an increase in usage. this may be due to quality problem causing more wastage.

The increase in wages has caused the rate to be 5865 A, but there was some efficiency savings but these didn't equal the overspend due to the wages increase.

Fixed overheads these were all adverse, the saving on labour efficiency reduced the hours working - therefore the absorbed calculation was lower. Also Overheads were higher then budget - these are normally uncontrollable.

Unit 5
Answer Bank

SECTION 1

RFB plc

Task 1

	Total £	Prime cost £	Production expense £	Admin. expense £	Selling and distribution expense £
Wages of assembly employees	6,750	6,750			
Wages of stores employees	3,250		3,250		
Tyres for toy wheels	1,420	1,420			
Safety goggles for operators	810		810		
Job advert for new employees	84			84	
Depreciation of salesmen's cars	125				125
Depreciation of production machines	264		264		
Cost of trade exhibition	1,200				1,200
Computer stationery	130			130	
Course fee for AAT training	295			295	
Royalty for the design of wheel 1477	240	240			
	14,568	8,410	4,324	509	1,325

Task 2

(a) (i) and (ii)

Invoice number 3275	Your order number 57623
Date 1.11.94	
	£
50 coils @ £132	6,600
Standard cost of actual quantity (50 × £120)	6,000
Material price variance	600 (A)

Invoice number 4517	Your order number 58127
Date 17.11.94	
	£
150 coils @ £108	16,200
Standard cost of actual quantity (150 × £120)	18,000
Material price variance	1,800 (F)

Invoice number 5178	Your order number 60173
Date 17.11.94	
	£
100 coils @ £120	12,000
Standard cost of actual quantity (100 × £120)	12,000
Material price variance	- (-)

VARIANCE ACCOUNT

(b)

1.11.94	Purchase	600	00	17.11.94	Purchase	1,800	00

(c) The adverse variance may have been due to careless purchasing by the purchasing department or an unexpected price increase or the loss of a quantity discount because a smaller quantity than standard was purchased. The favourable variance may be due to greater care taken in purchasing by the purchasing department, an unexpected price decrease or an increased quantity discount because a larger quantity than standard was purchased. (The fact that there is no variance when 100 coils are purchased and that there is an adverse variance when less are purchased and a favourable variance when more are purchased implies that the standard purchase quantity is 100 coils and that the variances are the result of changes to quantity discounts.)

To avoid adverse variances, the purchasing manager should ensure that the cheapest price for material is obtained (although quality of material should not be jeopardised). Material should, if at all possible, be purchased in quantities that ensure the standard discount is received, although care must be taken to ensure that the costs of holding stock are not greater than any quantity discounts received. The responsibility for this lies with the purchasing manger and the stores manager.

Task 3

(a)

	Bending	Cutting	Assembly
Budgeted overheads	£120,000	£90,000	£60,000
Budgeted activity level	10,000 machine hours	3,000 machine hours	15,000 labour hours
Standard overhead absorption rate	£12 per machine hour	£30 per machine hour	£4 per labour hour

(b)

STANDARD COST CARD			
Toy car wheels Part number 5917B			Date: X. X. XX
Standard quantity 100 wheels			
	Performance standard	Standard rate/price	Standard cost £
Direct materials			
Tyres	100	10p each	10.00
Steel strip	50	£10.40 per 100	5.20
Wire	1000	2p each	20.00
			35.20
Direct labour	hours	£	
Bending	0.8	4.00	3.20
Cutting	0.5	6.00	3.00
Assembly	1.2	5.00	6.00
			12.20
Overheads			
Bending	0.4	12.00	4.80
Cutting	0.5	30.00	15.00
Assembly	1.2	4.00	4.80
			24.60
TOTAL COST			72.00

Task 4

REFINING COST STATEMENT		
		November 1994
	Quantity (Kilos)	*Cost* (£)
Input material (chemical)	60	12,000
Labour		2,000
Overheads		8,000
	60	22,000
Output (refined product)	55	*21,228
Normal loss (60 × 0.05)	3	-
Abnormal loss	2	** 772
	60	22,000

Cost per unit $= \dfrac{22,000}{(60-3)} = £385.96$

* 55 × £385.96

** 2 × £385.96

AMP plc

Task 1

Stores Record Card									
Material: Paper								*Code:* 1564A	
		Receipts		Issues			Stock		
Date	Details	Sheets	£	Sheets	Price	£	Sheets	Price	£
	Opening stock						10,000	0.30	3,000
3 May	Purchase	4,000	1,600				14,000	0.33	4,600
6 May	Issue			7,000	0.33	2,310	7,000	0.33	2,290
12 May	Purchase	10,000	3,100				17,000	0.32	5,390
15 May	Issue			6,000	0.32	1,920	11,000	0.32	3,470
22 May	Issue			7,200	0.32	2,304	3,800	0.32	1,166
25 May	Purchase	10,000	3,200				13,800	0.32	4,366

Task 2

(a)

		Singh £	*Smith* £
Basic pay	(38 hrs × £4.50)	171.00	
	(38 hrs × £4.00)		152.00
Overtime pay	(1½ × 1⅓ × £4.50)	9.00	
	((1 × 1⅓ × £4.00) + (2 × 1½ × £4.00))		17.33
Production bonus	(£0.10 × (10,500/100))	10.50	
	(£0.10 × (10,900/100))		10.90
Gross wages		190.50	180.23

(b) Gross wages of Singh = £190.50

Piecework rate is per 100 sheets and 10,500 sheets produced.
∴ Piecework rate would be paid 105 (10,500/100) times.

£190.50/105 = £1.81

Piecework rate = £1.81 per 100 sheets

Task 3

Departmental Operating Account					

Month: May 1994 **Budget hours**: 320 **Department**: Binding
Date prepared: 10.6.94 **Actual hours**: 290 **Manager**: Mrs Jones

Actual Costs	£	Standard Costs			*Total Variance* £
		Output (Manuals)	*Unit Cost* £	*Total Cost* £	
Direct materials	1,200	1,200	0.90	1,080	120 (A)
Direct labour:					
290 hours	1,300	1,200	1.00	1,200	100 (A)
Variable overheads	580	1,200	0.50	600	20 (F)
Fixed overheads	1,920	1,200	1.50	1,800	120 (A)
Total	5,000			4,680	320 (A)

Task 4

(a)

	£
290 hours should have cost (× £4)	1,160
but did cost	1,300
Direct labour rate variance	140 (A)
1,200 manuals should have taken (× ¼ hr)	300 hrs
but did take	290 hrs
Direct labour efficiency variance (in hours)	10 hrs (F)
× standard rate per hour	× £4
	£40 (F)

Total variance = £140(A) + £40(F) = £100(A)

(b) The rate variance arose because labour were paid more than the standard £4.00 per hour perhaps because of a wage rate increase following strike action.

The efficiency variance arose because labour worked more efficiently than the rate specified in the standard and hence output was produced more quickly than expected, perhaps because better quality equipment or materials were used than those set in the standard.

If the wage rate has increased and the increase is permanent then the standard needs to be changed to reflect this since variances will always be adverse if it is not.

A favourable variance should be encouraged and the labour force should continue to use higher quality materials and/or equipment unless their use causes, for example, larger adverse material price variances.

(c) The change of the standard would be the responsibility of the accountant and/or his assistant although wage rates are the responsibility of the personnel department which should feed information about wage rates changes through to the appropriate members of staff.

Pears plc

Task 1

OVERHEAD ANALYSIS SHEET   DATE   17.4.X3

	TOTAL	PRODUCTION			SERVICE	
		Cutting	Sewing	Finishing	Stores	Maintenance
	£	£	£	£	£	£
Overheads	603,000	187,000	232,000	106,000	28,000	50,000
(a) Apportion Stores (W1) (Base: Material issued)	-	9,333	11,667	4,667	(28,000)	2,333
(b) Apportion Maintenance (W2) (Base: Machine hours)	-	19,625	32,708	-	-	(52,333)
	603,000	215,958	276,375	110,667		

Workings

1   Total material issued = £'000 (200 + 250 + 100 + 50)
            = £600,000

Issued to		*% of total*	*Share of overhead* £
Cutting	200/600	33¹/₃	9,333
Sewing	250/600	41²/₃	11,667
Finishing	100/600	16²/₃	4,667
Maintenance	50/600	8¹/₃	2,333
		100	28,000

2   Total machine hours = 15,000 + 25,000 = 40,000.

Worked in		*% of total*	*Share of overhead* £
Cutting	15,000/40,000	37¹/₂	19,625
Sewing	25,000/40,000	62¹/₂	32,708
			52,333

Task 2

(a)

Department	Basis of absorption	Hours	Overhead £	Overhead absorption rate
Cutting	Machine hours	15,000	215,958	£14.40 per mach hr
Sewing	Machine hours	25,000	276,375	£11.06 per mach hr
Finishing	Labour hours	12,000	110,667	£9.22 per labour hr
			603,000	

(b) Machine hour rates should be used in the cutting and sewing departments because activity levels and output depend on the number of machine hours worked in the department. Absorption rates should therefore be based on machine hours.

Task 3

<table>
<tr><td colspan="6">STANDARD PRODUCT COST SHEET
PRODUCT : 'XL'

Date: 17.4.X3</td></tr>
<tr><td></td><td></td><td></td><td></td><td>£</td><td>£</td></tr>
<tr><td>Direct Material Cost</td><td></td><td></td><td></td><td></td><td>4.32</td></tr>
<tr><td></td><td colspan="2">Hours</td><td>Rate
£</td><td>1.00</td><td></td></tr>
<tr><td>Direct Labour Cost</td><td colspan="2"></td><td></td><td>3.00</td><td></td></tr>
<tr><td>- cutting</td><td colspan="2">¼</td><td>4.00</td><td>2.50</td><td></td></tr>
<tr><td>- sewing</td><td colspan="2">1</td><td>3.00</td><td></td><td></td></tr>
<tr><td>- finishing</td><td colspan="2">½</td><td>5.00</td><td></td><td></td></tr>
<tr><td>Total Labour Cost</td><td></td><td></td><td></td><td></td><td>6.50</td></tr>
<tr><td></td><td colspan="2">Hours</td><td>Rate
£</td><td>3.60</td><td></td></tr>
<tr><td>Overhead Cost</td><td colspan="2"></td><td></td><td>11.06</td><td></td></tr>
<tr><td>- cutting</td><td colspan="2">¼</td><td>14.40</td><td>4.61</td><td></td></tr>
<tr><td>- sewing</td><td colspan="2">1</td><td>11.06</td><td></td><td></td></tr>
<tr><td>- finishing</td><td colspan="2">½</td><td>9.22</td><td></td><td></td></tr>
<tr><td>Total Overhead Cost</td><td></td><td></td><td></td><td></td><td>19.27</td></tr>
<tr><td>TOTAL COST</td><td></td><td></td><td></td><td></td><td>30.09</td></tr>
</table>

Task 4

(a) (i) *Material price variance*

	£
50 metres should have cost (× £3.00)	150
but did cost (× £2.00)	100
Material price variance	50 (F)

(ii) *Material usage variance*

20 garments should have used (× 2m)	40 m
but did use	50 m
Material usage variance (in metres)	10 m (A)
× standard cost per metre	× £3
Material usage variance (in £)	£30 (A)

(iii) *Total material cost variance*

	£
20 garments should have cost (× £3.00 × 2m)	120
but did cost	100
Total material cost variance	20 (F)

(b) Price variance - purchasing manager
Usage variance - production manager

(c) Providing the quality of the product was unaffected, the material should have been bought because the overall cost variance was favourable. The adverse variance arising from the use of substandard material was more than compensated for by the favourable price variance arising from the use of cheaper material.

McHugh Ltd

Task 1

To complete Task 1 you have to allocate to the five departments those overheads which are directly associated with the departments.

	Forming £	Colouring £	Assembly £	Maintenance £	General £	Total £
Directly allocated overheads:						
Repairs, maintenance	800	1,800	300	200	100	3,200
Departmental expenses	1,500	2,300	1,100	900	1,500	7,300
Indirect labour	3,000	5,000	1,500	4,000	2,000	15,500
	5,300	9,100	2,900	5,100	3,600	26,000

Task 2

This task involves apportioning the remaining overheads (those which have not been directly allocated) to the five departments.

		Forming £	Colouring £	Assembly £	Maintenance £	General £	Total £
Directly allocated overheads:							
Repairs, maintenance		800	1,800	300	200	100	3,200
Departmental expenses		1,500	2,300	1,100	900	1,500	7,300
Indirect labour		3,000	5,000	1,500	4,000	2,000	15,500
		5,300	9,100	2,900	5,100	3,600	26,000
Apportionment of other overheads:							
Rent, rates	1	1,600	3,200	2,400	400	400	8,000
Power	2	200	450	75	25	0	750
Light, heat	1	1,000	2,000	1,500	250	250	5,000
Dep'n of plant	3	2,500	6,000	750	750	0	10,000
Dep'n of F & F	4	50	25	100	50	25	250
Insurance of plant	3	500	1,200	150	150	0	2,000
Insurance of buildings	1	100	200	150	25	25	500
		11,250	22,175	8,025	6,750	4,300	52,500

Basis of apportionment:

1   floor area
2   effective horsepower
3   plant value
4   fixtures and fittings

Task 3

To complete this task you had to use the information provided on the number of hours work the two service departments are budgeted to do for the other departments (and each other).

	Forming £	Colouring £	Assembly £	Maintenance £	General £	Total £
Allocated and apportioned o'hds	11,250	22,175	8,025	6,750	4,300	52,500
	1,350	3,375	1,350	(6,750)	675	
					4,975	
	995	2,985	498	497	(4,975)	
	99	249	99	(497)	50	
	10	30	5	5	(50)	
	1	3	1	(5)		
	13,705	28,817	9,978			52,500

Task 4

The forming and assembly departments are labour intensive. The overhead absorption rate for these two departments should therefore be based on labour hours. The colouring department, on the other hand, is machine intensive. Machine hours should therefore be used as the basis of the overhead absorption rate.

Department			OAR
Forming	$\dfrac{£13,705}{27,400}$	=	£0.50 per labour hour
Colouring	$\dfrac{£28,817}{14,400}$	=	£2.00 per machine hour
Assembly	$\dfrac{£9,978}{20,000}$	=	£0.50 per labour hour

Task 5

The under-/over-absorbed overhead is calculated as the difference between the overhead actually incurred and the overhead absorbed. The overhead absorbed is the OAR × actual number of the basis of the absorption rate.

	Overhead incurred £		Overhead absorbed £	(Under)-/over-absorbed overhead £
Forming	14,580	(30,000 × £0.50)	15,000	420
Colouring	30,050	(16,000 × £2.00)	32,000	1,950
Assembly	9,840	(18,500 × £0.50)	9,250	(590)
Over-absorbed overhead				1,780

Task 6

MEMORANDUM

To: Jenny Chang, Production Manager
From: Cost accountant
Date: January 19X4
Subject: Costing methods

Following our telephone conversation earlier today, I set out below the reasons why job costing is not an appropriate costing method for McHugh Ltd, and the reasons why process costing is more suitable.

(a) Job costing is used when production is carried out in accordance with a customer's special requirements. At McHugh Ltd, however, we decide in advance how many units of N–17T to produce regardless of the identity of the customer who will eventually buy the product.

(b) As job costing is used when production is carried out to customers' specific requirements, it is usual for each job to differ in one or more respects from every other job. We produce one product, N–17T, each unit of N–17T being identical to all of the others.

(c) If job costing applies, each job is separately identifiable during its manufacture. It is, however, impossible to distinguish one N–17T from another.

(d) When job costing is used, each job differs in one or more respects from every other job and so separate records are maintained to show the details of each particular job. In our organisation we maintain records, not for particular units of output, but for the three processes (forming, colouring and assembly).

We calculate the cost to be attributed to a unit of N–17T for each process as the total of the costs incurred in that process divided by the number of units processed in that process.

(e) Other features of our production which mean that job costing is not appropriate are as follows.

(i)   There is often a loss in process due to spoilage, wastage, evaporation and so on.

(ii) The continuous nature of the production process means that there is closing work in process at the end of our accounting period which has to be valued.

I hope this memorandum proves useful but if you have any further questions please do not hesitate to contact me.

Task 7

KJ53 will either be a joint product or a by-product depending on its sales value. If it has a relatively low sales value in comparison with N–17T it will be classed as a by-product but if its sales value is substantial (either at its point of separation from N–17T or after further processing) then it is a joint product.

Task 8

Since the sales value of the KJ53 is not insignificant when compared to that of the N–17T, they are joint products.

With the information provided, we can split the common processing costs on the basis of physical measurement or on the basis of sales value less post-separation costs. Note that we are given no information about weightings so we cannot use the weighted units method to split the costs. Neither do we know the sales value (if there is one) of N–17T at the end of the forming process, and so we cannot use the sales value at split-off point method.

Physical measurement

	KJ53		N–17T
$\dfrac{10,000}{40,000} \times £3,725,000 =$	£931,250	$\dfrac{30,000}{40,000} \times £3,725,000 =$	£2,793,750

Sales value less post-separation costs

	KJ53		N–17T
	£		£
Sales value (£100 × 10,000)	1,000,000	(£120 × 30,000)	3,600,000
Post-separation costs	-		1,750,000
	1,000,000		1,850,000
Split costs (1,000:1,850)	1,307,018		2,417,982

Jasperino Ltd

Task 1

STORES LEDGER CONTROL ACCOUNT

	£		£
Balance b/f	8,000	Work in progress a/c	34,000
Cash/creditors	75,000	Production overhead a/c	4,000
		Balance c/f	45,000
	83,000		83,000

Task 2

WORK IN PROGRESS CONTROL ACCOUNT

	£		£
Balance b/f	15,000	Finished goods control a/c	
Stores ledger control a/c	34,000	(balancing figure)	77,500
Wages control account(18,000 – 2,500)	15,500		
Production overhead account			
(200% of £15,500)	31,000	Balance c/f	18,000
	95,500		95,500

Task 3

To calculate the under- or over-absorbed overhead we need to prepare a production overhead control account.

PRODUCTION OVERHEAD CONTROL ACCOUNT

	£		£
Prepayments b/f	1,000	Work in progress control a/c	31,000
Stores ledger control a/c	4,000	Under-absorbed overhead a/c	
Wages control a/c		(balancing figure)	3,500
Direct workers	2,500		
Indirect workers	11,000		
Cash/creditors	16,000		
	34,500		34,500

The under-absorbed overhead is £3,500.

Task 4

FINISHED GOODS CONTROL ACCOUNT

	£		£
Balance b/f	22,000	Cost of goods sold a/c	65,000
Work in progress control a/c	77,500	Scrap - P&L a/c	2,000
		Balance c/f	32,500
	99,500		99,500

Task 5

PROFIT AND LOSS ACCOUNT

	£		£
Cost of goods sold a/c	65,000	Sales	110,000
Selling and dist'n o'hd	12,000		
Finished goods a/c - scrap	2,000		
Under-absorbed o'hd a/c	3,500		
Profit c/f	27,500		
	110,000		110,000

Task 6

	Straight-line		Reducing balance
	£		£
Cost	17,580		17,580
Depreciation (year 1) (£17,580 ÷ 5)	(3,516)	(£17,580 × 25%)	(4,395)
	14,064		13,185
Depreciation (year 2)	(3,516)	(£13,185 × 25%)	(3,296)
	10,548		9,889
Depreciation (year 3)	(3,516)	(£9,889 × 25%)	(2,472)
	7,032		7,417
Depreciation (year 4)	(3,516)	(£7,417 × 25%)	(1,854)
	3,516		5,563
Depreciation (year 5)	(3,516)	(£5,563 × 25%)	1,391
	-		4,172

Task 7

JOB 212/A

	£		£
Balance b/f	11,022	Materials transfer	3,500
Materials	3,122	Cost of sales	16,410
Labour	1,922		
Production overhead			
(200% of direct wages)	3,844		
	19,910		19,910

JOB 219/C

	£		£
Materials	4,003	Cost of sales	29,268
Materials transfer	3,500		
Labour	7,255		
Production overhead			
(200% of direct wages)	14,510		
	29,268		29,268

Task 8

	212/A	219/C
	£	£
Factory cost	16,410	29,268
Administration and marketing overheads	2,462	4,390
Cost of sale	18,872	33,658
Invoice value	20,500	28,750
Profit/(loss)	1,628	(4,908)

SECTION 2

Group A

1   £72.00 = 90%

∴ 100% = £72/90% × 100% = £80

∴ Selling price per 100 wheels = £80

2   The steps in determining the standard labour hours for producing 100 wheels are as follows.

(a)   Study the operations involved in the task.

(b)   Establish the most efficient methods of performing the operations.

(c)   Ascertain the grades of labour and types of machine required to perform the operations.

(d)   Determine the time for each individual operation, building in allowances for rest, relaxation, calls of nature, fluctuating performance, machine breakdowns and so on.

3   The costs of the stores department could be apportioned to other cost centres using one of the following bases.

(a)   Number of material requisitions per cost centre
(b)   Value of requisitions per cost centre

The costs of the personnel department could be apportioned to other cost centres using the number of employees per cost centre.

4   The value of the abnormal loss should be credited to the refining cost centre and debited to the cost profit and loss account.

5   Closing stock   = 150 pairs × (100 + 200 – 150) × £1.90 (purchase price on 7.11.94)
                       = £285

6   *Minutes*
   A   200 × 4 =   800
   B   350 × 2 =   700
   C   300 × 3 =   900
                    ‾2,400‾

Standard hours produced = 2,400 ÷ 60 = 40 standard hours.

7   The reorder level is influenced by rate of usage and lead time (delivery time).

8   Significant overhead costs incurred by an international firm of management consultants could include the following.

(a)   Rent
(b)   Travelling expenses
(c)   Support staff (secretaries and so on)
(d)   Publicity/advertising
(e)   Entertaining
(f)   Depreciation of computers, wordprocessors and so on

9   (a)   Possible cost units would include a kilogram of crops (such as wheat or barley or oats) or an individual cow/calf/bull.

(b)   Possible cost centres include an area (such as a field or an acre), a herd of cattle, the dairy, ploughing activities and harvesting activities.

10   (a)   If overheads are over absorbed, the amount over absorbed should be debited to the cost centre overhead account and credited to the cost profit and loss account

(b)   Over-absorbed overhead increases cost profit for a period.

11   Piecework is an incentive scheme in that the more output you produce the more you are paid. Differential piecework pays a different rate for different levels of production, for example as follows.

Up to 100 units a day   20p per unit
101 to 150 units a day   22p per unit
151 to 200 units a day   25p per unit
Over 200 units a day   30p per unit

12   It is true that a standard cost is a 'guess' although it may be a very accurate one determined in a highly scientific manner. It is *not* true that standard costs are not relevant once actual costs are known. Standard costs are used not only for planning in advance, but also for measuring actual performance and deciding whether changes need to be made.

Group B

1   Holding large quantities of paper in stock could cause the following problems.

(a)   Larger stocks require more storage space and possibly extra staff and equipment to control and handle them.

(b)   When material becomes out-of-date and is no longer required, existing stocks must be thrown away and written off to the profit and loss account.

2   Overtime premium is analysed as departmental overheads except in the following circumstances.

(a)   If overtime is worked at the specific request of a customer to get his order completed, the overtime premium is a direct cost of the order.

(b)   If overtime is worked regularly by a production department in the normal course of operations, the overtime paid to direct workers could be incorporated into an average direct labour hourly rate (though it does not need to be).

3   One overhead variance which one would expect to find in the binding department is a fixed overhead expenditure variance. This would be adverse since the budgeted fixed overhead (1,200 × £1.50 = £1,800) is less than the actual overhead (£1,920).

4   The company should use current/expected standards rather than ideal standards since ideal standards are based on the most favourable operating conditions (no wastage, idle time, breakdowns and so on) and are therefore likely to have an unfavourable motivational impact. Employees will often feel that the goals are unattainable and not work so hard.

5   We need to calculate an overhead absorption rate.

$$\text{Absorption rate} = \frac{\text{budgeted overheads}}{\text{budgeted activity level}} = \frac{£5,995}{550 \text{ hrs}}$$

= £10.90 per machine hour

	£
Actual overheads	6,500
Absorbed overheads (540 hrs × £10.90)	5,886
Under-absorbed overheads	614

Under-absorbed overheads reduce the profit for the period.

6   (a)   With activity based costing, cost drivers are a means of establishing the overhead cost of activities.

(b)   A suitable cost driver for the purchasing department of a large manufacturing company would be the number of orders handled in the period.

7   (a)   The joint products of the process are products B and D. Products A and C are by-products since their sales values per kg are relatively low in comparison with those of B and D.

(b)   There are four ways of treating the sales values of products A and C (by-products) in the cost accounts.

(i)   Income (minus any post-separation further processing or selling costs) from the sales of the by-products may be added to sales of the main product, thereby increasing sales turnover for the period.

(ii)   The sales of the by-product may be treated as a separate, incidental source of income against which are set only post-separation costs (if any) of the by-products. The revenue would be recorded in the profit and loss account as 'other income'.

(iii) The sales income of the by-products may be deducted from the cost of production or cost of sales of the main product.

(iv) The net realisable value of the by-products may be deducted from the cost of production of the main products. Any closing stock valuation of the main product or joint products would therefore be reduced.

8 One would expect (a) a paint manufacturer and (d) the chemical industry to use process costing.

9 (a) Depreciable amount = £(3,000 – 200) = £2,800.
      Expected life = 4 years.
      Annual depreciation charge = £2,800/4 = £700.

   (b)

	£
Depreciation charged = 3 × £700	2,100
Amount which should have been charged	3,000
Obsolescence charge	900

   It is normal practice to charge a loss resulting from obsolescence to the costing profit and loss account.

10 | *Cost pool* | *Cost driver* |
    |---|---|
    | Production scheduling costs | Number of production runs |
    | Despatch costs | Number of orders delivered |

11 It is usually regarded as better to calculate the materials price variance at the time of receipt of stock, so that it can be eliminated and stocks can be valued at standard. The advantage is that this reduces clerical work in issuing stocks. All issues are valued at standard, and it is not necessary to calculate a variance as each issue is made.

12 Batch costing is a form of costing that is similar to job costing, except that costs are collected for a batch of items. The cost unit is the batch. A cost per unit is calculated by dividing the total batch cost by the number of units in the batch.

Group C

1 Minimum stock levels are established for each type of material in a stock control system to allow for unexpected rises or falls in demand and for severe shortages of supply.

2 (a) A stores requisition is used to request and authorise an issue of stock from stores to production.

   (b) A purchase requisition is used to instruct and authorise the purchasing department to obtain supplies.

3 In a period of rising prices the LIFO method (c) of pricing issues would place the lowest value on closing stocks, because we assume that the newest stock is used first and the residue is the oldest (and hence cheapest) stock.

4 Two advantages of paying employees by the results achieved are as follows.

   (a) Output should be higher.
   (b) Employees can receive higher wages.

5 The majority of employees are paid on the basis of time rather than by results achieved since it can be difficult to measure work done and because quality can suffer if employees try to rush production.

6 *Tutorial note.* Either method of allocating joint costs would be acceptable as an answer to this question.

   By output

	Total	A	B	C
	£	£	£	£
Sales	16,000	4,000	6,000	6,000
Joint cost (see below)	14,400	1,600	3,200	9,600
	1,600	2,400	2,800	(3,600)

	Output Kgs	Share of cost	Apportioned joint cost £
A	1,000	1/9	1,600
B	2,000	2/9	3,200
C	6,000	6/9	9,600
	9,000	1	14,400

By sales value

	Total £	A £	B £	C £
Sales	16,000	4,000	6,000	6,000
Joint cost (see below)	14,400	3,600	5,400	5,400
	1,600	400	600	600

	Sales value £	Share of of cost	Apportioned joint cost £
A	4,000	4/16	3,600
B	6,000	6/16	5,400
C	6,000	6/16	5,400
	16,000	1	14,400

7

	Kgs	
Input	100	
Output	89	
Normal loss (10% of input)	10	$(100 \times 10\%)$
Abnormal loss	1	$(100 - 89 - 10)$
Total	100	

8 Strictly speaking this is false. Indirect materials costs are called indirect materials costs! Indirect expenses are indirect costs other than materials or labour. In practice, however, terms like 'cost', 'expense' and 'overhead' are used very loosely.

9 The workforce of Casios Ltd have been working at a less efficient rate than standard to produce a given output. The result is an *adverse* fixed overhead *usage variance*.

The total number of hours worked was, however, more than originally budgeted. The effect is measured by a *favourable* fixed overhead *capacity* variance.

10 Economic order quantity (EOQ) $= \sqrt{\dfrac{2cd}{h}}$, where

c = cost of ordering $= £18$

d = annual demand $= 200,000$

h = cost of carrying one unit in stock for one year $= £3.20$

$\therefore \text{EOQ} = \sqrt{\dfrac{2 \times 18 \times 200,000}{3.20}} = 1,500 \text{ units}$

11 False.

	£
Overheads incurred	9,322
Overheads absorbed ($£5 \times 1,753$)	8,765
Under-absorbed overhead	557

12 B

Group D

1 By charging as many costs as possible to cost units rather than treating them as overheads, arbitrary overhead apportionment, resulting in a less accurate cost per unit, is avoided.

2   (a)   Changing from FIFO to LIFO during a period of rapidly rising prices would result in lower stock valuations.

    (b)   Changing from FIFO to LIFO during a period of rapidly rising prices would result in higher costs of materials charged to production.

3   Additional payments to production workers for weekend working would be treated as a production overhead and not a direct cost since it would be unfair if an item made during overtime hours was more costly just because, by chance, it was made during hours in which employees do not normally work.

4   (a)   A building contractor should treat each contract as a cost unit.

    (b)   An airline should treat each passenger mile (or 100 or 1,000 passenger miles) as a cost unit.

5   (a)   The variance account affected would be the overhead capacity variance account.

    (b)   Unit costs of production would increase because costs would have to be spread over a smaller number of units and therefore each unit would have to bear a larger share of the production overhead.

6   When deciding the optimum level of stock of component parts to be held in a store serving a mass production assembly line, the following factors should be considered.

    (a)   The economic order quantity
    (b)   Deterioration/obsolescence
    (c)   Space taken up by stores
    (d)   Cost of capital tied up in stocks
    (e)   Continuity of supplies

7   (a)   Canteen costs: number of employees per production cost centre or labour hours worked in each production cost centre

    (b)   Heating and lighting: floor area per production cost centre or volume of space occupied by each cost centre

    (c)   Building maintenance: valuation of production cost centre building or number of hours spent on maintenance jobs undertaken or actual cost of work undertaken

8   The overhead absorption rate is calculated by dividing the budgeted/estimated overheads which have been apportioned to the particular production cost centre by the budgeted/estimated number of hours machines in that production cost centre will be running. Each unit of output is therefore charged with overhead on the basis of the number of machine hours it requires in that cost centre. The machine hour basis should be used if production is highly mechanised such that a large proportion of overhead expenditure is likely to be more closely related to machine utilisation than to direct labour input.

9   Activity based costing, a recent development in cost accounting, attempts to absorb overheads into product costs on a more realistic basis than that used by traditional absorption costing. The basic idea is that instead of arbitrarily choosing an absorption base for all overheads, overhead costs are grouped according to what drives them or causes them to be incurred. These costs drivers are then used as an absorption basis.

    For example, costs associated with handling orders are driven by the number of orders. The cost driver for such costs is therefore the number of orders. Costs relating to production run set-ups are driven by the number of set-ups, costs associated with machine activity are driven by the number of machine hours and costs related to labour activity are driven by the number of labour hours.

10 The reorder level is the level to which stocks should be allowed to fall before an order is placed. The maximum stock level indicates the level above which it becomes wasteful to hold stocks whereas the minimum level indicates the level below which stocks should never be allowed to fall. The reordering level is fixed between the maximum and minimum levels and is usually just slightly higher than the minimum level, to cover such emergencies as abnormal usage of material or unexpected delay in delivery of fresh supplies.

11 Advantage   Variances from ideal standards are useful for pinpointing areas where a close examination may result in large savings.

Disadvantage   They are likely to have an unfavourable motivational impact. Employees will often feel that the goals are unattainable and not work so hard.

12 (a)   Process costing
    (b)   Job costing
    (c)   Batch costing
    (d)   Process costing
    (e)   Process costing
    (f)   Job costing

Group E

1   This is term used to express the way in which the cause of one variance may be wholly or partly explained by the cause of another variance. For instance, if the purchasing department buys a cheaper material which is poorer in quality than the expected standard, the material price variance will be favourable, but there may be material wastage and an adverse usage variance.

2   When using absorption costing, a time-based overhead absorption rate is generally favoured over any other because of the belief that most items of overhead expenditure tend to increase with time. A direct wages percentage rate is to an extent time based, but if differential wage rates exist, this can lead to inequitable overhead absorption. The direct labour hour rate does not suffer from this disadvantage.

Note that ABC is based on the idea that most items of overhead expenditure do not increase with time.

3   *Statement A* is correct. Job costs are identified with a particular job, whereas process costs (of units produced and work in process) are averages, based on equivalent units of production.

Statement B is also correct. The direct cost of a job to date, excluding any direct expenses, can be ascertained from materials requisition notes and job tickets or time sheets.

Statement C is correct. Without data about units completed and units still in process, losses and equivalent units of production cannot be calculated.

Statement D is incorrect, because the cost of normal loss will usually be incorporated into job costs as well as into process costs. In process costing, this is commonly done by giving normal loss no cost, leaving costs to be shared between output, closing stocks and abnormal loss/gain. In job costing, it can be done by adjusting direct materials costs to allow for normal wastage, and direct labour costs for normal reworking of items or normal spoilage.

4   The cost accounting entry is as follows.

    DR   Material price variance account
    CR   Stores ledger control account

5   An equivalent unit calculation is necessary when there are partially completed stocks at either the beginning or the end of the process in order to establish the cost of a completed unit of production.

6   Costs per equivalent unit

	£	*Equivalent units (W)*	£
Materials	5,520	3,680	1.50
Labour	1,840	3,680	0.50
	7,360		

Closing WIP		£
Materials (480 (W) × £1.50)		720
Labour (480 (W) × £0.50)		240
		960

Working

Units completed	3,200
Total units	4,000
WIP	800

WIP is 60% complete, so total equivalent units come to 3,200 + (800 × 60%) = 3,680, and equivalent units for closing WIP is 800 × 60% = 480.

7   Usage and efficiency variances are quantity variances. They measure the difference between the actual physical quantity of materials used or hours taken and the quantities that should have been used or taken for the actual volume of production. The physical differences are then converted into money values by applying the appropriate standard cost.

8   The company spent £500 more on fixed production overheads than budgeted, which is probably not very significant. Units were produced in an average of 2.25 hours each which is a good deal faster than standard. The company also managed to operate for 100 hours longer than expected, and produced 100 extra units. Apart from the slight overspending and assuming the extra units can be sold, all of this is good.

If you calculated the variances you should have got the following figures.

	£
Price	500 (A)
Efficiency	1,200 (F)
Capacity	800 (F)
Total	1,500 (F)

9   (a)   Cost centres: a ward, an operating theatre, a doctor, a sister, a bed
    (b)   Cost units: a patient/day, an operation, an outpatient visit

10   The maximum stock level depends on the reorder level, the reorder quantity, the rate of usage and the delivery time.

11   The main advantages are:

    (a)   the system is unambiguous;

    (b)   the system saves time. Descriptions can be time-consuming;

    (c)   the chances of issuing the wrong stock are reduced;

    (d)   computer processing is made easier;

    (e)   the system is designed to be flexible, and can be expanded to include more stock items as necessary.

12   (a)   The purchasing manager
     (b)   The production manager

PRACTICE CENTRAL ASSESSMENT 1: DOWRA LTD

SECTION 1

Task 1

DOWRA LTD					
Overhead analysis sheet					
Department	Cutting £	Assembly £	Finishing £	Design £	Stores £
Allocated overheads	138,250	141,080	170,140	194,150	22,000
Factory overheads (W1)	35,420	60,260	49,680	22,080	16,500
Stores (W2)	14,679	16,427	6,757	697	(38,560)
Design	72,309	72,309	72,309	(216,927)	-
Total	260,658	290,076	298,886	-	-
Machine hours	180,000	85,000	240,000		
Absorption rate per machine hour	£1.45	£3.41	£1.25		

Workings

1   Overhead per square metre

$$= \frac{£184,000}{(770 + 1,310 + 1,080 + 480 + 360)}$$

$$= \frac{£184,000}{4,000} = £46$$

2   Overhead per £ of requisition

$$= \frac{£38,560}{(97,760 + 109,400 + 45,000 + 4,640)}$$

$$= \frac{£38,560}{256,800} = £0.1501557$$

Task 2

<table>
<tr><td colspan="4" align="center">Standard Cost Card
Wooden Duck on Wheels</td></tr>
<tr><td>*Materials*</td><td align="center">*Quantity*</td><td align="center">*Price*
£</td><td align="center">*Value*
£</td></tr>
<tr><td>5 mm board</td><td align="center">0.2 sq m</td><td align="center">4.60 per m^2</td><td align="center">0.92000</td></tr>
<tr><td>4 cm diameter wheels</td><td align="center">4</td><td align="center">18.20 per 100</td><td align="center">0.72800</td></tr>
<tr><td>Box</td><td align="center">1</td><td align="center">16.00 per 100</td><td align="center">0.16000</td></tr>
<tr><td>**Subtotal:**</td><td></td><td></td><td align="center">**1.80800**</td></tr>
<tr><td>*Labour*</td><td align="center">*Time*</td><td align="center">*Rate*
£</td><td align="center">*Value*
£</td></tr>
<tr><td>Cutter</td><td align="center">1.5 mins</td><td align="center">7.50 per hr</td><td align="center">0.18750</td></tr>
<tr><td>Assembler</td><td align="center">3 mins</td><td align="center">6.80 per hr</td><td align="center">0.34000</td></tr>
<tr><td>Painter</td><td align="center">4 mins</td><td align="center">8.20 per hr</td><td align="center">0.54667</td></tr>
<tr><td>Packer</td><td align="center">30 secs</td><td align="center">5.00 per hr</td><td align="center">0.04167</td></tr>
<tr><td>**Sub total:**</td><td></td><td></td><td align="center">**1.11584**</td></tr>
<tr><td>*Production overheads*</td><td align="center">*Time*</td><td align="center">*Rate*
£</td><td align="center">*Value*
£</td></tr>
<tr><td>Cutting</td><td align="center">1.5 mins</td><td align="center">1.45 per hr</td><td align="center">0.03625</td></tr>
<tr><td>Assembly</td><td align="center">3 mins</td><td align="center">3.41 per hr</td><td align="center">0.17050</td></tr>
<tr><td>Finishing</td><td align="center">4.5 mins</td><td align="center">1.25 per hr</td><td align="center">0.09375</td></tr>
<tr><td>**Subtotal:**</td><td></td><td></td><td align="center">**0.30050**</td></tr>
<tr><td>**GRAND TOTAL**</td><td></td><td></td><td align="center">**3.22434**</td></tr>
</table>

Task 3

MEMORANDUM

TO: Sales manager/production manager
FROM: A Technician
DATE: X.X.XX
SUBJECT: Overhead apportionment

As a result of falling demand for many of our popular products I have reviewed the method used by Dowra Ltd to apportion production overheads (unallocated factory costs, stores overheads and design overheads) to different products. The results of my investigation and my conclusions are set out in the following paragraphs.

(a) *Unallocated factory overheads*

At present unallocated factory overheads are apportioned to the five cost centres on the basis of floor area. Unless the size of *all* the overheads which have been allocated to the overall factory cost centre can be related in some way to floor area, such a method of apportionment will not be fair. The costs of heating and lighting could be apportioned on the basis of floor area because the greater the floor area of a cost centre, the greater (in general) will be the consumption of heating and lighting within that cost centre. Other costs (such as canteen costs) could perhaps be apportioned on a more suitable basis, such as number of employees per cost centre.

Instead of grouping all unallocated factory overheads together they should be analysed in more detail and individual overheads apportioned to the cost centres using bases appropriate to the overhead in question.

(b) *Stores overheads*

Stores overheads are currently apportioned to the other four cost centres according to the *value* of materials requisitions. Apportionment on the basis of the *number* of materials requisition may be more appropriate. Using value, the assembly cost centres bears the largest share of the overhead. Using the number of requisitions, on the other hand, it would bear the second smallest share. The choice of method will depend on whether, in general, the value of requisitions varies because of the value of individual items requisitioned or because requisitions with a higher value are made up of more items. It is only fair to charge the stores overhead to the cost centres on the basis of the amount of work the stores cost centre does for each department. A requisition involving a great many items will involve more work than a requisition made up of just one expensive item.

(c) *Design overheads*

Using the present system, design overheads are apportioned in equal proportions to the three production departments and then applied to products using machine hours as a basis, a totally inaccurate representation of the usage of design costs by products. At present the costs are applied to products whenever one unit is produced whereas in reality the costs are incurred, just once, when the product is designed. Absorption costing is therefore unsuitable and consideration should be given to the use of activity based costing, which is particularly appropriate for support overheads.

Conclusion

The introduction of activity based costing may well improve the fairness of the apportionment of all production overheads. This should produce more accurate product costs which will, in turn, enable sensible pricing decisions to be made.

Task 4

(a) (i)

	£
25 sq m should have cost (× £4.50)	112.50
but did cost	110.00
Materials price variance	2.50 (F)

120 ducks should have used (× 0.2 sq m)	24 sq m
but did use	25 sq m
Materials usage variance in sq m	1 sq m (A)
× standard cost per sq m	× £4.50
Materials usage variance in £	£4.50 (A)

(ii)

	£
2.75 hours should have cost (× £7.20)	19.80
but did cost	22.00
Wage rate variance	2.20 (A)

120 ducks should have taken (× 1.5 mins)	180 mins
but did take (2.75 × 60)	165 mins
Labour efficiency variance in mins	15 mins (F)
× standard rate per minute (£7.20 ÷ 60)	× £0.12
Labour efficiency variance in £	£1.80 (F)

(b) The favourable material price variance may be due to unforeseen discounts received or greater care taken in purchasing or the purchase of lower quality material.

The adverse material usage variance may be due to defective material, excessive waste, theft or stricter quality control.

There could be an interrelationship between the favourable material price variance and the adverse usage variance. Cheaper material than standard could have been purchased, which proved to be more difficult to work with than anticipated, causing greater waste than standard.

The adverse wage rate variance could have been caused by the use of workers with a rate of pay higher than standard or an unexpected wage rate increase.

The favourable labour efficiency variance means that the ducks were produced more quickly than expected which might be due to worker motivation or the use of better quality materials or machines.

There could be a link between the labour rate and efficiency variances. The use of more skilled, and hence more expensive, labour could result in production at a rate quicker than standard.

SECTION 2

1   Work in progress at Dowra Ltd could include (two of) timber that has been cut to shape (but not assembled), assembled toys (before being painted and varnished) or painted and varnished toys (before being packed).

2   Indirect materials in the design department could include pencils and paper (the cost of these being too insignificant to allocate to individual products).

3   String and wire are treated as indirect materials because their cost per toy is too insignificant to justify the administrative effort of allocating them to individual products.

4   Standard labour times would have been set by using time and motion study. Individual operations (cutting head for example) would be observed and timed with a stop watch.

5   In order to cost at the most realistic valuation (that is, a valuation which represents the current cost of the materials used), LIFO (last in, first out) could be used since stocks are issued from stocks at a price which is close to current market value. (Replacement cost *should* be used if available but this is unlikely.)

6   Some production overheads can be allocated directly to cost centres because the overhead can be associated in total with that particular cost centre. For example, the salary of the foreman in the cutting department can be charged direct to that department.

7   The idle time variance identifies the cost of idle time (that is, the time when the labour force, although being paid, were unable to work due to machine breakdowns, bottlenecks in production, or shortage of customer orders). The labour efficiency variance will then relate only to the productivity of the labour force during the time spent *actively* working.

8   Under a good bonus payments system, employees are paid more for their efficiency but, in spite of the extra labour cost, the unit cost of output is reduced and the profit earned per unit of sale is increased. The profits arising from productivity improvements are therefore shared between the company and employees.

9   *Reorder level.* When stocks reach this level action should be taken to replenish stocks.

Minimum level. This is a warning level to draw management attention to the fact that stocks are approaching a dangerously low level and that stockouts are possible. It is essentially a buffer stock.

10 (a)   Stockholding costs include (two of) the following.

      (i)   Costs of storage and stores operations
      (ii) Interest charges
      (iii) Insurance
      (iv) Risk of obsolescence
      (v) Deterioration
      (vi) Theft

(b)   Ordering costs include (two of) the following.

      (i)   Clerical and administrative costs associated with purchasing, accounting for and receiving goods

      (ii) Transport costs

      (iii) Production run costs

11 Although computerised stock control systems hold records on stock levels at all times, stocktaking will still be necessary to ensure that there are no discrepancies between the physical amount of an item in stock and the amount shown in the stock records. Just because the stock control system is computerised does not mean that the following types of discrepancies will not occur.

(a)   Suppliers deliver a different quantity of goods to that shown on the goods received note. Since this note is used to update stock records, a discrepancy will arise.

(b)   The quantity of stock issued to production is different from that shown on the materials requisition note.

(c)   Excess stock is returned from production without documentation.

(d)   Clerical errors may occur in the stock records such as an entry having been made in the wrong stock account.

(e)   Breakages in stores may go unrecorded.

(f)   Employees may steal stock.

12   The copyright fee should be classified as a direct expense because each fee of £1 will be incurred as a direct consequence of making one unit of the model.

PRACTICE CENTRAL ASSESSMENT 2: SOUTHWOOD COLLEGE

SECTION 1

Task 1

STORES LEDGER CARD								
PHOTOCOPY PAPER								
Date	*Receipts*			*Issues*			*Balance*		
	Quantity	*Price*	*Value*	*Quantity*	*Price*	*Value*	*Quantity*	*Price*	*Value*
		£	£		£	£		£	£
Oct 2							84	23.00	1,932.00
Oct 2				70	23.00	1,610.00	14	23.00	322.00
Oct 5	100	21.60	2,160.00				100	21.60	2,160.00
							114		2,482.00
Oct 9				14	23.00	322.00			
				66	21.60	1,425.60	34	21.60	734.40
Oct 12	80	26.25	2,100.00				80	26.25	2,100.00
							114		2,834.40
Oct 26				34	21.60	734.40			
				36	26.25	945.00	44	26.25	1,155.00

Task 2

Method	Closing stock valuation		
	Reams	*Price* £	*Value* £
FIFO	44	26.25	1,155.00
LIFO	14	23.00	322.00
	20	21.60	432.00
	10	26.25	262.50
	44		1,016.50
Standard cost	44	24.00	1,056.00

Task 3

MEMORANDUM

TO: Chief Accountant
FROM: A Technician
DATE: X.X.XX
SUBJECT: Stock valuation methods - photocopy paper

(a) *FIFO*

FIFO costs stock issues at the price of the earliest purchased stock. Stock is thus valued at the most recent purchase price. Stock is therefore valued realistically; however, if there is inflation, issues will be underpriced.

(b) *LIFO*

LIFO costs stock issues at the price of the most recently purchased stock. Stock is thus valued at the price of the earliest purchased stock. Stock will therefore be undervalued in a time of inflation but issues costed at a realistic price.

(c) *Standard cost*

Under standard costing, stock is costed at standard cost, the cost forecast and budgeted for by the organisation. Such a system may undercost or overcost depending on how the actual cost differs from the standard cost. Standard costs are most useful at a time of relatively stable prices.

(d) *Method to use*

Use of the LIFO method will ensure that the cost of courses is not understated. However, stocks cannot be valued at LIFO for financial accounting purposes, and therefore a different system (probably FIFO) will have to be used for the financial accounts. Standard costing is not really suitable as the price of paper appears to be rising.

Task 4

MEMORANDUM

TO: Administration Manager
FROM: A Technician
DATE: 5 December 1995
SUBJECT: Material price variance photocopy paper - October

(a) *Material price variance*

	£
Actual cost of purchases	4,260
Standard cost of purchases (180 × £24)	4,320
Variance	60 (F)

(b) *Explanation of variance*

The reason for the favourable variance is the purchase of 100 reams of paper at a 10% quantity discount. However, this was offset by an increase in the basic price to £26.25 per ream of the other 80 units bought during the month.

Task 5

REPORT

THE POSSIBLE BULK BUYING OF PHOTOCOPY PAPER

Advantages

Bulk buying will reduce:

(a)   the basic cost of the material being purchased;

(b)   the ordering costs (since fewer orders will be required during the year).

Disadvantages

Bulk buying will increase stockholding costs since more of the material will have to be stored.

Information required

The information that will be required to calculate the optimum purchase quantity is:

(a)   ordering costs. These include stationary, postage, telephone and buying department wages;

(b)   holding costs. These include rent and rates, insurance, light and heat, wage costs and obsolescence and deterioration;

(c)   annual demand for paper.

Task 6

Course:	AAT Recording Cost Information (Classroom B)	
Duration:	10 days @ 7 hours per day	
Estimated students	20	
		£
Direct costs:		
Teaching time 70 hours at £30		2,100
Photocopy costs 20 × 0.1 × £30		60
Food and drink 20 × 10 × £3		600
Indirect costs:		
Catering 20 × 10 × £7.75		1,550
Administration		800
Other overhead costs 20 × 10 × £4.46		892
Total cost		6,002

Workings

	Classroom A	Classroom B	Classroom C	Admin	Catering	Total
	£	£	£	£	£	£
Wages	-	-	-	76,000	48,000	-
Heating and lighting (£40 per m2)	10,000	8,000	6,000	8,000	8,000	40,000
Depreciation of equipment	2,400	3,600	36,000	12,000	6,000	60,000
Total	12,400	11,600	36,000	96,000	62,000	
Student days	3,800	2,600	1,600	-	8,000	
Courses	-	-	-	120	-	
Absorption rates						
Catering (per student day)					7.75	
Admin (per course)				800.00		
Other overheads (per student day)	3.26	4.46	22.50			

SECTION 2

1   Materials costing £642 were requisitioned for the job, by material requisition 648.

2   The consultant's fee would have been directly related to this job, and this job alone.

3   The information on the labour hours would have come from timesheets identifying the jobs worked on by different employees.

4   £880/80 hours = £11 per direct labour hour.

5   Materials costing £68 were returned by the job to the stores (recorded on materials return note 214).

6   The treatment of overtime premium will depend on the circumstances. It will be a direct cost if it occurs because of a specific request by the customer to ensure speedy completion of the job. Otherwise it will generally be indirect, as there is no reason other than chance that means a specific job will be worked on during an employee's overtime.

7   The cost should be allocated to the land and buildings fixed asset account. The reason is that the labour is being used to create a fixed asset, not to produce what is sold by the organisation. It is therefore capital expenditure, and not a cost of sale.

8   (a)   This represents the amount of direct wages incurred by the company for that period on manufacturing the product.

    (b)   This represents the amount of indirect production wages for the period, for example wages of supervision staff, overtime rates or bonus payments.

9   Lead time is the time between the issue of a purchase order and the receipt of goods. Re-order level must be set so that it is greater than maximum usage of stock × maximum lead time, otherwise the company may run out of stock.

10   The connection between the variances may be that the company is using cheaper material, but of poorer quality leading to higher wastage.

11   Significant variances are those whose size is worth investigating (eg ± 10% of budget).

Variances reported to a manager should be controllable by that manager. For example the purchasing manager may be responsible for the material price variance, unless there is a universal price over which he/she can have no influence.

12   A variable cost.

PRACTICE CENTRAL ASSESSMENT 3: WHITEWALL LTD

SECTION 1

Task 1

(a)

STORES LEDGER RECORD
MATERIAL: EXON

Date	Receipts			Issues			Balance		
	Kgs	Price £	Value £	Kgs	Price £	Value £	Kgs	Price £	Value £
May 1							30,000	2.00	60,000
May 7	10,000	2.25	22,500				40,000		82,500
May 14	12,000	2.50	30,000				52,000		112,500
May 18				30,000	2.00				
				5,000	2.25	71,250	17,000		41,250

STORES LEDGER RECORD
MATERIAL: DELTON

Date	Receipts			Issues			Balance		
	Kgs	Price £	Value £	Kgs	Price £	Value £	Kgs	Price £	Value £
May 1							25,000	3.00	75,000
May 8	9,000	3.20	28,800				34,000		103,800
May 15	8,000	3.40	27,200				42,000		131,000
May 19				8,000	3.40				
				9,000	3.20				
				3,000	3.00	65,000	22,000		66,000

(b) (i)   FIFO and LIFO are used as methods of pricing issues because it is not possible to identify which specific units of material such as Exon and Delton are being issued at any issue. Hence reasonable assumptions such as FIFO or LIFO need to be made about the price of the units being issued.

(ii)   The stores supervisor's understanding of FIFO and LIFO is incorrect. FIFO and LIFO are methods of pricing, they are not methods of stock control. As individual stock units cannot be precisely identified, the physical movement of stock will not normally be related to the pricing of stock issues.

Task 2

LABOUR COST CARD			
JOB: WHEELBASE Date: May 1996			
	Assembly	*Moulding*	*Finishing*
Actual wage cost £	26,970	34,020	36,540
Standard hours produced	6,000	7,500	7,600
Actual hours worked	6,200	7,000	7,000
Standard hours saved	-	500	600
Actual wage rate per hour £	-	4.86	5.22
Bonus £	-	1,215	1,566
Total labour cost £	26,970	35,235	38,106

Task 3

(a)

OVERHEAD ANALYSIS SHEET

		Assembly	*Moulding*	*Finishing*
Budgeted total overheads	£	3,249,000	3,950,400	3,419,900
Budgeted machine hours		90,000	120,000	110,000
Budgeted overhead absorption rate	£	36.10	32.92	31.09

(b)

JOB OVERHEAD ANALYSIS CARD

		Assembly	*Moulding*	*Finishing*
Job machine hours		6,000	6,800	6,600
Budgeted overhead absorption rate	£	36.10	32.92	31.09
Overhead absorbed by job	£	216,600	223,856	205,194

(c)

MEMORANDUM

To: Job Wheelbase Supervisor
From: A Technician
Date: 18 June 1996
Subject: Overhead absorption rates

(i)   *Purpose of overhead absorption*

The purpose of overhead absorption is to allow overheads to be absorbed by a cost unit on a predetermined basis, so that all costs are recovered by budgeted output.

(ii) *Reasons for using machine hours*

The overhead absorption rate should mean that cost units are charged with a level of overheads that reflects the resources that have been used in producing them. Machine hours will probably have been used as machine usage is felt to have the most direct relationship to overheads incurred.

(iii) *Your suggested approach*

Your suggested approach is not appropriate as the overheads charged to a cost unit will not reflect the overheads incurred in making that unit. Consequently some jobs will bear too many overheads, others too few and hence pricing will be distorted.

Task 4

JOB COST CARD
JOB: WHEELBASE   Date: May 1996

	Total
	£
Material	
Exon	71,250
Delton	65,000
	136,250
Labour	
Assembly	26,970
Moulding	35,235
Finishing	38,106
	100,311
Overhead	
Assembly	216,600
Moulding	223,856
Finishing	205,194
	645,650
Total cost	882,211
Profit	294,070
Job price	1,176,281

Task 5

(a) (i)

Total labour cost variance assembly department	£
6,000 hours should have cost (× £4.50)	27,000
but did cost	26,970
Total labour cost variance	30 (F)

(ii)

Labour efficiency variance		
Work should have taken	6,000	hrs
but did take	6,200	hrs
Labour efficiency variances in hrs	200	hrs (A)
× Standard rate per hour	× £4.50	
Labour efficiency variance in £	£900	(A)

(iii)

Labour rate variance	£
Work should have cost 6,200 × 4.50	27,900
but did cost	26,970
Labour rate variance	930 (F)

(b)

MEMORANDUM

To: Production Manager
From: A Technician
Date: 18 June 1996
Subject: Labour cost variance: Assembly Department

Actual labour costs are £30 lower than standard labour costs. The £30 favourable variance is made up of two elements:

(a) A £930 favourable labour wage rate variance, possibly explained by cheaper than budgeted labour being used.

(b) A £900 adverse labour efficiency variance. This may be due to cheaper labour being used. Investigation will be needed of whether use of cheaper labour has had any adverse effects on the quality of products.

Task 6

Finishing department	Data
Budgeted total overheads	£3,419,900
Budgeted machine hours	110,000
Budgeted overhead absorption rate per machine hour	£31.09
Actual machine hours	108,000
Overhead absorbed (108,000 × 31.09)	£3,357,720
Actual overheads	£3,572,000
Over/(under) absorption of overheads	£214,280

REPORT

To: Cost Accountant
From: A Technician
Date: 18 June 1996
Subject: Finishing department overheads

(a) *Consequence of results*

There has been an under-absorption of overheads of £214,280. In consequence the budgeted profit for Whitewall will be reduced by this sum.

(b) *Possible causes*

One cause of the under-absorption is that the actual capacity of 108,000 hours is less than the budgeted capacity 110,000 hours. Other possible causes include:

(i)   too low a level of overheads being budgeted;

(ii)   too slack a rate of recovery being set;

(iii) a lack of control over overhead costs;

(iv)   an absorption basis being used that does not reflect how overheads are incurred within the finishing department.

(c) *Effect on costing*

The underrecovery of overheads on costing such jobs as Wheelbase will mean that the job is underpriced. This will adversely affect Whitewall's profitability.

(d) *Possible remedial action*

One way to reflect better the overheads incurred in the finishing department would be to base overhead recovery on the activities that drive costs in the department rather than machine hours.

SECTION 2

1   The FIFO method prices issues with the oldest material price first, whereas the LIFO method uses the most recent material price first. As a result, stock will be valued using the price of most recent receipts if FIFO is used. If LIFO is used, stock will be valued using the price of the earliest receipts.

2   (i)   Any two of the following.

Rent and rates, light and heat, insurance, wage costs, obsolescence, deterioration and security.

(i)   Any two of the following.

Stationery, postage, wages and telephone.

3   A stocktake is a count of physical stock on hand, to check against the balance shown by stock records to see if there has been any theft or deterioration.

4   (i)   Periodic.
    (ii)   Continuous stocktaking.

5   A standard hour is the predetermined output from one worker for one hour as a result of detailed study of the operations involved in a task.

6   Any two from:

Timesheets, job cards, clock cards and route cards.

7   $\dfrac{\text{Standard hours produced}}{\text{Actual hours}} \times 100\%$

Standard hours produced are divided by actual hours and a % derived to measure the efficiency of actual production.

8

		Debit £	Credit £
DEBIT	Profit and loss account	214,280	
CREDIT	Production overheads		214,280

9   Service cost centre overheads are apportioned on the basis of the service they provide to production cost centres and other service centres (eg catering services may be apportioned on the basis of the number of workers in other departments).

10   A direct expense can be traced directly to the job concerned, whilst overheads are incurred for a number of jobs/cost centres, and shared to each job/cost centre on a predetermined basis.

11   Administration costs

Light and heat (many other examples are possible).

12   (a)   A cost driver is the factor that causes the costs associated with an activity/output.
     (b)   An example of a possible cost driver is production runs.

PRACTICE CENTRAL ASSESSMENT 4: TAMWORTH LTD

SECTION 1

Task 1

(a)

Department	Cutting	Moulding	Finishing	Packaging
Average number of workers	164	173	162	195
Workers leaving during the year	35	14	11	13
% staff leaving 1996	21.3%	8.1%	6.8%	6.7%
% staff leaving 1995	12.1%	7.8%	7.3%	7.4%

(b)

MEMO

To: Production Manager
From: A Technician
Date: 3 December 1996
Re: STAFF RETENTION RATES

Departmental rates

The staff turnover rates for the moulding, finishing and packaging departments in 1996 are similar to the 1995 rates. However, the cutting department's turnover rate has increased significantly from 12.1% to 21.3%. In 1995, the staff turnover rate in the cutting department was one and a half times as large as the next most rapid rate. In 1996, the staff turnover rate in the cutting department was two and a half times the size of the next most rapid rate.

Causes of high staff turnover

Causes may include:

(i)   low wages;
(ii)   poor conditions;
(iii) long or uncongenial hours;
(iv)   poor relationships between management and staff;
(v)   lack of opportunity for advancement;
(vi)   poor recruitment procedures.

Costs and consequences for the company

These include:

(i)   costs of recruitment;

(ii)   inefficiency of new labour;

(iii) costs of training;

(iv)   lost output arising from staff shortages because of gaps between staff leaving and joining;

(v)   increased waste due to lack of skills of new staff.

Task 2

(a)

Department	Cutting	Moulding	Finishing	Packaging
Budgeted production (hours)	37,900	44,500	48,280	25,000
Actual labour hours worked	37,214	41,213	45,874	24,315
Standard hours produced	37,640	44,150	48,550	24,855
Capacity ratio	98.2%	92.6%	95.0%	97.3%
Efficiency ratio	101.1%	107.1%	105.8%	102.2%

(b)

NOTE

To: Packaging Department Manager
From: A Technician
Date: 3 December 1996
Re: CAPACITY AND EFFICIENCY RATIOS

The capacity ratio shows that only 97.3% of hours budgeted were worked. The efficiency ratio demonstrates that actual production was 102.2% of production that should have been produced in the actual hours worked.

Reasons for capacity being less than budgeted might include:

(i)   production being less than planned;

(ii) stoppages occurring which were not accounted for separately as idle time;

(iii) actual staff numbers employed being less than budgeted staff;

(iv) staff being more efficient than expected (this explanation would be borne out by the efficiency ratio).

Task 3

Report

To: Production Manager
From: A Technician
Date: 3 December 1996
Re: DEPRECIATION OF CUTTING MACHINE

Method of depreciation

The method of depreciation that should be used is the reducing balance method. Using this method, a % depreciation rate is charged on the net book value of the machine at the start of the accounting year. Thus the amount charged to the profit and loss account will be higher in earlier years when the net book value is higher.

Reason for using reducing balance method

The main reason for using this method is that it approximates to what is actually happening, ie the machine is losing most value and having most usage early on in its life.

Calculation of rate

Using a rate of 40% would mean that the cutting machine was depreciated to a value within the range of possible scrap values, as demonstrated below.

	Balance Sheet £	Profit and loss account £
Capital costs	180,000	
Year 1 charge c/f	(72,000)	72,000
	108,000	
Year 2 charge c/f	(43,200)	43,200
	64,800	
Year 3 charge c/f	(29,920)	25,920
	38,880	
Year 4 charge c/f	(15,552)	15,552
	23,328	
Year 5 charge	(9,331)	9,331
	13,997	
Final value		

> *Tutorial note.* Any rate that produces a final value between £10,000 and £15,000 would be acceptable. The range of possible rates is between 39.2% and 44%.

Task 4

Department	Cutting	Moulding	Finishing	Packaging
Actual overheads incurred	£1,234,736	£1,156,347	£938,463	£834,674
Budgeted absorption rate per labour hour	£33.82	£26.80	£20.25	£29.62
Actual labour hours worked	37,214	41,213	45,874	24,315
Overheads absorbed	£1,258,577	£1,104,508	£928,948	£720,210
(Under) / over absorbed overheads	£23,841	(£51,839)	(£9,515)	(£114,464)

Task 5

Standard material prices

Standard material price is the price at which the material issues and closing stock will be priced. It is the price expected to be paid for materials delivered.

Ascertaining standard material prices

Standard material prices will be set taking account of:

(i)   past prices;
(ii) contracted purchase terms;
(iii) expectations of price rises;
(iv) availability of discounts.

Advantages of standard material prices

(i)   All issues are made at a constant price, and therefore comparisons can easily be made.

(ii) It is easier to use and administer than FIFO and LIFO, because under FIFO and LIFO it is necessary to take into account previous stock movements when pricing materials.

Disadvantages of standard material prices

(i)   Standards may not reflect actual prices paid because of inflation or unexpected developments. Hence significant variances may occur.

(ii) Determination of standards can be difficult and time-consuming.

(iii) Altering standards frequently can cause confusion.

SECTION 2

1   Records of leavers maintained by the personnel department.

2   The wage rate may have been set, taking account of:

   (a)   past pay rates, together with an allowance for increases due to inflation;
   (b)   amounts other businesses are paying for this type of work;
   (c)   what management consider the work 'to be worth'.

3   (a)   Overtime
   (b)   Holiday pay
   (c)   Idle time

4   (a)   The costs of the stores department would be apportioned to the production department on a fair basis, such as the value of requisitions.

   (b)   The costs of each production department (including the allocated stores costs) would be absorbed by the cost units on the basis of labour or machine hours required to produce each unit.

5   Under activity-based costing, overheads are assigned to a product on the basis of consumption of activities; under more traditional methods, overheads are generally assigned using measures of production volume such as labour hours or machine hours.

6   Re-order level   = maximum usage x maximum delivery time
                     = 5,000 x 4
                     = 20,000 units

7   A normal loss is an unavoidable loss expected during the normal course of operations, whilst an abnormal loss is an unexpected loss. The costs of a normal loss will be spread across the expected units of good output; the costs of an abnormal loss will be written off to the profit and loss account.

8   One of the four production departments (Cutting, Moulding, Finishing, Packaging).

9   (a)   Allocation is the assignment of directly attributable costs to cost units or cost centres. Apportionment is the process of spreading costs jointly incurred by a number of cost centres over individual centres on the basis of benefits received.

    (b)   (i)   Salary of supervisor.
          (ii) Share of cleaning costs.

10 (a)   No, it means actual overheads are greater than absorbed overheads by £151,977.
    (b)   Under-absorption will mean actual profit is less than budgeted profit.

11 Costs are coded in order to provide a succinct reference which contains the key characteristics (cost nature, type, relevant cost centre) of the cost.

12

Date	Description	FIFO £	LIFO £
25 Nov	Total issue value	5,800	6,000
30 Nov	Total closing stock value	1,400	1,200

PRACTICE CENTRAL ASSESSMENT 5: BRAMWELL LTD

SECTION 1

Task 1

(a)

Production (bars) % of Capacity Costs	5,400,000 90% £	5,700,000 95% £	6,000,000 100% £
Direct Material	270,000	285,000	300,000
Direct Labour	225,000	237,500	250,000
Direct Expenses	180,000	190,000	200,000
Prime Cost	675,000	712,500	750,000
Variable Overheads	135,000	142,500	150,000
Fixed Overheads	300,000	300,000	300,000
Total Cost	1,110,000	1,155,000	1,200,000
Total Cost Per Bar (to 4 decimal places)	0.2056	0.2026	0.2000

WORKINGS

	90%	95%
Direct material	0.9 x 300,000 = 270,000	0.95 × 300,000 = 285,000
Direct labour	0.9 x 250,000 = 225,000	0.95 × 250,000 = 237,500
Direct expenses	0.9 x 200,000 = 180,000	0.95 × 200,000 = 190,000
Variable overheads	0.9 x 150,000 = 135,000	0.95 × 150,000 = 142,500

(b)

MEMO

To: Account Manager
From: A Technician
Date: 17 June 1997
Subject: Trends in cost per bar

The total cost per bar decreases as production increases.

The major reason for this decrease is the fact that the total cost per unit is made up of variable cost per unit *and* absorbed fixed cost per unit. Total variable costs will vary according to the number of units produced, ie variable cost per unit will be the same whatever the level of production. By contrast total fixed costs will be unchanged over the whole range of production. Hence, the more that is produced, the greater the number of units over which fixed costs are spread, and the less fixed costs per unit will be.

Task 2

Workings

	£
Material price variance	
93,500 kgs should cost (× £0.415)	38,803
but did cost	40,205
Material price variance	1,402 (A)

Material usage variance		
850,000 bars should use	89,250	kgs
but did use	93,500	kgs
Material usage variance in kgs	4,250	kgs (A)
× standard cost per kg	£0.415	
Material usage variance in £	£1,764	(A)

REPORT TITLE: Material variances   **PERIOD: 11**

	£	
Material price variance	1,402	Adverse
Material usage variance	1,764	Adverse
Total material cost variance	3,166	Adverse

POSSIBLE REASONS FOR THE CAUSES OF THESE VARIANCES

Adverse material price variance

An adverse material price variance may be caused by:

(a)   purchase of higher quality materials than was anticipated when the standards were set;

(b)   material price increases being greater than expected;

(c)   obtaining less favourable terms than was expected when standards were set (due to lack of availability of discounts, different suppliers having to be used)

Adverse material usage variance

An adverse material usage variance may be caused by :

(a)   inferior quality material being purchased;

(b)   excessive waste of material;

(c)   theft of material;

(d)   rejection of material by quality control procedures that were more stringent than expected.

Task 3

WORKINGS

Amount of time 168 units should take

	168 x 0.25	=	42 hours
at a cost of:	42 x £6	=	£252

Labour bonus

$$(42 - 35) \text{ hours x £6 x } 0.5 = £21$$

REPORT

To: Production Manager

From: A Technician

Date: 17 June 1997

Subject: BONUS SCHEMES

The main characteristic of a standard hours saved bonus scheme is that it compensates employees who are paid under a time based system for their inability to increase earnings by working more efficiently. Under the scheme a target is set, actual performance is compared with target, and employees are paid more for their efficiency.

From the employee's viewpoint, using the figures indicated, employees will be paid £210 (35 hours at £6), plus an additional £21 (7 hours at £3), to take account of the fact that output of 168 units should have taken 42 hours to produce. Their total remuneration will therefore increase by 10% to £231.

From the company's viewpoint, the standard cost of 168 units will be £252 (42 hours at £6) but the actual cost will be £231 as explained above. Hence profitability will be greater than budgeted.

The principal concerns with the scheme are:

(a)   production may be rushed and quality suffer;
(b)   increases in labour efficiency may be limited by factors outside labour's control (for example machinery problems) and this may be de-motivating.

Task 4

Budgeted production overhead schedule

	Basis	Total £	Processing £	Quality Assurance £	Packing £	Stores £	Factory Maintenance £
Rent & Rates	Area	320,000	166,400	51,200	32,000	32,000	38,400
Canteen Costs	Personnel	169,000	114,400	10,400	26,000	10,400	7,800
Depreciation of Machinery	Machine usage	273,000	189,000	8,400	75,600	—	—
Total		762,000	469,800	70,000	133,600	42,400	46,200

SECTION 2

1   Buffer stock is a quantity of stock which a business holds in order to be able to cope with unexpected events, for example demand being higher than predicted or supplies not being delivered.

2   Use of standard costs means that stock issues and stock remaining will be priced at a single price, the standard price, set according to the price the business expects to pay for materials.

3   With FIFO, stock issues will be valued at the prices of the oldest items in stock, and hence stock remaining will be valued at the prices of the most recent purchases. With LIFO stock issues will be valued at the prices of the most recently purchased items; hence stock remaining will be valued at the prices of the oldest items.

4   (a)   Standard labour hours produced.

(b) Budgeted labour hours are the amount of labour hours expected to be incurred in producing the budgeted output. Standard labour hours produced are a quantity of work, the output that employees would have produced given normal conditions in the hours worked.

5

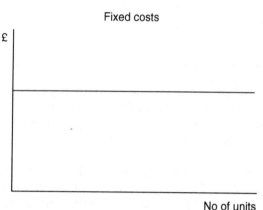

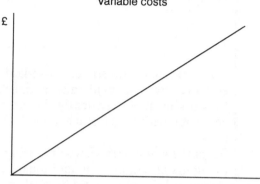

6 Apportionment is the process of spreading costs jointly incurred by a number of cost centres over individual cost centres on the basis of benefit received. Absorption is the process of adding costs, which have been allocated or apportioned to production cost centres, to unit, job or process costs.

7 (a) The budgeted costs of the service departments will need to be apportioned to the production departments according to how much each production department uses each service department. The costs of the maintenance department will be allocated according to the number of maintenance hours of each production department for example.

(b) The costs of service departments are apportioned to production departments because only production departments are involved directly in manufacture. In order to ensure service department overheads are reflected in unit costs, all service department overheads must therefore be apportioned to production departments.

8 Under-absorption means the overheads actually incurred are greater than overheads charged to costs. Under-absorption may arise because actual overheads were greater than expected, or because actual activity was less than expected, or a combination of the two.

9 Bramwell Ltd uses process costing because it is not worthwhile trying to ascertain the direct costs of producing each individual chocolate bar because of the continuous nature of the production process, the low cost per unit, and the fact that each bar will be sold at the same price. Instead, costs are averaged out over the units produced. Job costing is used when it is important to ascertain the costs of each job, generally because each job will be individually priced.

10 (a) Normal loss = 5% x 4,000

= 200 kgs

Abnormal loss = Input – Normal loss – Output

= 4,000 – 200 – 3,700

= 100 kgs

(b) Debit: Abnormal loss account

Credit: Process account

with the abnormal loss, costed at the full cost per unit of output.

11

	Description	DR	CR
0001	Variance account	1,764	
0002	Work in progress account		1,764
	with material usage variance		

PRACTICE CENTRAL ASSESSMENT 6: EDWARDS LTD

SECTION 1

Task 1

(a)

MATERIAL BITCOM									
JOB: 548								**MONTH: NOV 97**	
Date	Receipts			Issues			Stock		
	Qty (Units)	*Unit Price* £	*Value* £	*Qty* (Units)	*Unit Price* £	*Value* £	*Qty* (Units)	*Unit Price* £	*Value* £
Bal 1 Nov							50	40	2,000
2 Nov	450	50	22,500				500	50 × 40 450 × 50	24,500
6 Nov				240	50	12,000	260	50 × 40 210 × 50	12,500
12 Nov	360	60	21,600				620	50 × 40 210 × 50 360 × 60	34,100
14 Nov				290	60	17,400	330	50 × 40 210 × 50 70 × 60	16,700
20 Nov	300	90	27,000				630	50 × 40 210 × 50 70 × 60 300 × 90	43,700
23 Nov				320	300 × 90 20 × 60	28,200	310	50 × 40 210 × 50 50 × 60	15,500
30 Nov				280	50 × 60 210 × 50 20 × 40	14,300	30	40	1,200

(b)

MEMO	
To:	Cost Clerk
From:	Accounting Technician
Date:	2 December 1997
Subject:	Costing stock issues

FIFO costs issues at the oldest purchase price and stock at the most recent purchase price. LIFO costs issues at the most recent purchase price and stock at the oldest purchase price.

The consequences of the change in policy is that by using LIFO, issues to Job 548 have been costed at £71,900 during November and closing stock is valued at £1,200; whilst using FIFO, issues have been costed at £70,400 whilst closing stock has been valued at £2,700.

Task 2

LABOUR VARIANCE REPORT		
Job: 548	**Period: Nov 1997**	
	£	
Labour efficiency variance	340	(F)
Labour wage rate variance	3,120	(A)
Labour cost variance	2,780	(A)

The possible causes for the variances are that a higher grade of labour may have been used, reflected in the adverse wage rate and the favourable efficiency variance. The wage rate variance is significantly higher than the labour efficiency variance, leading to the significant labour cost variance. Other reasons that may have caused the adverse wage-rate variance are that excessive overtime might have been worked, or that the standard wage-rate was set too low.

Workings

Labour efficiency variance	$(4,200 - 4,160) \times £8.50 =$	£340 F
Wage rate variance	$(9.25 - 8.50) \times 4,160 =$	£3,120 A

Task 3

JOB COST CARD	
JOB: 548	**MONTH: NOVEMBER 97**
	£
Direct material	71,900
Direct labour	38,480
Direct expenses	2,925
Production overhead	94,016
Production cost	**207,321**
Administration overhead	69,107
Total cost	**276,428**
Profit (33 1/3% of job price)	138,214
Job price	**414,642**

Workings

$$\text{Production overhead} = \frac{1,324,925}{58,625} = £22.60 \text{ per labour hour}$$

$22.60 \times 4,160 = £94,016$

Task 4

OVERHEAD SUMMARY			
MONTH: NOVEMBER 1997		COST CENTRE: JOB 548	
	Overhead absorbed	*Overhead incurred*	*(Under)/Over absorption of overhead*
	£	£	£
Production overhead	94,016	99,328	(5,312)
Administration overhead	69,107	74,269	(5,162)

Notes

The factory underabsorbed production overheads by £5,312 and administration overheads by £5,162. The consequences for Job 548 are that it has been undercosted by £10,474 and the job profit has been overstated by this amount.

SECTION 2

1   Individual product produced as a single order.

    or

    Job 548 will be carried out in accordance with the special requirements of the customer.

2   Direct Expenses (i)   Hire of tools and equipment used on Job 548.
                      (ii) Cost of special designs, or drawings.

    Overheads   (i)   Factory rent.
                      (ii) Factory insurance.

3   Machine hours.

4   Time-based absorption methods such as machine hours and direct labour hours reflect more accurately the cause of overheads than methods such as labour cost as many overheads are incurred on a time basis (rent, rates, insurance etc).

5   A material requisition will be placed with stores to secure the issue of Bitcom to Job 548. Once stocks of Bitcom are running low the stores department will place a purchase requisition with the purchasing department to order Bitcom from suppliers.

6   A lead time of 10 days for the material Bitcom means that there is a 10 day delay between the ordering of goods and delivery. A buffer stock of 25 units means that this is the minimum level of stock that the company will hold in order to avoid stock-out.

7   (a)   The physical counting at a certain date of stock in hand and checking against the balance shown in the records.

    (b)   (i)   Periodic stocktake,
            (ii) Continuous stocktake

8   (a)   Standard labour hours produced

$$= \frac{35,700}{8.50} = \quad 4,200$$

        Actual hours worked = 4,160

        Standard hours saved =   40

    (b)   Bonus = (75% of 40 hours) × £9.25 = £277.50

9   (i)   Current and past wage rates.
    (ii)   Market conditions for labour within the locality.

10   (a)   Idle time is time that workers are paid for that is non-productive and for which the workers are not responsible.

    (b)   (i)   Non-productive time due to a machine breakdown.
            (ii) Non-productive time due to a stocktake of materials.

11

Under/Overabsorbed Overheads A/C

	£		£
Production overheads	5,312		
Administration overheads	5,162	Profit and loss account	10,474
	10,474		10,474

SUGGESTED ANSWERS TO THE SAMPLE CENTRAL ASSESSMENT

SECTION 1

Task 1

Costs Units	1998 BUDGETED PRODUCTION COSTS		
	750,000	1,000,000	1,250,00
Variable costs	£	£	£
Material	2,250,000	3,000,000	3,750,000
Labour	2,437,500	3,250,000	4,062,500
Overhead	2,062,500	2,750,000	3,437,500
Total	**6,750,000**	**9,000,000**	**11,250,000**
Fixed costs			
Labour	1,100,000	1,100,000	1,100,000
Overhead	1,750,000	1,750,000	1,750,000
Total	**2,850,000**	**2,850,000**	**2,850,000**
Total production cost	**9,600,000**	**11,850,000**	**14,100,000**
Cost per unit	**12.80**	**11.85**	**11.28**

Task 2

WAGE SCHEDULE				
Blowing dept: Team Alpha			Month: January 1998	
	Team	*Master Blower*	*Blower*	*Gen Assistant*
Wage rate (£)		8.60	6.40	4.20
Hrs worked	155	155	155	155
Total wage (£)		**1,333.00**	**992.00**	**651.00**
Standard hours produced	179			
Standard hours saved	24			
Bonus (£)		103.20	76.80	50.40
Total wage + bonus (£)		**1,436.20**	**1,068.80**	**701.40**

Task 3

STORE CARD										
Material: Silica Sand									MONTH: NOV 97	
Date	Receipts			Issues			Stock			
Nov	Qty '000 kg	Cost per kg £	Value £'000	Qty '000 kg	Cost per kg £	Value £'000	Qty '000 kg	Cost per kg £	Value £'000	
Bal 1							1,470	2.00	2,940	
5	860	2.15	1,849				1,470 860	2.00 2.15	4,789	
9				1,060	860 @ 2.15 200 @ 2.00	2,249	1,270	2.00	2,540	
14	1,100	2.25	2,475				1,270 1,100	2.00 2.25	5,015	
18	1,050	2.20	2,310				1,270 1,100 1,050	2.00 2.25 2.20	7,325	
21				2,300	1,050 @ 2.20 1,100 @ 2.25 150 @ 2.00	5,085	1,120	2.00	2,240	
23	1,430	2.40	3,432				1,120 1,430	2.00 2.40	5,672	
25				1,540	1,430 @ 2.40 110 @ 2.00	3,652	1,010	2.00	2,020	
28				820	2.00	1,640	190	2.00	380	

Task 4

(a)

Budgeted Production Overhead Schedule							
Year: 1998							
Cost centre Cost	Blowing £'000	Cutting £'000	Engraving £'000	Quality control £'000	Stores £'000	Maintenance £'000	Total £'000
Allocated overhead	876	534	413	278	374	292	2,767
Apportioned overhead	1,138	793	541	311	416	324	3,523
Sub-total	**2,014**	**1,327**	**954**	**589**	**790**	**616**	**6,290**
Maintenance	280	145	95	48	48	(616)	
Stores	486	178	131	43	(838)		
Quality control	420	140	120	(680)			
Total budgeted overheads	**3,200**	**1,790**	**1,300**				**6,290**

(b)

	Blowing	Cutting	Engraving
Total budgeted overheads (£)	3,200,000	1,790,000	1,300,000
Budgeted labour hours	48,000	35,800	32,500
Budgeted overhead absorption rate £ per labour hour	66.67	50.00	40.00

(c)

Department	Time	Budgeted overhead absorption rate per labour hour	Overhead absorbed
	Minutes	£	£
Blowing	9	66.67	10.00
Cutting	7½	50.00	6.25
Engraving	12	40.00	8.00
Total			24.25

SECTION 2

Task 1

The cost per unit has moved downwards from £12.80 at 750,000 units to £11.28 at 1,250,000 units. The reason for this is that fixed overheads have remained the same with changes in the level of output. As a consequence, as more units are produced, fixed overheads will be spread over a greater number of units, which will reduce the unit cost. The variable overhead will remain the same at all levels of production.

Task 2

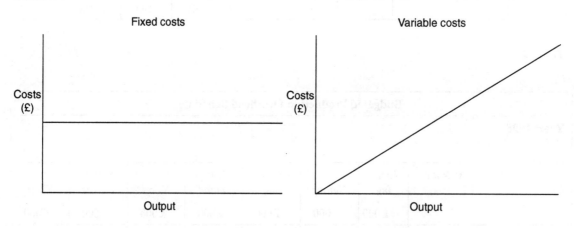

Task 3

Classification: Semi-variable cost
Example: Telephone costs

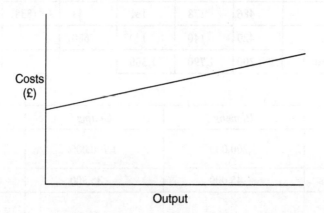

Task 4

(a) Benefits to workers

The wage payment that they receive can be increased within the normal working week if the conditions for the bonus are met. If a bonus is not earned, the basic wage based on time attendance will be received.

(b) Benefits to employers

Employers should have a motivated workforce with the introduction of a bonus system. The labour cost per unit will be reduced because only part of the cost is given to the employee as a bonus, and overheads per unit will be reduced as, ideally, more units will be produced.

Task 5

A time and motion study will have been undertaken to establish realistic times allowed for each operation that makes up the manufacture of the vases. These will then be aggregated to arrive at the standard times for the blowing team.

Task 6

(i) Clock cards
(ii) Time sheets

Task 7

LIFO was chosen as the method to cost issues of silica sand in Task 3 of Section 1 as it is the method that costs issues to production at the most recent price, which is what the company wants.

Task 8

The weaknesses of LIFO as a method of costing issues and valuing stock include

(i) Stock is valued at out-of-date costs.
(ii) The method is not recognised by the Inland Revenue for tax purposes
(iii) The method is considered appropriate for external reporting purposes

Task 9

Holding cost	Ordering cost
(i) Warehouse costs	(i) Purchase department salaries
(ii) Financing costs	(ii) Purchase department overheads (telephone etc)

Task 10

(a) Economic order quantity.

(b) This method sets out to minimise the cost of ordering and holding stock by deriving an optimum order quantity and number of orders per year, given the level of demand by the company for that item of stock.

Task 11

Blowing department allocated overhead:	Supervisor's salary
Blowing department apportioned overhead:	Rent and rates

Task 12

Supervisors' salaries are allocated to a cost centre when they can be directly attributed to that cost centre. Overheads are apportioned to a cost centre when the cost centre has had the partial benefit of an overhead that has benefited a number of cost centres but cannot be directly attributable to any one particular cost centre. An example of this is rent and rates.

Section 3

Task 1

VARIANCE SCHEDULE			
Blowing dept			**January 1998**
		£	£
Material variance			
Material usage			4,236 (A)
Material price			1,125 (F)
Total			**3,111 (A)**
Labour variance			
Labour efficiency			1,750 (F)
Labour wage-rate			5,865 (A)
Total			**4,115 (A)**
Fixed overhead variance			
Expenditure			16,520 (A)
	Capacity	10,050 (A)	
	Efficiency	5,360 (F)	
Volume			4,690 (A)
Total			**21,210 (A)**

REPORT

The total material, labour and overhead variances are all adverse, as are all the sub-variances with the exception of the material price variance, fixed overhead efficiency variance and labour efficiency variance, which are favourable. In particular, the material usage variance, labour wage rate variance and all the fixed overhead sub-variances are significant as they are in excess of £4,000.

The material variances could have come about from the change in supplier. The supplies of material are cheaper but the quality might not be up to standard, hence the significant material usage variance of £4,236. The significant wage rate variance of £5,865 looks as if it was brought about by not budgeting for the full wage increase. However, the effect of this is lessened by the favourable labour efficiency variance.

The adverse total fixed overhead variance means that overheads were under-absorbed by £21,210. The most significant reason for this is the expenditure variance, which is £16,520 adverse. This is worrying as it means that actual overheads were greater than those budgeted. It would be expected that actual overheads would be greater than budget if actual activity was greater than budgeted. However, this was not the case as the budgeted level of production was not achieved, which is shown by the adverse fixed overhead capacity variance. This sub-variance shows that fixed overheads were underabsorbed by £10,050 because actual production was less than budget. The effect of this is ameliorated by the favourable fixed overhead efficiency variance of £5,360, giving a total volume variance of £4,690 adverse.

ORDER FORM

Any books from our AAT range can be ordered by telephoning 0181-740 2211. Alternatively, send this page to our Freepost address or fax it to us on 0181-740 1184, or email us at **publishing@bpp.co.uk**. Or look us up on our Website: http://www.bpp.co.uk

All books are sent out within 48 hours of receipt of your order, subject to availability.

To: BPP Publishing Ltd, Aldine House, Aldine Place, London W12 8AW

Tel: 0181-740 2211   **Fax: 0181-740 1184**   **Email: publishing@bpp.co.uk**

Mr / Ms (full name): _____

Day-time delivery address: _____

_____

Postcode: _____   Daytime Tel: (for queries only):_____

Please send me the following quantities of books:

	5/98 Interactive Text	8/98 DA Kit	8/98 CA Kit
FOUNDATION			
Unit 1 Cash Transactions		(5/98) ☐	☐
Unit 2 Credit Transactions			
Unit 3 Payroll Transactions	(6/98)	☐	
Unit 19 Data Processing (Windows) *	(8/98)		
Unit 21-25 Business Knowledge			

* Contains hands-on tuition and assignments; you will need access to Sage accounting software and BPP data disks

INTERMEDIATE			
Unit 4 Financial Records and Accounts		(5/98) ☐	☐
Unit 5 Cost Information			
Unit 6 Reports and Returns		(5/98) ☐	
Unit 20 Information Technology			
Unit 22: see below			
TECHNICIAN			
Unit 7/8 Core Managing Costs and Allocating Resources			☐
Unit 9 Core Managing Accounting Systems		(5/98) ☐	☐
Unit 10 Option Drafting Financial Statements			
Unit 14 Option Cash Management and Credit Control			
Unit 15 Option Evaluating Activities			
Unit 16 Option Implementing Auditing Procedures			
Unit 17 Option Business Taxation Computations	(8/98)	date TBC	
Unit 18 Option Personal Taxation Computations	(8/98)	date TBC	

TOTAL BOOKS ☐ + ☐ + ☐ = ☐

@ £9.95 each = £ ☐

Postage and packaging:

UK: £2.00 for each book to maximum of £10

Europe (inc ROI & CD): £4.00 for each book ————————— P & P £ ☐

Rest of the World: £6.00 for each book

Unit 22 Maintaining a Healthy Workplace Interactive Text (postage free)   Quantity ☐   @ £3.95   £ ☐

GRAND TOTAL £ ☐

I enclose a cheque for £ _____ (cheques to BPP Publishing Ltd) or charge to Access/Visa/Switch

Card number ☐☐☐☐☐☐☐☐☐☐☐☐☐☐☐☐☐☐☐

Start date _____   **Expiry date** _____   **Issue no. (Switch only)**___

Signature _____

REVIEW FORM & FREE PRIZE DRAW

All original review forms from the entire BPP range, completed with genuine comments, will be entered into one of two draws on 31 January 1999 and 31 July 1999. The names on the first four forms picked out on each occasion will be sent a cheque for £50.

Name: _____   Address: _____

_____

_____

How have you used this Devolved Assessment Kit?
(Tick one box only)

☐ Home study (book only)

☐ On a course: college _____

☐ With 'correspondence' package

☐ Other _____

Why did you decide to purchase this Devolved Assessment Kit? *(Tick one box only)*

☐ Have used BPP Interactive Texts in the past

☐ Recommendation by friend/colleague

☐ Recommendation by a lecturer at college

☐ Saw advertising

☐ Other _____

During the past six months do you recall seeing/receiving any of the following?
(Tick as many boxes as are relevant)

☐ Our advertisement in *Accounting Technician* magazine

☐ Our advertisement in *Pass*

☐ Our brochure with a letter through the post

Which (if any) aspects of our advertising do you find useful?
(Tick as many boxes as are relevant)

☐ Prices and publication dates of new editions

☐ Information on Interactive Text content

☐ Facility to order books off-the-page

☐ None of the above

Have you used the companion Interactive Text for this subject?   ☐ Yes   ☐ No

Your ratings, comments and suggestions would be appreciated on the following areas

	Very useful	Useful	Not useful
How to use this Devolved Assessment Kit section	☐	☐	☐
Standards of Competence	☐	☐	☐
Assessment Strategy	☐	☐	☐
Practice Devolved Assessments	☐	☐	☐
Trial Run Devolved Assessments	☐	☐	☐
AAT Sample Simulation	☐	☐	☐
Quality of solutions	☐	☐	☐
Layout of pages	☐	☐	☐
Structure of book and ease of use	☐	☐	☐

	Excellent	Good	Adequate	Poor
Overall opinion of this Kit	☐	☐	☐	☐

Do you intend to continue using BPP Assessment Kits/Interactive Texts? ☐ Yes   ☐ No

Please note any further comments and suggestions/errors on the reverse of this page.

Please return to: Clare Donnelly, BPP Publishing Ltd, FREEPOST, London, W12 8BR

REVIEW FORM & FREE PRIZE DRAW (continued)

Please note any further comments and suggestions/errors below

FREE PRIZE DRAW RULES

1 Closing date for 31 January 1999 draw is 31 December 1998. Closing date for 31 July 1999 draw is 30 June 1999.

2 Restricted to entries with UK and Eire addresses only. BPP employees, their families and business associates are excluded.

3 No purchase necessary. Entry forms are available upon request from BPP Publishing. No more than one entry per title, per person. Draw restricted to persons aged 16 and over.

4 Winners will be notified by post and receive their cheques not later than 6 weeks after the relevant draw date. Lists of winners will be published in BPP's *focus* newsletter following the relevant draw.

5 The decision of the promoter in all matters is final and binding. No correspondence will be entered into.